SUNDAY CELEBRATIONS

CELEBRACIONES DOMINICALES

LEADER'S EDITION

EDICION PARA LOS QUE DIRIGEN LA ASAMBLEA

CELEBRACIONES DOMINICALES EN LA AUSENCIA DE UN PRESBITERO

EDICION PARA LOS QUE DIRIGEN LA ASAMBLEA

**APROBADO PARA USO EN LAS
DIOCESIS DE LOS ESTADOS UNIDOS DE AMERICA
POR LA CONFERENCIA NACIONAL DE OBISPOS CATOLICOS**

Preparado por el Comité Episcopal de Liturgia
Conferencia Nacional de Obispos Católicos

A Liturgical Press Book

THE LITURGICAL PRESS
Collegeville, Minnesota

SUNDAY CELEBRATIONS IN THE ABSENCE OF A PRIEST

LEADER'S EDITION

**APPROVED FOR USE IN THE
DIOCESES OF THE UNITED STATES OF AMERICA
BY THE NATIONAL CONFERENCE OF CATHOLIC BISHOPS**

Prepared by the Committee on the Liturgy
National Conference of Catholic Bishops

A Liturgical Press Book

THE LITURGICAL PRESS
Collegeville, Minnesota

Cover design by Ann Blattner. Cross by Frank Kacmarcik, Obl.S.B.

Concordat cum originali:
Reverend James P. Moroney, Executive Director
Secretariat for the Liturgy
National Conference of Catholic Bishops

Published by authority of the Committee on the Liturgy, National Conference of Catholic Bishops (Publicado por la autoridad del Comité de Liturgia de la Conferencia Nacional de Obispos Católicos).

ACKNOWLEDGMENTS

Excerpts from the English translation of the *Directory for Sunday Celebrations in the Absence of a Priest* © 1988, International Committee on English in the Liturgy, Inc. (ICEL), 1522 K Street, NW, Suite 1000, Washington, DC 20005-1202 USA; excerpts from the English translation of *Documents on the Liturgy, 1963–1979: Conciliar, Papal, and Curial Texts* © 1982, ICEL; excerpts from the English translation of *Holy Communion and Worship of the Eucharist outside Mass* © 1974, ICEL; excerpts from *The Roman Missal (Sacramentary)* © 1973, ICEL; excerpts from *The Liturgy of the Hours* © 1970, 1973, 1975, ICEL. Excerpts from the English translation of the *Rite of Christian Initiation of Adults* © 1985, ICEL. All rights reserved.

The Psalms: A New Translation © The Grail, (England) 1963.

The Complete Psalms first published in 1963 by and available through Wm. Collins Sons & Co., Limited — In North America through the Paulist Press Inc. and Collins + World.

Excerpts of the Spanish translation of *Ordinario de la Misa* © 1989, United States Catholic Conference.

Oración del Día and Oración después de la Comunión from *Misal Romano* © 1993, Obra Nacional de la Buena Prensa, A.C., Mexico City, Mexico.

Excerpts of the Spanish translation of *La Liturgia de las Horas* © 1980, Comisión Episcopal Española de Liturgia.

Excerpts of the Spanish translation of *Ritual de la Sagrada Comunión y del Culto a la Eucaristía fuera de la Misa* © 1974, Comisión Episcopal Española de Liturgia.

English and Spanish texts of *Prayers of Thanksgiving* Appendix II, Part V, © 1993, United States Catholic Conference.

Excerpts from the *New American Bible,* © 1970, with *Revised New Testament,* © 1986, and *Revised Psalms,* © 1991, Confraternity of Christian Doctrine, 3211 Fourth Street, NE, Washington, DC 20017-1194 USA. All rights reserved.

Spanish Biblical Texts from *La Biblia, Latinoamericano,* Copyright © 1972, Ramon Riccardi and Bernardo Hurault.

"Father We Thank Thee": words by permission of the Church Pension Fund.

"O Radiant Light": words © 1973, Fides Publishers, Inc., Notre Dame, Indiana, from *Morning Praise and Evensong.* Used by permission.

The English translation of the "Apostles' Creed," the "Nicene Creed," Benedictus, Magnificat, Gloria, and Glory to the Father by the International Consultation on English Texts (ICET).

The arrangement, introduction, rubrics and original texts in *Sunday Celebrations in the Absence of a Priest: Leader's Edition* © 1993 United States Catholic Conference (USCC), 3211 Fourth Street, NE, Washington, DC 20017-1194 USA. All rights reserved.

Copyright © 1997 by The Order of St. Benedict, Inc., Collegeville, Minnesota. All rights reserved.

Printed in the United States of America.

ISBN 0-8146-2416-2

INDICE GENERAL

TABLE OF CONTENTS

CONFERENCIA NACIONAL DE OBISPOS CATOLICOS DE LOS ESTADOS UNIDOS DE AMERICA

DECRETO

De acuerdo con las provisiones del núm. 41 del *Directorio para las Celebraciones Dominicales en la Ausencia de un Presbítero*, promulgado por la Congregación del Culto Divino el 2 de junio de 1988, la publicación *Celebraciones Dominicales en la Ausencia de un Presbítero: Edición para Los que Dirigen la Asamblea* fue aprobada por los miembros de la Conferencia Nacional de Obispos Católicos en asamblea plenaria el 7 de noviembre de 1989 para uso en las Diócesis de los Estados Unidos de América.

El 1° de enero de 1994 *Celebraciones Dominicales en la Ausencia de un Presbítero: Edición para Los que Dirigen la Asamblea* puede ser publicada y usada en aquellas diócesis donde el obispo diocesano ha dado el permiso para llevar a cabo celebraciones dominicales cuando el sacerdote está ausente.

Dado en el Secretariado General de la Conferencia Nacional de Obispos Católicos, Washington, DC, el 14 de septiembre de 1993, la fiesta de la Santa Cruz.

✠ William H. Keeler
Arzobispo de Baltimore
Presidente
Conferencia Nacional de Obispos Católicos

Robert N. Lynch
Secretario General

NATIONAL CONFERENCE OF CATHOLIC BISHOPS

UNITED STATES OF AMERICA

DECREE

In accordance with the provisions of no. 41 of the *Directory for Sunday Celebrations in the Absence of a Priest,* promulgated by the Congregation for Divine Worship on 2 June 1988, *Sunday Celebrations in the Absence of a Priest: Leader's Edition* was approved for use by the members of the National Conference of Catholic Bishops in plenary assembly on 7 November 1989.

On 1 January 1994 *Sunday Celebrations in the Absence of a Priest: Leader's Edition* may be published and used in those dioceses where the diocesan bishop has given authorization for Sunday celebrations in the absence of a priest.

Given at the General Secretariat of the National Conference of Catholic Bishops, Washington, DC, on 14 September 1993, the feast of the Holy Cross.

✠ William H. Keeler
Archbishop of Baltimore
President
National Conference of Catholic Bishops

Robert N. Lynch
General Secretary

PRESENTACION

A la luz de las necesidades expresadas por muchas conferencias nacionales de obispos para ofrecer celebraciones litúrgicas en aquellos lugares donde no hay un sacerdote para celebrar la Misa cada domingo, la Congregación para el Culto Divino ha publicado un *Directorio para Celebraciones Dominicales en la Ausencia de un Presbítero* (2 de junio de 1988).[1] Este Directorio recuerda la enseñanza de la Iglesia sobre el significado del domingo, indica las condiciones cuando tales celebraciones pueden realizarse legítimamente, y ofrece pautas para llevarlas a cabo correctamente.

Puesto que es la responsabilidad de las conferencias de obispos, según lo sugieran las circunstancias, el determinar estas normas con mayor detalle y adaptarlas a la cultura y condiciones de sus feligreses, la Conferencia Nacional de Obispos Católicos ha preparado esta publicación, *Celebraciones dominicales en la Ausencia de un Presbítero: Edición para Los que Dirigen la Asamblea,* para que la usen los diáconos y los laicos que han de dirigir tales celebraciones.[2]

Para preparar este ritual, el Comité Episcopal de Liturgia hizo una encuesta en las diócesis de los Estados Unidos a fin de determinar la necesidad de celebraciones dominicales en la ausencia de un sacerdote y con qué frecuencia se tienen hoy día esas celebraciones. Basados en ese estudio, el Comité descubrió que tales celebraciones son una necesidad pastoral presente en muchas diócesis y que pueden llegar a ser aun más necesarias en los próximos años.

Antes de que comiencen las celebraciones dominicales en la ausencia de un sacerdote en cualquier diócesis o parroquia, es esencial que se tenga una catequesis a nivel diocesano sobre la naturaleza de estas celebraciones y la necesidad de promover vocaciones al sacerdocio a fin de que, eventualmente, no le falte a ninguna comunidad la celebracion de la Misa dominical.

✠ Monseñor Donald W. Trautman
Obispo de Erie
Presidente, Comité Episcopal de Liturgia

---

[1] Congregación para el Culto Divino, *Directorio para Celebraciones Dominicales en la Ausencia de un Presbítero* (en adelante se citará como *Directorio*) (2 de junio de 1988).

[2] Véase *Directorio*, núm. 7.

FOREWORD

In light of the need expressed by many conferences of bishops for the provision of liturgical celebrations for those places where a priest is not available to celebrate the eucharist each Sunday, the Congregation for Divine Worship has published a *Directory for Sunday Celebrations in the Absence of a Priest* (June 2, 1988).[1] This Directory recalls the Church's teaching on the meaning of Sunday, indicates the conditions when such celebrations may legitimately take place, and provides guidelines for carrying out such celebrations correctly.

Since it is the responsibility of the conferences of bishops, as circumstances suggest, to determine these norms in greater detail and to adapt them to the culture and conditions of their people, the National Conference of Catholic Bishops has prepared *Sunday Celebrations in the Absence of a Priest: Leader's Edition* for use by deacons and laypersons who will lead such celebrations.[2]

In the process of preparing this ritual book, the Bishops' Committee on the Liturgy surveyed the dioceses of the United States in order to determine the need for Sunday celebrations in the absence of a priest and the frequency of such celebrations at the present time. On the basis of that study, the Committee discovered that such services are a present pastoral necessity in many dioceses and may become even more necessary in the coming years.

Before Sunday celebrations in the absence of a priest are begun in any diocese or parish, it is essential that there be diocesan-wide catechesis on the nature of these celebrations and the necessity of fostering vocations to the priesthood so that eventually no community will be denied the Sunday celebration of the eucharist each week.

☩ Most Reverend Donald W. Trautman
Bishop of Erie
Chairman, Bishops' Committee on the Liturgy

---

[1] Congregation for Divine Worship, *Directory for Sunday Celebrations in the Absence of a Priest* (hereafter *Directory*) (2 June 1988).

[2] See *Directory*, no. 7.

INTRODUCCION

INTRODUCTION

INTRODUCCION

EL DOMINGO Y SU OBSERVANCIA

1   "La Iglesia, por una tradición apostólica que trae su origen del mismo día de la resurrección de Cristo, celebra el misterio pascual cada ocho días, en el día que con razón es llamado 'Día del Señor' o 'domingo'".[1]

2   El Nuevo Testamento y los Padres de la Iglesia ofrecen amplia evidencia de que en la Iglesia primitiva el domingo era el "Día del Señor". Ya que el Señor conquistó el pecado y la muerte y resucitó a una nueva vida el domingo. En nuestros tiempos, el Concilio Vaticano II nos ha recordado: "En este día, los fieles deben reunirse a fin de que, escuchando la palabra de Dios y participando en la Eucaristía, recuerden la pasión, la resurrección y la gloria del Señor Jesús y den gracias a Dios, que los 'hizo renacer a la viva esperanza por la resurrección de Jesucristo de entre los muertos'" (1 Pedro 1:3).[2]

3   La celebración litúrgica del domingo se caracteriza en su totalidad por la reunión de los fieles. Esta reunión manifiesta la Iglesia, ya que no se reúnen los fieles simplemente por su iniciativa propio sino por el llamado divino. El Pueblo de Dios es convocado a formar un organismo presidido por un sacerdote que actúa en la persona de Cristo. Por medio de la celebración de la liturgia de la Palabra, la asamblea de los fieles es instruida en el misterio pascual por la proclamación de las Escrituras que son luego explicadas por un sacerdote o diácono en la homilía. Y por medio de la celebración de la liturgia de la eucaristía, por la cual el misterio pascual se efectúa sacramentalmente, la asamblea participa en el mismo sacrificio de Cristo.[3]

4   La catequesis pastoral sobre la importancia del domingo debe hacer hincapié en que el sacrificio de la Misa es la única verdadera actualización del misterio pascual del Señor[4] y es la más completa manifestación de la Iglesia: "Por esto, el domingo es la fiesta primordial, que debe presentarse e inculcarse a la piedad de los fieles . . . No se le antepongan otras solemnidades, a no ser que sean, de veras, de suma importancia, puesto que el domingo es el fundamento y el núcleo de todo el año litúrgico".[5]

---

[1] Concilio Vaticano II, Constitución sobre la Sagrada Liturgia *Sacrosanctum Concilium* (en adelante SC), art. 106: DOL 1, núm. 106. Véase también *Ibíd.,* Apéndice, Declaración del Segundo Concilio Ecuménico del Vaticano sobre la Revisión del Calendario: DOL 1, núm. 131.

[2] Véase *Directorio*, núm. 8; véase SC, art. 106: DOL 1, núm. 106.

[3] Véase *Directorio*, núm. 12.

[4] Véase Pablo VI, Alocución dirigida a los obispos del centro de Francia, el 26 de marzo de 1977: AAS 69 (1977), 465; "La meta siempre debe ser la celebración del sacrificio de la Misa, la única verdadera actualización del misterio pascual del Señor" (tr., DOL 449, núm. 38.2).

[5] Véase SC, art. 106: DOL 1, núm. 106.

INTRODUCTION

SUNDAY AND ITS OBSERVANCE

1 "By a tradition handed down from the apostles and having its origin from the very day of Christ's resurrection, the Church celebrates the paschal mystery every eighth day, which, with good reason, bears the name of the Lord's Day or Sunday."[1]

2 The New Testament and the Fathers of the Church give ample evidence that for the early Church Sunday was the "Lord's Day." For it was on Sunday that the Lord conquered sin and death and rose to new life. In our own time, the Second Vatican Council has reminded us: "On this day Christ's faithful must gather together, so that, by hearing the word of God and taking part in the eucharist, they may call to mind the passion, resurrection, and glorification of the Lord Jesus and may thank God, who 'has begotten them again unto a living hope through the resurrection of Jesus Christ from the dead'" (1 Peter 1:3).[2]

3 The complete liturgical celebration of Sunday is characterized by the gathering of the faithful to manifest the Church, not simply on their own initiative but as called together by God, that is, as the people of God in their organic structure, presided over by a priest, who acts in the person of Christ. Through the celebration of the liturgy of the Word the assembled faithful are instructed in the paschal mystery by the Scriptures which are proclaimed and which are then explained in the homily by a priest or deacon. And through the celebration of the liturgy of the eucharist, by which the paschal mystery is sacramentally effected, the assembly participates in the very sacrifice of Christ.[3]

4 Pastoral catechesis on the importance of Sunday should emphasize that the sacrifice of the Mass is the only true actualization of the Lord's paschal mystery[4] and is the most complete manifestation of the Church: "Hence the Lord's Day is the first holy day of all and should be proposed to the devotion of the faithful and taught to them . . . Other celebrations, unless they be truly of greatest importance, shall not have precedence over the Sunday, the foundation and core of the whole liturgical year."[5]

---

[1] Vatican Council II, Constitution on the Liturgy *Sacrosanctum Concilium* (hereafter, *SC*), art. 106: DOL 1, no. 106. See also *Ibid.*, Appendix, Declaration of the Second Vatican Ecumenical Council on Revision of the Calendar: DOL 1, no. 131.

[2] See *Directory*, no. 8; see *SC*, art. 106: DOL 1, no.106.

[3] See *Directory*, no. 12.

[4] See Paul VI, Address to bishops of central France, 26 March 1977: AAS 69 (1977), 465; "The goal must always be the celebration of the sacrifice of the Mass, the only true actualization of the Lord's paschal mystery" (tr., DOL 449, no. 38:2).

[5] See *SC*, art. 106: DOL 1, no. 106.

5   En la asamblea del domingo, como también en la vida de la comunidad cristiana, los fieles deben encontrar tanto una participación activa como un verdadero espíritu de comunidad, así como la oportunidad de renovarse espiritualmente guiados por el Espíritu Santo.[6]

CELEBRACIONES DOMINICALES EN LA AUSENCIA DE UN SACERDOTE

6   Ha habido y todavía hay muchos fieles en los Estados Unidos para quienes la participación en la Misa requiere en gran sacrificio debido a la falta de sacerdotes o por otras razones serias.[7]

7   Además, debido a la escasez de sacerdotes en ciertas áreas, los sacerdotes tienen que celebrar varias Misas los domingos en muchas iglesias muy distantes unas de otras.[8] A estos sacerdotes se les debe alabar por su dedicación y celo pastoral.

8   Cuando se dieren las circunstancias que dificulten seriamente la celebración de la Misa, los obispos locales pueden juzgar necesario proveer otras celebraciones dominicales en la ausencia de un sacerdote, para que de la mejor manera posible la reunión semanal de los fieles pueda continuarse y la tradición cristiana con respecto al domingo pueda conservarse.[9]

9   Cuando en un domingo particular ni siquiera este tipo de celebración fuera posible, se exhorta encarecidamente a los fieles a que se dediquen a la oración "por un buen tiempo, bien sea individualmente o con la familia, o, si es posible, con un grupo de familias."[10]

CONDICIONES PARA LA CELEBRACION DOMINICAL EN LA AUSENCIA DE UN PRESBITERO

10   Cuando no pueda celebrarse la Misa un domingo, el Día del Señor, es muy importante que la comunidad, sea parroquial o sea de una misión, se reúna a celebrar la resurrección del Señor. Si, a juicio del obispo diocesano, no es práctico ni posible que la comunidad participe en la celebración de la Misa en una iglesia cercana,[11] se deben reunir para un rito dominical en su propia comunidad bajo el líderazgo de la persona que el obispo y el párroco hayan asignado para dirigirlos en oración. En tal caso, la celebracion debe hacerse en una de las formas que se encuentran en este ritual.

---

[6] Véase *Directorio*, núm. 15.

[7] Véase *Ibíd.*, núm. 2; véase *Codex Iuris Canonici*, 1983 (en adelante *CIC*), canon 1248, §2.

[8] Véase *Ibíd.*, núm. 5.

[9] Véase *Ibíd.*, núm. 6.

[10] Véase *Ibíd.*, núm. 32; véase *CIC*, canon 1248, §2.

[11] Véase *Ibíd.*, núm. 18.

---

5   In the Sunday assembly, as also in the life of the Christian community, the faithful should find both active participation and a true spirit of community, as well as the opportunity to be renewed spiritually under the guidance of the Holy Spirit.[6]

SUNDAY CELEBRATIONS IN THE ABSENCE OF A PRIEST

6   There have been and still are many of the faithful in the United States for whom, because of the lack of a priest or some other serious reason, participation in the eucharistic celebration demands a great sacrifice.[7]

7   In addition, because of the shortage of priests in certain areas, priests must celebrate Mass several times on Sundays in many widely scattered churches.[8] They are to be commended for their dedication and pastoral zeal.

8   In circumstances in which there is no reasonable opportunity to provide for the celebration of Mass, local bishops may judge it necessary to provide for other Sunday celebrations in the absence of a priest, so that in the best way possible the weekly gathering of the faithful can be continued and the Christian tradition regarding Sunday preserved.[9]

9   When on a particular Sunday even this kind of celebration is not possible, the faithful are strongly urged to devote themselves to prayer "for a suitable time either individually or with the family or, if possible, with a group of families."[10]

CONDITIONS FOR HOLDING SUNDAY CELEBRATIONS IN THE ABSENCE OF A PRIEST

10   When a priest cannot be present for the celebration of Mass on the Lord's Day, it is of paramount importance that the parish or mission community still come together to celebrate the resurrection of the Lord. If, in the judgment of the diocesan bishop, it is not practical or possible for the community to participate in the celebration of Mass in a church nearby,[11] they should assemble for Sunday worship in their own community under the leadership of the person the bishop and pastor have designated to lead them in prayer. In such a case the celebration takes one of the forms found in this ritual.

---

[6] See *Directory*, no. 15.
[7] See *Ibid.*, no. 2; see *Codex Iurs Canonici*, 1983 (hereafter, *CIC*), can. 1248, §2.
[8] See *Ibid.*, no. 5.
[9] See *Ibid.*, no. 6.
[10] See *Ibid.*, no. 32; see *CIC*, can. 1248, §2.
[11] See *Ibid.*, no. 18.

11   Antes que se dé comienzo a las celebraciones dominicales en la ausencia de un sacerdote, se debe explicar a los fieles que aunque estas celebraciones susti-tuyen la celebración dominical de la Misa, no se deben considerar como la solu-cion ideal a las circunstancias presentes ni como una forma de dejarse llevar por la mera conveniencia.[12] Normalmente debe haber solo una asamblea de este tipo en cada lugar y cada domingo donde esto suceda.[13]

12   Cuidadosamente debe evitarse cualquier confusión en la mente de los fieles entre este tipo de asamblea y lana celebración de la Misa. Estas celebraciones deben aumentar el deseo de los fieles de estar presentes y de participar en la cele-bración de la Misa.[14]

13   Con este fin, es necesario que los fieles comprendan que el sacrificio eucarís-tico no puede tenerse sin un sacerdote y que la comunión eucarística que ellos reciben en este tipo de asamblea está conectado íntimamente con el sacrificio de la Misa.[15]

OFICIOS Y MINISTERIOS

EL OBISPO

14   Es responsabilidad del obispo diocesano, después de consultar a su consejo presbiteral y, si es apropiado, a otros grupos consultativos, decidir si las celebra-ciones dominicales en la ausencia de un sacerdote deben celebrarse de un modo ocasional o regular dentro de su diócesis. El debe fijar normas generales y partic-ulares para tales celebraciones. Deben celebrarse solamente cuando y donde estén aprobadas por el obispo y solamente bajo el ministerio pastoral de un sacerdote que tiene la responsabilidad de esa comunidad particular.[16]

15   Antes de que el obispo decida tener celebraciones dominicales, debe consid-erar la posibilidad de recurrir a sacerdotes, aún sacerdotes religiosos, que no están directamente asignados a la cura de almas. Al mismo tiempo, debe considerar la frecuencia de las Misas en las diferentes parroquias e iglesias de su diócesis con vistas a liberar a un sacerdote para que celebre la Misa con una comunidad que no tiene sacerdote propio.[17] Se debe respetar la preeminencia de la celebración de la Misa, particularmente los domingos, sobre otras actividades pastorales.[18]

---

[12] Véase Pablo VI, Alocución dirigida a los obispos del centro de Francia, el 26 de marzo de 1977: AAS 69 (1977); "Procedan juiciosamente, pero sin multiplicar este tipo de asamblea dominical, como si fuera la solución ideal y la última oportunidad" (tr., DOL 449, núm. 3842).

[13] Véase *Directorio*, núm. 21.

[14] Véase *Ibíd.*, núm. 22.

[15] Véase *Ibíd.*, núm. 23.

[16] Véase *Ibíd.*, núm. 24.

[17] Véase *Ibíd.*, núm. 25; véase *SC* Ritos, Instrucción *Eucharisticum mysterium* (25 de mayo de 1967), núm. 26: AAS 59 (1967), 555; DOL 179, núm. 1255.

[18] Véase *Ibíd.*, núm. 25.

11   Before Sunday celebrations in the absence of a priest are begun, it should be explained to the faithful that although these celebrations substitute for the Sunday celebration of the eucharist, they should not be regarded as the ideal solution to present circumstances nor as a surrender to mere convenience. There should normally be only one assembly of this kind in each place on any given Sunday.[13]

12   Any confusion in the minds of the faithful between this kind of assembly and a eucharistic celebration must be carefully avoided. These celebrations should increase the desire of the faithful to be present at and participate in the celebration of the eucharist.[14]

13   To this end, the faithful need to understand that the eucharistic sacrifice cannot take place without a priest and that the eucharistic communion which they may receive in this kind of assembly is closely connected with the sacrifice of the Mass.[15]

OFFICES AND MINISTRIES

BISHOP

14   It is the responsibility of the diocesan bishop, after having received the advice of the diocesan presbyteral council and, if appropriate, other consultative bodies, to decide whether Sunday celebrations in the absence of a priest should be held on an occasional or regular basis in his diocese. He is to set out general and particular norms for such celebrations. They are to be held only when and where approved by the bishop and only under the pastoral ministry of a priest who has the responsibility for the particular community.[16]

15   Before the bishop decides on having such Sunday celebrations, he should consider the possibility of recourse to priests, even religious priests, who are not directly assigned to the care of souls. At the same time, he should consider the frequency of Masses in the various parishes and churches of the diocese with a view toward freeing a priest to celebrate Mass with a community without its own priest.[17] The preeminence of the celebration of the eucharist, particularly on Sunday, over other pastoral activities is to be respected.[18]

---

[12] See Paul VI, Address to bishops of central France, 26 March 1977: AAS 69 (1977); "Proceed judiciously, but without multiplying this type of Sunday assembly, as though it were the ideal solution and the last chance" (tr., DOL 449, no. 3842).

[13] See *Directory*, no. 21.

[14] See *Ibid.*, no. 22.

[15] See *Ibid.*, no. 23.

[16] See *Ibid.*, no. 24.

[17] See *Ibid.*, no. 25; see *SC* Rites, Instruction *Eucharisticum mysterium* (25 May 1967), no. 26: AAS 59 (1967), 555; DOL 179, no. 1255.

[18] See *Ibid.*, no. 25.

16   El obispo debe nombrar un delegado o un comité especial para asegurar que los ministros que han de dirigir la asamblea sean instruidos apropiadamente y que estas celebraciones se lleven a cabo correctamente. También debe procurar que los fieles de una parroquia o comunidad reciban la instrucción necesaria. Pero el obispo debe siempre velar que dichos fieles tengan la oportunidad de participar en la celebracion de la Misa tan frecuentemente como sea posible, y por lo menos varias veces al año.[19]

EL PÁRROCO

17   El párroco tiene la responsabilidad de informar al obispo de la necesidad de tales celebraciones en el área bajo su cuidado pastoral, preparar a los fieles, visitarles durante la semana, y en un momento conveniente celebrar los sacramentos con ellos, particularmente el sacramento de la penitencia. De esta manera dichas comunidades se darán cuenta que su asamblea dominical no es una asamblea "sin un sacerdote", sino una asamblea "en la ausencia de un sacerdote" o, dicho mejor, una asamblea "en espera de un sacerdote".[20]

EL DIÁCONO

18   Como ministro de la Palabra, que también es responsable de algunos sacramentos, el diácono está llamado de una manera especial a presidir estas asambleas dominicales. Puesto que el diácono ha sido ordenado para alimentar espiritualmente y hacer crecer el pueblo de Dios, a el le pertenece dirigir las oraciones, proclamar el evangelio, predicar la homilía y distribuir la comunión.[21]

19   Cuando un diácono preside la celebración dominical en ausencia de un sacerdote, actúa de la manera acostumbrada en lo que toca a saludos, oraciones, lectura del evangelio y homilía; también en lo que toca a dar la comunión, despedir y bendecir. Usa los ornamentos propios de su ministerio, esto es, el alba con la estola, y, si las circunstancias lo sugieren, la dalmática. Se sienta en la silla presidencial.[22]

20   El diácono siempre ha de ser ayudado por otros ministros quienes proclaman las Escrituras, le ayudan en la distribucion de la sagrada comunión, cantan salmos y otros himnos, proveen música instrumental, y preparan el lugar para la celebración.[23]

LOS LAICOS

21   En la ausencia tanto de un sacerdote como de un diácono, bajo la petición y recomendación del párroco, el obispo debe asignar a personas, laicas o religiosas,

---

[19] Véase *Ibíd.*, núm. 26.

[20] Véase *Ibíd.*, núm. 27.

[21] Véase *Ibíd.*, núm. 29; Véase Pablo VI, Motu proprio *Ad pascendum* (del 15 de agosto de 1972), núm. 1: MS 64 (1972), 534; DOL 319, núm. 2576.

[22] Véase *Ibíd.*, núm. 38.

[23] Véase *Ibíd.*, núm. 40.

16   The bishop should appoint a delegate or a special committee to insure that the ministers who will lead the assembly are properly instructed and that these celebrations are carried out correctly. He is also to see to it that the people of the parish or community receive the necessary instruction. But the bishop's concern should always be that the faithful involved have the opportunity to participate in the celebration of the eucharist as often as possible, and at least several times a year.[19]

PASTOR

17   The pastor has the responsibility of informing the bishop about the need for such celebrations in the area under his pastoral care, to prepare the faithful for them, to visit them during the week, and at a convenient time to celebrate the sacraments with them, particularly the sacrament of penance. In this way the communities involved will come to realize that their assembly on Sunday is not an assembly "without a priest," but an assembly "in the absence of a priest," or, better still, an assembly "in expectation of a priest."[20]

DEACON

18   As a minister of the Word, who also has a responsibility for the sacraments, the deacon is called in a special way to lead these Sunday assemblies. Since the deacon has been ordained for the nurture and increase of the people of God, it belongs to him to lead the prayers, to proclaim the gospel, to preach the homily, and to give communion.[21]

19   When a deacon presides at a Sunday celebration in the absence of a priest, he acts in the usual manner in regard to the greetings, the prayers, the gospel reading and homily, the giving of communion, and the dismissal and blessing. He wears the vestments proper to his ministry, that is, the alb with stole, and, as circumstances suggest, the dalmatic. He uses the presidential chair.[22]

20   The deacon is always to be assisted by other ministers who will proclaim the Scriptures, assist him in the distribution of holy communion, sing the psalms and other songs, provide instrumental music, and prepare the place for the celebration.[23]

LAYPERSONS

21   In the absence of both a priest and a deacon, upon the request and recommendation of the pastor, the bishop is to appoint persons, lay or religious, who

---

[19] See *Ibid.*, no. 26.

[20] See *Ibid.*, no. 27.

[21] See *Ibid.*, no. 29; see Paul VI, Motu proprio Ad pascendum (15 August 1972), no. 1: AAS 64 (1972), 534; DOL 319, no. 2576.

[22] See *Ibid.*, no. 38.

[23] See *Ibid.*, no. 40.

a quienes se les confíe el ministerio de dirigir estas celebraciones, es decir, hacer las oraciones, proclamar la palabra, y, cuando se incluya en la celebración, distribuir la sagrada comunión.

Estos ministros cumplen con sus responsabilidades en virtud de su bautismo y confirmación.[24] Se debe escoger a tales personas teniendo en cuenta su constancia en el modo de vivir según el evangelio y suponiendo que sean aceptadas por la comunidad de los fieles. El obispo hace el nombramiento de tales ministros y los asigna por un tiempo determinado. Se da a conocer su nombramiento a la comunidad por medio de una celebración litúrgica en la cual se ora en favor de los que han sido nombrados. Puede usarse con este fin el "Rito de la Bendición de Aquellos que Ejercen un Ministerio Pastoral"[25] que se encuentra en el *Bendicional*.

El párroco proporciona la instrucción apropiada y continua de estos ministros laicos y así como ayudarles en la preparación de celebraciones dignas.[26]

22   Los laicos nombrados para este ministerio deben de ver en el oficio confiado a ellos no tanto un honor cuanto una responsabilidad y, sobre todo, un servicio a sus hermanos y hermanas bajo la autoridad del párroco.[27] Ellos "deben hacer todo, y solamente, aquellas partes que les pertenecen por ese oficio".[28] Deben llevar a cabo su oficio con devoción sincera y con el decoro que exige tal responsabilidad y que por derecho espera de ellos el pueblo de Dios.[29]

23   El líder laico usa las fórmulas especiales indicadas en los ritos de saludo y bendición, no usa las palabras que le son propias a un sacerdote o diácono, y omite aquellos ritos, gestos, y textos que pueden asociarse fácilmente con la Misa y que pudieran dar la impresión que un/a laico/a es un ministro ordenado.[30]

24   El laico usa un vestido apropiado para su función o la vestidura prescrita por el obispo.[31] Un/a laico/a no se sienta en la silla presidencial.[32] Puesto que el altar es la mesa del sacrificio y del banquete pascual, en estas celebraciones solamente se usa para el rito de la comunión, cuando las hostias consagradas se colocan sobre él al principio de este rito.

Otros ministros asisten el líder en la proclamación de las escrituras, en la distribución de la sagrada comunión, en el canto de los salmos y otras canciones, con la música instrumental, y la preparación del lugar para la celebración.[33]

---

[24] Véase *CIC*, can. 230, §3.

[25] Véase El Ritual Romano, *Bendicional*, Parte VI, Capítulo 60.

[26] Véase *Directorio*, núm. 30.

[27] Véase *Ibíd.*, núm. 27; véase *CIC*, can. 230, §3.

[28] Véase *SC*, art. 28: DOL 1, núm. 28.

[29] Véase *Directorio*, núm. 31; véase *SC*, art. 29: DOL 1, núm. 29.

[30] Véase *Ibíd.*, núm. 39; véase *Instrucción General para la Liturgia de las Horas* (en adelante *IGLH*), núm. 258: DOL 426, núm. 3688; véase también El Ritual Romano, *Bendicional*, núms. 48, 119, 130, 181.

[31] Véase El Ritual Romano, *Ritual de la Sagrada Comunión y del Culto a la Eucaristia fuera de la Misa* (en adelante *SCCEFM*), núm. 20: DOL 266, núm. 2098.

[32] "El o ella no usarán la silla presidencial, sino otra silla preparada fuera del presbiterio" (*Directorio*, núm. 40). Véase también *IGLH*, núm. 258: DOL 426, núm. 3688.

[33] Véase *Directorio*, núm. 40.

are to be entrusted with the care of leading these celebrations, namely, with leading the prayers, with the ministry of the word, and, when it is to be included in the celebration, with giving holy communion.

These ministers carry out their responsibilities in virtue of their baptism and confirmation.[24] Such persons are to be chosen in view of the consistency of their way of life with the Gospel and in the expectation of their being acceptable to the community of the faithful. The appointment of such ministers is made by the bishop for a definite time. Their appointment is to be made known to the community by means of a liturgical celebration in which prayers are offered to God on behalf of those appointed. The Order for the Blessing of Those Who Exercise Pastoral Service[25] contained in the *Book of Blessings* may be used for this purpose.

The pastor is to see to the suitable and continuous instruction of these laypersons and to assist them in the preparation of worthy celebrations.[26]

22   The laypersons appointed as leaders should regard the office entrusted to them not so much as an honor but as a responsibility and, above all, as a service to their brothers and sisters under the authority of the pastors.[27] They "should do all of, but only, those parts which pertain to that office."[28] They should carry out their office with sincere devotion and the decorum demanded by such a responsibility and rightly expected of them by God's people.[29]

23   The leader who is a layperson uses the special forms indicated in the rites for the greeting and blessing, does not use words that are proper to a priest or deacon, and omits those rites, gestures, and texts that are too readily associated with the Mass and which might give the impression that the layperson is a sacred minister.[30]

24   The layperson wears vesture that is suitable for his or her function or the vesture prescribed by the bishop.[31] A layperson does not use the presidential chair.[32] Since the altar is the table of sacrifice and of the paschal banquet, its only use in one of these celebrations is for the rite of communion, when the eucharist is placed on it at the beginning of the communion rite.

The leader is always to be assisted by other ministers who will proclaim the Scriptures, assist in the distribution of holy communion, sing the psalms and other songs, provide instrumental music, and prepare the place for the celebration.[33]

---

[24] See *CIC*, can. 230, §3.

[25] See The Roman Ritual, *Book of Blessings,* Part VI, Chapter 60.

[26] See *Directory,* no. 30.

[27] See *Ibid.,* no. 27; see *CIC,* can. 230, §3.

[28] See *SC*, art. 28: DOL 1, no. 28.

[29] See *Directory,* no. 31; see *SC,* art. 29: DOL 1, no. 29.

[30] See *Ibid.,* no. 39; see *General Instruction of the Liturgy of the Hours* (hereafter *GILH*), no. 258: DOL 426, no. 3688; see also The Roman Ritual, *Book of Blessings,* nos. 48, 119, 130, 181.

[31] See The Roman Ritual, *Holy Communion and Worship of the Eucharist outside Mass* (hereafter *HCWEOM*), no. 20: DOL 266, no. 2098.

[32] "He or she does not use the presidential chair, but another chair prepared outside the sanctuary" (*Directory,* no. 40). See also *GILH,* no. 258: DOL 426, no. 3688.

[33] See *Directory,* no. 40.

FORMAS QUE PUEDE TOMAR LA CELEBRACION DOMINICAL

25   Un rasgo común de los ritos litúrgicos de la celebración dominical en la ausencia de un sacerdote es la proclamacion de la Palabra de Dios. Esta norma tiene por fin que se provea la riqueza de la Sagrada Escritura y de la oración de la Iglesia a los fieles reunidos el domingo aún fuera de la Misa. No se debe privar a los fieles de las lecturas que se leen en la Misa durante el curso del año, ni tampoco de las oraciones propias de los tiempos litúrgicos.[34]

26   Una segunda norma de las celebraciones que se proveen a continuación es la distribución de la sagrada comunión. Aunque los fieles no pueden participar en la celebración misma de la Misa, sin embargo pueden ser alimentados de la mesa del Señor, uniéndose espiritualmente a la comunidad de la cual se trajo la sagrada eucaristía para la celebración dominical.

No siempre se puede tener la distribución de la sagrada comunión durante la celebración dominical. Cuando este sea el caso, debe advertirse a los que están reunidos que, aún así, Cristo está verdaderamente presente tanto en la asamblea reunida como las Escrituras proclamadas.[35]

LITURGIA DE LAS HORAS

27   El primer modo que se da para la celebración dominical en la ausencia de un sacerdote es el de la Oración de la Mañana (Laudes) o de la Tarde (Vísperas) de *La Liturgia de las Horas*.[36] Porque "cuando se invita al pueblo a la liturgia de las horas y se reúne en unidad de corazón y de voz, muestran a la Iglesia en su celebración del misterio de Cristo".[37] Se puede distribuir la Sagrada Comunión al final de la Oración de la Mañana o de la Tarde.[38]

28   Aquellos que son responsables de la preparación y celebración de la Oración de la Mañana y de la Tarde deben estar familiarizados tanto con la *Instrucción General de la Liturgia de las Horas*[39] como con la estructura y contenido de *La Liturgia de las Horas*.[40]

29   Los textos provistos para la Oración de la Mañana (núms. 52–86) y para la Oración de la Tarde (núms. 87–121) se ofrecen como una forma común y a modo de ejemplo. Deben usarse siempre los textos propios de cada domingo contenidos en *La Liturgia de las Horas*. En circunstancias especiales, será necesario adaptar el rito. Cuando se hace esto, se sigue el rito de la celebración y se conservan los

---

[34] Véase *Ibíd.*, núm. 19.

[35] Véase *SC*, núm. 7: DOL 1, núm. 7.

[36] Véase *La Liturgia de las Horas* (en adelante *LDLH*).

[37] Véase *IGLH*, núm. 22: DOL 426, núm. 3452.

[38] Véase *Directorio*, núm. 33.

[39] Véase *LDLH*.

[40] Véase *Ibíd.*

FORMS THE SUNDAY CELEBRATION MAY TAKE

25 A common feature of the liturgical rites provided for the Sunday celebration in the absence of a priest is the proclamation of the Word of God. The aim of this provision is that the riches of Sacred Scripture and of the Church's prayer be amply provided to the faithful gathered on Sundays in various ways even apart from Mass. For the faithful should not be deprived of the readings that are read at Mass in the course of a year, nor of the prayers of the liturgical seasons.[34]

26 A second provision of the services which follow is the distribution of holy communion. Although the faithful cannot share in the actual celebration of the Mass, they nevertheless may be fed at the table of the Lord and be spiritually united to the community from which the holy eucharist was brought to the Sunday celebration.

According to circumstances, it may not always be possible to have the distribution of holy communion during the Sunday celebration. When this is the case, those present should be made to realize that, nevertheless, Christ is truly present in the gathered assembly and in the Scriptures that are proclaimed.[35]

LITURGY OF THE HOURS

27 The first form given for the Sunday celebration in the absence of a priest is that of Morning or Evening Prayer from *The Liturgy of the Hours*.[36] For "when the people are invited to the liturgy of the hours and come together in unity of heart and voice, they show forth the Church in its celebration of the mystery of Christ."[37] Holy communion may be given at the end of either Morning or Evening Prayer.[38]

28 Those responsible for the preparation and celebration of Morning or Evening Prayer should be familiar with the *General Instruction of the Liturgy of the Hours*[39] as well as the structure and contents of *The Liturgy of the Hours*.[40]

29 The texts provided for Morning Prayer (nos. 52–86) and Evening Prayer (nos. 87–121) are given as a common form and by way of example. The texts proper to each Sunday contained in *The Liturgy of the Hours* may always be used. In particular circumstances, it may be necessary to adapt the rite. When this is done,

---

[34] See *Ibid.*, no. 19.

[35] See *SC*, no. 7: DOL 1, no. 7.

[36] See *The Liturgy of the Hours* (hereafter *LOTH*), New York: Catholic Book Publishing Company, 1975–1976.

[37] See *GILH*, no. 22: DOL 426, no. 3452.

[38] See *Directory*, no. 33.

[39] See *LOTH*.

[40] See *Ibid.*

elementos esenciales, conforme a los esquemas que se ofrecen antes de la Oración de la Mañana y de la Tarde.

30 La música es parte esencial del oficio divino y siempre debe ser parte de cada celebración. Lo que se cante y el tipo de música que se use dependerá de los recursos musicales que se tengan y de la habilidad de los miembros de la asamblea para cantar.

31 Tanto la Oración de la Mañana como la Oración de la Tarde tienen la misma estructura y los siguientes elementos:

Ritos introductorios—Estos ritos (introducción e himno) sirven para que los fieles se constituyan en comunidad de culto.

Salmodia—El canto o la recitación de salmos y cánticos bíblicos, junto con sus respectivas antífonas y oraciones después de los salmos, permiten que la asamblea una su alabanza y acción de gracias a la de Cristo, nuestro abogado y sumo sacerdote.

Liturgia de la Palabra—La proclamación de las Sagradas Escrituras a los que están reunidos en la fe, les trae el mensaje de la buena nueva de salvación y redención en Cristo. La respuesta de la asamblea a la Palabra de Dios es una combinación de acción de gracias (Cántico de Zacarías o Cántico de María) por la bondad de Dios para nosotros, y de intercesión (Preces) por las necesidades de la Iglesia y del mundo.

[*Rito de Comunión*—La asamblea se une al misterio pascual de Cristo en la sagrada comunión. También es un signo y expresión de la unión de la asamblea con aquellos que pueden celebrar la Santa Misa en ese mismo día.]

Rito Conclusivo—Después de haber escuchado la Palabra de Dios (y de haberse alimentado con el Cuerpo y la Sangre de Cristo en la sagrada comunión) se despide a la asamblea con la bendición de Dios para que viva cristianamente.

LITURGIA DE LA PALABRA

32 Entre las formas de celebración en la tradición litúrgica, cuando no es posible tener Misa, se recomienda de manera especial la celebración de la Palabra de Dios.[41] Esta celebración puede concluir con la comunión eucarística, cuando sea posible. De este modo los fieles son alimentados tanto con la Palabra de Dios como con el cuerpo de Cristo. "Porque oyendo la Palabra de Dios conocen que las maravillas divinas que se proclaman culminan en el misterio pascual, cuyo memorial se celebra sacramentalmente en la Misa, y en el cual participan por la comunión".[42] Aún más, en ciertas circunstancias, la celebración dominical puede combinarse con la celebración del bautismo, del matrimonio, o bendiciones apropiadas a las necesidades de cada comunidad.[43]

---

[41] Véase *SC*, art. 35, 4: DOL 1, núm. 35.

[42] Véase *SCCEFM*, núm. 26.

[43] Véase *Directorio*, núm. 20.

the order of the celebration and the essential elements, as given in the outlines before Morning and Evening Prayer, are to be maintained.

30   Music is an essential part of the divine office and should always be a part of each celebration. The amount of singing and the type of music used will depend on the musical resources that are available and the abilities of the members of the assembly to sing.

31   Morning and Evening Prayer both have the same structure and the following elements:

Introductory Rites—These rites (Introduction and Hymn) serve to gather the faithful into a worshiping community.

Psalmody—The singing or recitation of psalms and scriptural canticles, along with their respective antiphons and psalm-prayers, permits the assembly to join its praise and thanksgiving to God to that of Christ, who is our great high priest and advocate.

Liturgy of the Word—The proclamation of the Scriptures to those gathered in faith brings them the message of the good news of salvation and redemption in Christ. The response of the assembly to the Word of God is a combination of thanksgiving (Canticle of Zechariah or Canticle of Mary) for God's goodness to us, and of intercession (Intercessions) for the needs of the Church and the world.

[*Communion Rite*—The assembly unites itself to the paschal mystery of Christ in holy communion. It is also a sign and expression of the assembly's union with those who are able to celebrate the eucharist on that particular day.]

Concluding Rite—After having heard the Word of God (and having been nourished by the body and blood of Christ in holy communion), the assembly is sent forth with God's blessing to live the Christian life.

LITURGY OF THE WORD

32   Among the forms of celebration found in liturgical tradition when Mass is not possible, a celebration of the Word of God is particularly recommended.[41] This celebration may be concluded by eucharistic communion, when possible. In this way the faithful can be nourished by both the Word of God and the body of Christ. "By hearing the Word of God the faithful learn that the marvels it proclaims reach their climax in the paschal mystery, of which the Mass is a sacramental memorial and in which they share by communion."[42] Further, in certain circumstances the Sunday celebration may be combined with the celebration of baptism, marriage, or blessings in ways that are suited to the needs of each community.[43]

---

[41] See *SC*, art. 35, 4: DOL 1, no. 35.
[42] See *HCWEOM*, no. 26.
[43] See *Directory*, no. 20.

33   El rito que ha de seguirse en esta forma de celebración dominical consiste en la celebración de la Palabra de Dios y puede también incluir la distribución de la sagrada comunión. Nada de lo que es propio de la Misa, y en particular la presentación de las ofrendas y la plegaria eucarística, puede incluirse en la celebración.[44]

34   Los textos de las oraciones y las lecturas de cada domingo, solemnidad, o fiesta del Señor están tomados del *Misal Romano (Sacramentario)* y del *Leccionario para la Misa*. Esto permite que los fieles sigan el ciclo del año litúrgico y oren y escuchen la Palabra de Dios en comunión con otras comunidades de la Iglesia.[45] Las oraciones del *Sacramentario* se incluyen en este ritual en el **Apéndice III**.

35   Las personas que son responsables de la preparación de esta forma de la celebración dominical deben estar familiarizadas con los principios que se encuentran en la Instrucción General del Misal Romano[46] y en la Introducción del *Leccionario para la Misa*.[47]

36   Lo que sigue es un esquema de los elementos de la celebración:

Ritos Introductorios—El fin de estos ritos es que los fieles se constituyan en una comunidad y que ellos se dispongan para la celebración.

Liturgia de la Palabra—Dios habla a su pueblo, les revela el misterio de la redención y salvación; el pueblo responde por medio de la profesión de fe y de las intercesiones generales.

Acción de Gracia—Se bendice a Dios por su gran gloria.

[*Rito de Comunión*—Este rito es una expresión y un cumplimiento de la comunión con Cristo y con sus miembros, especialmente con aquellos que en ese mismo día participan en el sacrificio de la Misa.]

Ritos Conclusivos—La bendición y la despedida hacen ver la conexión que existe entre la liturgia y la vida cristiana.[48]

---

[44] Véase *Ibíd.*, núm. 40.
[45] Véase *Ibíd.*, núm. 36.
[46] Véase *Misal Romano (Sacramentario)*.
[47] Véase *Leccionario para la Misa*, Nueva York: Centro Católico para Hispanos del Nordeste, 1982 y 1988.
[48] Véase *Directorio*, núm. 41.

33 The order to be followed in this form of the Sunday celebration consists of the celebration of the Word of God and may also include the giving of holy communion. Nothing that is proper to Mass, and particularly the presentation of the gifts and the eucharistic prayer, is to be inserted into the celebration.[44]

34 The texts of the prayers and readings for each Sunday, solemnity, or feast of the Lord are taken from *The Roman Missal (Sacramentary)* and the *Lectionary for Mass*. This allows the faithful to follow the cycle of the liturgical year and pray and listen to the Word of God in communion with the other communities of the Church.[45] The prayers from the *Sacramentary* are contained in **Appendix III** of this ritual.

35 Those who are responsible for the preparation and celebration of this form of the Sunday celebration should be familiar with the principles found in the General Instruction of the Roman Missal[46] and the Introduction of the *Lectionary for Mass*.[47]

36 The following is an outline of the elements of the celebration:

Introductory Rites—The purpose of these rites is to form the gathered faithful into a community and for them to dispose themselves for the celebration.

Liturgy of the Word—God speaks to his people, to disclose to them the mystery of redemption and salvation; the people respond through the profession of faith and the general intercessions.

Thanksgiving—God is blessed for his great glory.

[*Communion Rite*—This rite is an expression and accomplishment of communion with Christ and with his members, especially with those who on this same day take part in the eucharistic sacrifice.]

Concluding Rites—The blessing and dismissal point to the connection existing between the liturgy and the Christian life.[48]

---

[44] See *Ibid.,* no. 40.
[45] See *Ibid.,* no. 36.
[46] See *The Roman Missal (Sacramentary)*.
[47] See *Lectionary for Mass,* New York: Catholic Book Publishing Company, 1970.
[48] See *Directory,* no. 41.

ELEMENTOS INDIVIDUALES DE TODAS LAS CELEBRACIONES DOMINICALES

RITOS INICIALES

37   En la introducción al principio de la celebración, o en algún otro momento, el líder debe informar a la asamblea del sitio donde el párroco está celebrando la Misa ese domingo particular y animarla a unirse espiritualmente con esa comunidad.[49]

SALMODIA

38   El canto de salmos se incluye en cada celebración dominical. La salmodia constituye el corazón de la Oración de la Mañana y de la Tarde. Con el uso de los salmos la iglesia une la alabanza de la Iglesia en la tierra a la de los santos en el cielo. El salmo responsorial en la liturgia de la Palabra permite a la asamblea responder a la Palabra de Dios y meditarla.

LITURGIA DE LA PALABRA

39   Normalmente se hacen tres lecturas como en la Misa dominical. La primera va seguida de un salmo responsorial y la segunda de la aclamación antes del evangelio.

40   Las primeras dos lecturas son proclamadas por uno o dos lectores. El evangelio es proclamado por el líder. Cuando el líder es un/a laico/a, omite el saludo "El Señor esté con ustedes", antes del evangelio.

41   Para que la asamblea pueda recordar la Palabra de Dios, debe haber una explicación de las lecturas o un momento de silencio para reflexionar sobre lo que se ha escuchado. Ya que sólo un ministro ordenado puede predicar la homilía,[50] el párroco puede prepararla para que la lea el líder laico.[51] En otros casos cuando el obispo ha permitido predicar a un/a laico/a, esa persona puede ofrecer a los que están presentes una breve explicación del texto bíblico, para que entiendan por la fe el significado de la celebración.

42   La oración de los fieles incluye las intenciones que se indican en el **Apéndice I**.[52] Siempre se deben incluir las intenciones particulares propuestas por el obispo para toda la diócesis. Con frecuencia en esta oración se añaden peticiones por vocaciones al orden sagrado, por el obispo, y por el párroco.[53]

---

[49] Véase *Ibíd.*, núm. 42.
[50] Véase *CIC*, canones 766–767.
[51] Véase *Directorio*, núm. 43.
[52] Véase *IGMR*, núms. 45–47: DOL 208, núms. 1435–1437.
[53] Véase *Ibíd.*, núm. 44.

INDIVIDUAL PARTS OF ALL
SUNDAY CELEBRATIONS

INTRODUCTORY RITES

37   In the introduction at the beginning of the celebration, or at some other point, the leader should inform the assembly where the pastor is celebrating the eucharist on that particular Sunday and urge the assembly to unite itself in spirit with that community.[49]

PSALMODY

38   The singing of psalms is included in every Sunday celebration. Psalmody lies at the core of Morning and Evening Prayer. By the use of the psalms the Church unites the praise of the Church on earth to that of the saints. The responsorial psalm in the liturgy of the Word allows the assembly to respond to the Word of God and reflect upon it.

LITURGY OF THE WORD

39   Normally there are three readings as at the Sunday Mass. The first reading is followed by a responsorial psalm and the second reading is followed by the gospel acclamation.

40   The first two readings are proclaimed by one or two readers. The gospel is proclaimed by the leader. A layperson omits the greeting, "The Lord be with you," before the gospel.

41   In order that the assembly may retain the Word of God, there should be an explanation of the readings or a period of silence for reflection on what has been heard. Since only an ordained minister may give a homily,[50] the pastor may prepare a homily for the leader to read.[51] In other cases when a layperson has been permitted to preach by the bishop, he or she may give those present a brief explanation of the biblical text, so that they may understand through faith the meaning of the celebration.

42   The general intercessions follow the established series of intentions as is indicated in **Appendix I**.[52] Particular intentions for the whole diocese proposed by the bishop are always to be included. Intentions for vocations to sacred orders, for the bishop, and for the pastor should often be included in the general intercessions.[53]

---

[49] See *Ibid.*, no. 42.
[50] See *CIC*, can. 766–767.
[51] See *Directory*, no. 43.
[52] See *GIRM*, nos. 45–47: DOL 208, nos. 1435–1437.
[53] See *Ibid.*, no. 44.

ACCIÓN DE GRACIAS

43 En la celebración de la Oración de la Mañana y de la Tarde de *La Liturgia de las Horas,* se expresa la acción de gracias por medio de salmos y cánticos. Cuando se distribuye la sagrada comunión al final bien sea de la Oración de la Mañana o de la Tarde, un salmo, himno o letanía de alabanza y acción de gracias puede seguir al rito de la comunión.

44 En la celebración de una liturgia de la Palabra, acción de gracias forma parte de la respuesta comunitaria a la Palabra de Dios, y cuando se distribuye la comunión se expresa la gratitud por poder participar en este sacramento.

Mientras que el núm. 45 del *Directorio* ofrece varias posturas para la acción de gracias, la Conferencia Nacional de Obispos Católicos ha determinado que debe hacerse de la siguiente manera.

Después de la oración de los fieles, el líder invita a todos a dar gracias y entonces los fieles alaban la gloria y misericordia de Dios. Esto puede hacerse usando un salmo (por ejemplo, Salmos 99 [100], 112 [113], 117 [118], 135 [136], 146 [147], 150), un himno (por ejemplo, el *Gloria*), un cántico (por ejemplo, el Cántico de María [el Magníficat]), una letanía o una oración. El líder y los fieles están de pie y, de cara al altar, recitan juntos la acción de gracias. Textos adicionales para la acción de gracias se ofrecen en el **Apéndice II**.

A fin de evitar toda confusión entre la plegaria eucarística de la Misa y la oración de acción de gracias usada en estas celebraciones dominicales, estas oraciones de gratitud no deben tomar la forma de una plegaria eucarística ni de un prefacio.[54]

RITO DE COMUNIÓN

45 Cuando se distribuye la sagrada comunión, se deben observar las normas dictadas en *El Ritual Romano* para la comunión fuera de la Misa.[55] Se debe recordar con frecuencia a los fieles que aunque reciban la comunión fuera de la Misa están unidos al sacrificio eucarístico.[56]

46 Cuando no se puede celebrar la Misa, el párroco deberá procurar que haya frecuentes oportunidades de que se celebre el rito de la comunión. También debe proveer la celebración de la Misa a su debido tiempo en cada comunidad. Las hostias consagradas deben renovarse con frecuencia y reservarse en un lugar seguro.[57]

47 Para la comunión, si es posible, se debe usar el Pan eucarístico consagrado ese mismo domingo en una Misa celebrada en otro lugar. Un diácono o laico/a lo trae en un copón u otro recipiente y lo pone en el tabernáculo antes de la celebración. Puede usarse también el Pan eucarístico consagrado en la última Misa

---

[54] Véase *Ibíd.,* núm. 45.

[55] Véase *SCCEFM,* cap. 1: DOL 266, núms. 2092–2103.

[56] Véase *Directorio,* núm. 46.

[57] Véase *Ibíd.,* núm. 28.

ACT OF THANKSGIVING

43   At the celebration of Morning and Evening Prayer from *The Liturgy of the Hours,* thanksgiving is expressed by the psalms and canticles. When holy communion is distributed at the end of either Morning or Evening Prayer, a psalm, hymn, or litany of praise and thanksgiving may follow communion.

44   At a celebration of a liturgy of the Word, the act of thanksgiving is part of the communal response to the Word of God, and when communion is distributed it is an expression of gratitude for being able to participate in this sacrament.

While no. 45 of the *Directory* provides several positions for the thanksgiving, the National Conference of Catholic Bishops has determined that it should take place in the following manner.

After the general intercessions, the leader invites all to an act of thanksgiving, in which the faithful praise the glory and mercy of God. This can be done by use of a psalm (for example, Psalms 100, 113, 118, 136, 147, 150), a hymn (for example, the *Gloria*), a canticle (for example, the Canticle of Mary), a litany, or a prayer. The leader and the faithful stand and, facing the altar, together recite the thanksgiving. Additional texts for the act of thanksgiving are given in **Appendix II**.

In order to avoid all confusion between the eucharistic prayer of the Mass and the prayer of thanksgiving used in these Sunday celebrations, these prayers of thanksgiving are not to take the form of a eucharistic prayer or preface.[54]

COMMUNION RITE

45   When holy communion is to be given, the provisions given in *The Roman Ritual* for communion outside Mass are to be observed.[55] The faithful are to be frequently reminded that even when they receive communion outside Mass they are united to the eucharistic sacrifice.[56]

46   When Mass cannot be celebrated, the pastor will see to it that frequent opportunities are provided for giving holy communion. He is also to see to it that there is a celebration of the Eucharist in due time in each community. The consecrated hosts are to be renewed often and kept in a safe place.[57]

47   For communion, if at all possible, eucharistic Bread consecrated that same Sunday in a Mass celebrated elsewhere is used; a deacon or layperson brings it in a ciborium or another vessel and places it in the tabernacle before the celebration. Eucharistic Bread consecrated at the last Mass celebrated in the place of assembly

---

[54] See *Ibid.,* no. 45.
[55] See *HCWEOM,* ch. 1: DOL 266, nos. 2092–2103.
[56] See *Directory,* no. 46.
[57] See *Ibid.,* no. 28.

que se celebró en esa comunidad. Antes del Padrenuestro, el líder va al tabernáculo o lugar donde se ha reservado la eucaristía, toma el recipiente con el Cuerpo del Señor, y lo coloca sobre el altar.[58] El líder laico/a regresa entonces a su sitio y da comienzo al Padrenuestro. Después del saludo de la paz, el líder va al altar para invitar a la comunión.[59] Un diácono permanece cerca del altar para el Padrenuestro y el saludo de paz.

48   El Padrenuestro se recita siempre o se canta por todos, aunque no haya comunión. Se da el saludo de paz y, después de la comunión, "se puede observar algún momento de silencio, o se puede entonar algún salmo o cántico de alabanza".[60]

RITO DE CONCLUSIÓN

49   Antes de la conclusión de la celebración, se leen los anuncios u otras noticias relacionadas con la vida de la parroquia o de la diócesis.[61] La colecta de ofrendas monetarias por parte de la asamblea puede hacerse también en este momento.

PREPARACIONES PARA LA CELEBRACION DOMINICAL

50   El líder o alguna otra persona debe supervisar la preparación de la iglesia o del lugar donde se ha de tener la celebración. Se deben hacer los siguientes preparativos:

El *Leccionario* para la Misa se marca antes de la celebración. Puede ser llevado en la procesión de entrada, si la hay, o colocado en el ambón.

Cuando se celebra la Oración de la Mañana o de la Tarde o una liturgia de la Palabra sin la distribución de la sagrada comunión, se colocan velas prendidas cerca del ambón.

Las decoraciones de la iglesia o del lugar de la celebración deben estar de acuerdo con el tiempo litúrgico.

Cuando se distribuye la comunión en una iglesia u oratorio, se extiende un corporal sobre el altar, que debe de estar cubierto ya con un mantel. Cuando se distribuye la comunión en otros lugares, se prepara una mesa apropiada cubierta con un mantel. Se ponen velas prendidas en un lugar cercano o sobre el altar o mesa.[62]

51   Al preparar la celebración el párroco, junto con los diáconos y/o laicos/as que han sido nombrados, pueden hacer adaptaciones de acuerdo con el número de participantes en la celebración, la habilidad del líder y de los otros ministros, y la clase de instrumentos disponibles para la música y el canto.[63]

---

[58] Véase *Ibíd.*, núm. 47.

[59] Véase Carta de la Congregación para el Culto Divino y Disciplina de los Sacramentos, 24 de abril de 1991, Prot. N. CD 6/90.

[60] Véase *SCCEFM*, núm. 37.

[61] Véase *Directorio*, núm. 49.

[62] Véase *SCCEFM*, núm. 19: DOL 266, núm. 2097.

[63] Véase *Ibíd.*, núm. 37.

may also be used. Before the Lord's Prayer the leader goes to the tabernacle or place where the eucharist is reserved, takes the vessel with the body of the Lord, and places it upon the table of the altar.[58] A leader who is a layperson then returns to his or her chair and introduces the Lord's Prayer. After the sign of peace the leader goes to the altar for the invitation to communion.[59] A deacon remains at the altar for the Lord's Prayer and the sign of peace.

48   The Lord's Prayer is always recited or sung by all, even if there is to be no communion. The sign of peace may be exchanged. After communion, "a period of silence may be observed or a psalm or song of praise may be sung."[60]

CONCLUDING RITE

49   Before the conclusion of the assembly, announcements or notices relating to the life of the parish or the diocese are read.[61] The collection of monetary gifts of the assembly may also be done at this time.

PREPARATIONS FOR THE SUNDAY CELEBRATION

50   The leader or some other person should see to the preparation of the church or place where the celebration will take place. The following preparations are made:

The *Lectionary for Mass* is prepared before the celebration. It may be carried in the entrance procession, if there is one, or placed on the lectern.

When Morning or Evening Prayer or a liturgy of the Word is celebrated without the distribution of holy communion, lighted candles may be placed near the ambo.

The decorations of the church or place of celebration should be in accord with the liturgical season being celebrated.

When communion is given in a church or oratory, a corporal is to be placed on the altar, which is already covered with a cloth. When communion is given in other places, a suitable table is to be prepared and covered with a cloth. Lighted candles are placed on or near the altar or table.[62]

51   In preparing the celebration the pastor, together with the appointed deacons and/or laypersons, may make adaptations suited to the number of those who will take part in the celebration, the ability of the leader of the assembly and other ministers, and the kind of instruments available for the music and the singing.[63]

---

[58] See *Ibid.,* no. 47.

[59] See Letter from the Congregation for Divine Worship and the Discipline of the Sacraments, 24 April 1991, Prot. N. CD 6/90.

[60] See *HCWEOM,* no. 37.

[61] See *Directory,* no. 49.

[62] See *HCWEOM,* no. 19: DOL 266, no. 2097.

[63] See *Ibid.,* no. 37.

CAPITULO I

ORACION DE LA MAÑANA Y DE LA TARDE
[CON LA SAGRADA COMUNION]

CHAPTER I

MORNING AND EVENING PRAYER
[WITH HOLY COMMUNION]

ORACION DE LA MAÑANA
[CON LA SAGRADA COMUNION]

MORNING PRAYER
[WITH HOLY COMMUNION]

ESQUEMA DEL RITO

RITOS INTRODUCTORIOS
Introducción
Himno

SALMODIA
Antífona 1
Salmo
[Oración después del Salmo]
Antífona 2
Cántico del Antiguo Testamento
Antífona 3
Salmo
[Oración después del Salmo]

LITURGIA DE LA PALABRA
Primera Lectura
Salmo Responsorial
Segunda Lectura
Aclamación del Evangelio
Evangelio
Homilía o Reflexión sobre las Lecturas
Respuesta a la Palabra de Dios (Responsorio)
[Despedida de los Catecúmenos]
Cántico de Zacarías
Preces

	O RITO DE COMUNION
Padrenuestro	Padrenuestro
	El Saludo de Paz
	Invitación a Comulgar
	Comunión
Oración Conclusiva	Oración después de la Comunión

RITO DE CONCLUSION
Anuncios Breves
[Colecta de las Ofrendas Monetarias por parte de la Asamblea]
Bendición
Despedida

OUTLINE OF THE RITE

INTRODUCTORY RITES
    Introduction
    Hymn

PSALMODY
    Antiphon 1
    Psalm
    [Psalm-prayer]
    Antiphon 2
    Old Testament Canticle
    Antiphon 3
    Psalm
    [Psalm-prayer]

LITURGY OF THE WORD
    First Reading
    Responsorial Psalm
    Second Reading
    Gospel Acclamation
    Gospel
    Homily or Reflection on the Readings
    Response to the Word of God (Responsory)
    [Dismissal of Catechumens]
    Canticle of Zechariah
    Intercessions

	OR COMMUNION RITE
Lord's Prayer	Lord's Prayer
	Sign of Peace
	Invitation to Communion
	Communion
Concluding Prayer	Prayer after Communion

CONCLUDING RITE
    Brief Announcements
    [Collection of the Monetary Offerings of the Assembly]
    Blessing
    Dismissal

ORACION DE LA MAÑANA
[CON LA SAGRADA COMUNION]

52 Cuando la celebración dominical en la ausencia de un sacerdote toma la forma de la Oración de la Mañana de *La Liturgia de las Horas,* se puede usar lo siguiente como un texto común para todos los domingos. Sin embargo, cuando hay textos especiales para los domingos, solemnidades, y fiestas del Señor en *La Liturgia de las Horas,* se deben usar esos textos.

RITOS INTRODUCTORIOS

INTRODUCCIÓN

53 Cuando se ha reunido la asamblea, todos se ponen de pie mientras el líder, hace la señal de la cruz, canta o dice:

✛ **Dios mío, ven en mi auxilio.**

Todos responden:

Señor, date prisa en socorrerme.

Gloria al Padre, y al Hijo, y al Espíritu Santo.
Como era en el principio, ahora y siempre,
por los siglos de los siglos. Amén. (Aleluya.)

HIMNO

54 Se canta un himno apropiado. El siguiente himno es apropiado para los domingos en tiempo ordinario. En otros días se puede usar un himno apropiado al tiempo litúrgico o a la fiesta que se celebra.

1. **Oh criaturas del Señor,**
cantad con melodiosa voz:
¡Alabadle! ¡Aleluya!
Ardiente sol con tu fulgor,
oh, luna de suave esplendor:
¡Alabadle! ¡Alabadle!
¡Aleluya! ¡Aleluya! ¡Aleluya!

2. **Viento veloz, potente alud,**
nubes en claro cielo azul:
¡Alabadle! ¡Aleluya!
Suave dorado amanecer;

tu manto, noche al extender:
¡Alabadle! ¡Alabadle!
¡Aleluya! ¡Aleluya! ¡Aleluya!

3. **Fuentes de agua de cristal,**
a nuestro Creador cantad:
¡Alabadle! ¡Aleluya!
Oh, fuego eleva tu loor,
Tú que nos das luz y calor:
¡Alabadle! ¡Alabadle!
¡Aleluya! ¡Aleluya! ¡Aleluya!

MORNING PRAYER
[WITH HOLY COMMUNION]

52 When the Sunday celebration in the absence of a priest takes the form of *Morning Prayer* from *The Liturgy of the Hours,* the following may be used as a common text for all Sundays. However, when special texts for Sundays, solemnities, and feasts of the Lord are contained in *The Liturgy of the Hours* they may be used.

INTRODUCTORY RITES

INTRODUCTION

53 When the assembly has gathered, all stand while the leader, making the sign of the cross, sings or says:

✠ **God, come to my assistance.**

All respond:

Lord, make haste to help me.

Glory to the Father, and to the Son, and to the Holy Spirit: as it was in the beginning, is now, and will be for ever. Amen. (Alleluia.)

HYMN

54 A suitable hymn is sung. The following hymn is appropriate for the Sundays in Ordinary Time. On other days a hymn appropriate to the season or feast may be used.

On this day, the first of days,
God the Father's name we praise;
Who, creation's Lord and spring,
Did the world from darkness bring.

On this day the eternal Son
Over death his triumph won;
On this day the Spirit came
With his gifts of living flame.

Holy Spirit, you impart
Gifts of love to every heart;
Give us light and grace, we pray,
Fill our hearts this holy day.

4. Pródiga tierra maternal,
   que frutos brindas sin cesar:
   ¡Alabadle! ¡Aleluya!
   Rica cosecha, bella flor,
   magnificad al Creador:
   ¡Alabadle! ¡Alabadle!
   ¡Aleluya! ¡Aleluya! ¡Aleluya!

5. Con gratitud y con amor,
   cante la entera creación:
   ¡Alabadle! ¡Aleluya!
   Al Padre, al Hijo Redentor
   y al Eterno Consolador:
   ¡Alabadle! ¡Alabadle!
   ¡Aleluya! ¡Aleluya! ¡Aleluya!

SALMODIA

55 La antífona propia es entonada por el cantor, el coro, o toda la asamblea antes de cada salmo. La antífona es repetida por todos al final del salmo o después de cada estrofa. Todos pueden sentarse durante la salmodia.

El aleluya al final de la antífona se omite durante la Cuaresma.

Antífona 1   Por ti madrugo, Dios mío, para contemplar tu fuerza y tu gloria, (aleluya.)

Salmo 62 (63):2-9

Oh Dios, tú eres mi Dios, por ti madrugo,
mi alma está sedienta de ti;
mi carne tiene ansia de ti,
como tierra reseca, agostada, sin agua.
¡Cómo te contemplaba en el santuario
viendo tu fuerza y tu gloria!

Tu gracia vale más que la vida,
te alabarán mis labios.
Toda mi vida te bendeciré
y alzaré las manos invocándote.
Me saciaré como de enjundia y de manteca,
y mis labios te alabarán jubilosos.

En el lecho me acuerdo de ti
y velando medito en ti,
porque fuiste mi auxilio,
y a la sombra de tus alas canto con júbilo;

God, the blessed Three in One,
May thy holy will be done;
In thy word our souls are free.
And we rest this day with thee.

PSALMODY

55   The proper antiphon is sung by the cantor, the choir, or the entire assembly before each psalm. The antiphon may be repeated by all at the end of the psalm or after each strophe. All may be seated during the psalmody.

The alleluia at the end of an antiphon is omitted during Lent.

Antiphon 1   As morning breaks I look to you, O God, to be
            my strength this day, (alleluia.)

Psalm 63:2-9

O God, you are my God, for you I long;
for you my soul is thirsting.
My body pines for you
like a dry, weary land without water.
So I gaze on you in the sanctuary
to see your strength and your glory.

For your love is better than life,
my lips will speak your praise.
So I will bless you all my life,
in your name I will lift up my hands.
My soul shall be filled as with a banquet,
my mouth shall praise you with joy.

On my bed I remember you.
On you I muse through the night
for you have been my help;
in the shadow of your wings I rejoice.

mi alma está unida a ti,
y tu diestra me sostiene.

Gloria al Padre, y al Hijo, y al Espíritu Santo.
Como era en el principio, ahora y siempre,
por los siglos de los siglos. Amén.

ORACIÓN DESPUÉS DEL SALMO

56 Después de una breve pausa para orar en silencio, el líder puede ponerse de pie y decir:

Padre, creador de la luz eterna, concede esa misma luz a los que te invocan. Que nuestros labios te alaben, nuestras vidas proclamen tu bondad; nuestro trabajo te honre, y nuestras voces te celebren para siempre.

Se puede repetir la antífona.

Antífona 2   En medio de las llamas, los tres jóvenes, unánimes, cantaban: "Bendito sea el Señor", (aleluya).

Daniel 3:57-88, 56

**Criaturas todas del Señor, bendigan al Señor;
ensálcenlo con himnos por los siglos.
Ángeles del Señor, bendigan al Señor;
cielos, bendigan al Señor.
Aguas del espacio, bendigan al Señor;
ejércitos del Señor, bendigan al Señor.
Sol y luna, bendigan al Señor;
astros del cielo, bendigan al Señor.**

**Lluvia y rocío, bendigan al Señor;
vientos todos, bendigan al Señor.
Fuego y calor, bendigan al Señor;
fríos y heladas, bendigan al Señor.**

My soul clings to you;
your right hand holds me fast.

Glory to the Father, and to the Son, and to the Holy Spirit:
as it was in the beginning, is now, and will be for ever.
Amen.

PSALM-PRAYER

56   After a brief pause for silent prayer, the leader may stand and say:

Father, creator of unfailing light, give that same light to those
who call to you. May our lips praise you; our lives proclaim
your goodness; our work give you honor, and go our voices
celebrate you for ever.

The antiphon may be repeated.

Antiphon 2   From the midst of the flames the three young
men cried out with one voice: Blessed be God,
(alleluia).

Daniel 3:57-88, 56

Bless the Lord, all you works of the Lord.
Praise and exalt him above all forever.
Angels of the Lord, bless the Lord.
You heavens, bless the Lord.
All you waters above the heavens, bless the Lord.
All you hosts of the Lord, bless the Lord.
Sun and moon, bless the Lord.
Stars of heaven, bless the Lord.

Every shower and dew, bless the Lord.
All you winds, bless the Lord.
Fire and heat, bless the Lord.
Cold and chill, bless the Lord.

Rocíos y nevadas, bendigan al Señor;
témpanos y hielos, bendigan al Señor.
Escarchas y nieves, bendigan al Señor;
noche y día, bendigan al Señor.
Luz y tinieblas, bendigan al Señor;
rayos y nubes, bendigan al Señor.

Bendiga la tierra al Señor,
ensálcelo con himnos por los siglos.
Montes y cumbres, bendigan al Señor;
cuanto germina en la tierra, bendiga al Señor.
Manantiales, bendigan al Señor;
mares y ríos, bendigan al Señor.
Cetáceos y peces, bendigan al Señor;
aves del cielo, bendigan al Señor.
Fieras y ganados, bendigan al Señor;
ensálcenlo con himnos por los siglos.

Hijos de los hombres, bendigan al Señor;
bendiga Israel al Señor.
Sacerdotes del Señor, bendigan al Señor;
siervos del Señor, bendigan al Señor.
Almas y espíritus justos, bendigan al Señor;
santos y humildes de corazón, bendigan al Señor.
Ananías, Azarías y Misael, bendigan al Señor,
ensálcenlo con himnos por los siglos.

Bendigamos al Padre y al Hijo con el Espíritu Santo,
ensalcémoslo con himnos por los siglos.
Bendito el Señor en la bóveda del cielo,
alabado y glorioso y ensalzado por los siglos.

Se puede repetir la antífona.

Antífona 3   Que los hijos de Sión se alegren por su Rey,
(aleluya).

Dew and rain, bless the Lord.
Frost and chill, bless the Lord.
Ice and snow, bless the Lord.
Nights and days, bless the Lord.
Light and darkness, bless the Lord.
Lightnings and clouds, bless the Lord.

Let the earth bless the Lord.
Praise and exalt him above all forever.
Mountains and hills, bless the Lord.
Everything growing from the earth, bless the Lord.
You springs, bless the Lord.
Seas and rivers, bless the Lord.
You dolphins and all water creatures, bless the Lord.
All you birds of the air, bless the Lord.
All you beasts, wild and tame, bless the Lord.
You sons of men, bless the Lord.

O Israel, bless the Lord.
Praise and exalt him above all forever.
Priests of the Lord, bless the Lord.
Servants of the Lord, bless the Lord.
Spirits and souls of the just, bless the Lord.
Holy men of humble heart, bless the Lord.
Hananiah, Azariah, Mishael, bless the Lord.
Praise and exalt him above all forever.

Let us bless the Father, and the Son, and the Holy Spirit.
Let us praise and exalt him above all forever.
Blessed are you, Lord, in the firmament of heaven.
Praiseworthy and glorious and exalted above all forever.

The antiphon may be repeated.

Antiphon 3   Let the people of Zion rejoice in their King,
(alleluia).

Salmo 149

Canten al Señor un cántico nuevo,
resuene su alabanza en la asamblea de los fieles;
que se alegre Israel por su Creador,
los hijos de Sión por su Rey.
Alaben su nombre con danzas,
cántenle con tambores y cítaras.

Porque el Señor ama a su pueblo
y adorna con la victoria a los humildes.
Que los fieles festejen su gloria
y canten jubilosos en filas:
con vítores a Dios en la boca
y espadas de dos filos en las manos.

Para tomar venganza de los pueblos
y aplicar el castigo a las naciones,
sujetando a los reyes con argollas,
a los nobles con esposas de hierro.
Ejecutar la sentencia dictada
es un honor para todos sus fieles.

Gloria al Padre, y al Hijo, y al Espíritu Santo.
Como era en el principio, ahora y siempre,
por los siglos de los siglos. Amen.

ORACIÓN DESPUÉS DEL SALMO

57 Después de una breve pausa para orar en silencio, el líder puede ponerse de pie y decir:

Que Israel se regocije en ti, Señor, y te reconozca como
creador y redentor. Confiamos en tu fidelidad y proclamamos
tus maravillosas verdades de salvación. Que tu amorosa bon-
dad nos cubra ahora y siempre.

Se puede repetir la antífona.

Psalm 149

Sing a new song to the Lord,
his praise in the assembly of the faithful.
Let Israel rejoice in its maker,
let Zion's sons exult in their king.
Let them praise his name with dancing
and make music with timbrel and harp.

For the Lord takes delight in his people.
He crowns the poor with salvation.
Let the faithful rejoice in their glory,
shout for joy and take their rest.
Let the praise of God be on their lips
and a two-edged sword in their hand,

to deal out vengeance to the nations
and punishment on all the peoples;
to bind their kings in chains
and their nobles in fetters of iron;
to carry out the sentence pre-ordained;
this honor is for all his faithful.

Glory to the Father, and to the Son, and to the Holy Spirit:
as it was in the beginning, is now, and will be for ever.
Amen.

PSALM-PRAYER

57   After a brief pause for silent prayer, the leader may stand and say:

Let Israel rejoice in you, Lord, and acknowledge you as creator and redeemer. We put our trust in your faithfulness and proclaim the wonderful truths of salvation. May your loving kindness embrace us now and for ever.

The antiphon may be repeated.

LITURGIA DE LA PALABRA

58 Los domingos la Liturgia de la Palabra se celebra como en la Misa.

Las lecturas y el salmo son los que se han asignado en el *Leccionario para la Misa* para ese domingo particular.

Antes de que se proclamen las lecturas, se puede ofrecer una breve introducción con el fin de estimular la atención de los que escuchan, poner las lecturas dentro de su contexto, y hacer ver las conexiones entre las lecturas.

PRIMERA LECTURA

59 Un/a lector/a proclama la primera lectura.

SALMO RESPONSORIAL

60 Después de la primera lectura, se canta el salmo asignado en el Leccionario. Si es necesario, se puede escoger otro salmo que esté en armonía con el texto de la primera lectura.

SEGUNDA LECTURA

61 Si se tienen tres lecturas, el/la lector/a proclama luego la segunda lectura.

ACLAMACIÓN DEL EVANGELIO

62 Se canta la aclamación del evangelio que se da en el Leccionario antes de proclamar el evangelio.

EVANGELIO

63 Un diácono proclama el evangelio de la manera usual. Sin embargo, un/a laico/a omite el saludo "El Señor esté con ustedes", antes de leer el evangelio.

HOMILÍA O REFLEXIÓN SOBRE LAS LECTURAS

64 Cuando el líder es diácono, éste ofrece la homilía.

Cuando el líder es un/a laico/a que no ha sido delegado/a para predicar, el párroco puede preparar una homilía para que se lea durante la celebración.

En otros casos, cuando el/la laico/a ha sido delegado/a por el obispo para predicar, él o ella puede ofrecer a los presentes una breve explicación del texto bíblico, para que puedan comprender por la fe el significado de la celebración.

LITURGY OF THE WORD

58   On Sundays the Liturgy of the Word takes place as at Mass.

The readings and the psalm are those assigned in the *Lectionary for Mass* for that particular Sunday.

Before the readings are proclaimed, a brief introduction may be given in order to stimulate the attention of the listeners, to put the readings into context, and to point out connections between the readings.

FIRST READING

59   A reader proclaims the first reading.

RESPONSORIAL PSALM

60   After the first reading, the psalm assigned in the Lectionary is sung. If necessary, another psalm, which is in harmony with the text of the first reading, may be chosen.

SECOND READING

61   If there are to be three readings, a reader then proclaims the second reading.

GOSPEL ACCLAMATION

62   The gospel acclamation given in the Lectionary is sung before the proclamation of the gospel.

GOSPEL

63   A deacon proclaims the gospel in the usual manner. However, a layperson omits the greeting, "The Lord be with you," before reading the gospel.

HOMILY OR REFLECTION ON THE READINGS

64   A leader who is a deacon gives a homily.

When the leader is a layperson who has not been delegated to preach, the pastor may prepare a homily to be read during the celebration.

In other cases, when a layperson has been delegated to preach by the bishop, he or she may give those present a brief explanation of the biblical text, so that they may understand through faith the meaning of the celebration.

Después de la homilía hay un momento de silencio sagrado para reflexionar sobre la Palabra de Dios.

Respuesta a la Palabra de Dios (Responsorio)

65   Como respuesta a la Palabra de Dios se puede cantar un canto responsorial o un responsorio corto como se da más abajo. El responsorio se puede omitir. Pueden substituirse otros cantos que tengan el mismo propósito y carácter.

℣. **Cristo, Hijo de Dios vivo, ten piedad de nosotros.**
℟. Cristo, Hijo de Dios vivo, ten piedad de nosotros.

℣. **Tú que estás sentado a la derecha del Padre.**
℟. Ten piedad de nosotros.

℣. **Gloria al Padre, y al Hijo, y al Espiritu Santo.**
℟. Cristo, Hijo de Dios vivo, ten piedad de nosotros.

Despedida de los Catecúmenos

66   Si se va a distribuir la sagrada comunión y hay algunos catecúmenos presentes, se les puede despedir en este momento usando las opciones A o B; si tienen que quedarse para la conclusión de la Oración de la Mañana, se puede usar la opción C.

A   Para la despedida se puede usar la siguiente fórmula u otra parecida.

Catecúmenos, vayan en paz, y que el Señor los acompañe.

Catecúmenos:

Demos gracias a Dios.

B   Como otra fórmula opcional para despedir a los catecúmenos, el líder puede usar estas u otras palabras semejantes.

Mis queridos amigos, esta comunidad les envía ahora a reflexionar más profundamente sobre la palabra de Dios que han compartido con nosotros hoy. Pueden estar seguros de nuestro afecto, apoyo y oraciones por ustedes. Con gusto esperamos el día en que compartan plenamente de la Mesa del Señor.

After the homily there may be a period of sacred silence for reflection on the Word of God.

RESPONSE TO THE WORD OF GOD (RESPONSORY)

65   As a response to the Word of God a responsorial chant or short responsory, as given below, may be sung; however, the responsory may be omitted. Other chants with the same purpose and character may be substituted.

℣. **Christ, Son of the living God, have mercy on us.**
℟. Christ, Son of the living God, have mercy on us.

℣. **You are seated at the right hand of the Father,**
℟. have mercy on us.

℣. **Glory to the Father, and to the Son,
and to the Holy Spirit.**
℟. Christ, Son of the living God, have mercy on us.

DISMISSAL OF CATECHUMENS

66   If holy communion is to be distributed and there are catechumens present, they may be dismissed at this point by use of option A or B; if they are to remain for the conclusion of Morning Prayer, option C may be used.

A   For the dismissal the following or similar words are used.

Catechumens, go in peace, and may the Lord remain with you always.

Catechumens:

Thanks be to God.

B   As an optional formulary for dismissing the catechumens, the minister may use these or similar words.

My dear friends, this community now sends you forth to reflect more deeply upon the Word of God which you have shared with us today. Be assured of our loving support and prayers for you. We look forward to the day when you will share fully in the Lord's Table.

C   Si los catecúmenos tienen que quedarse durante la distribución de la sagrada comunión y la conclusion de la Oración de la Mañana, se les debe recordar que no pueden participar como lo hacen los bautizados. El líder les puede recordar esto con estas palabras u otras parecidas.

Aunque todavía no pueden ustedes participar de la sagrada comunión, quédense con nosotros como un signo de nuestra esperanza de que todos los hijos de Dios comerán y beberán con el Señor y trabajarán con su Espíritu para renovar la faz de la tierra.

CÁNTICO DE ZACARÍAS

67   Todos se ponen de pie y cantan el siguiente cántico evangélico.

La siguiente antífona, la antífona propia del día. u otro texto apropiado, puede cantarse antes del cántico, primero por el cantor o el coro, y luego por la asamblea. Puede repetirse después de cada estrofa o al final del cántico.

Antífona   Dios ha suscitado para nosotros un Salvador poderoso.

Lucas 1:68-79

✝ **Bendito sea el Señor, Dios de Israel,**
porque ha visitado y redimido a su pueblo,
suscitándonos una fuerza de salvación
en la casa de David, su siervo,
según lo había predicho desde antiguo
por boca de sus santos profetas.

Es la salvación que nos libra de nuestros enemigos
y de la mano de todos los que nos odian;
realizando la misericordia
que tuvo con nuestros padres,
recordando su santa alianza
y el juramento que juró a nuestro padre Abrahán.

C If the catechumens are to remain for the distribution of holy communion and the conclusion of Morning Prayer, they should be reminded that they cannot partake as the baptized do. They may be reminded of this by the minister in these or similar words.

Although you cannot yet partake of holy communion, stay with us as a sign of our hope that all God's children will eat and drink with the Lord and work with the Holy Spirit to re-create the face of the earth.

CANTICLE OF ZECHARIAH

67 All stand and sing the following gospel canticle.

The following antiphon, the antiphon proper to the day, or another suitable text, may be sung before the canticle, first by the cantor or the choir, and then by the people. It may be repeated after each strophe or at the end of the canticle.

Antiphon   God has raised up for us a mighty Savior.

Luke 1:68-79

✠ **Blessed be the Lord, the God of Israel;**
he has come to his people and set them free.

He has raised up for us a mighty savior,
born of the house of his servant David.

Through his holy prophets he promised of old
that he would save us from our enemies,
from the hands of all who hate us.

He promised to show mercy to our fathers
and to remember his holy covenant.

Para concedernos que, libres de temor,
arrancados de la mano de los enemigos,
le sirvamos con santidad y justicia,
en su presencia, todos nuestros días.

Y a ti, niño, te llamarán profeta del Altísimo,
porque irás delante del Señor
a preparar sus caminos,
anunciando a su pueblo la salvación,
el perdón de sus pecados.

Por la entrañable misericordia de nuestro Dios,
nos visitará el sol que nace de lo alto,
para iluminar a los que viven en tinieblas
y en sombra de muerte,
para guiar nuestros pasos
por el camino de la paz.

Gloria al Padre, y al Hijo, y al Espíritu Santo.
Como era en el principio, ahora y siempre,
por los siglos de los siglos. Amén.

Se puede repetir la antífona.

PRECES

68   Las preces siguen al cántico. El líder invita primero a la asamblea a orar,
luego otro ministro canta o recita las intenciones.

Se pueden usar las intenciones propias dadas en *La Liturgia de las Horas* en
lugar de las siguientes, o se pueden añadir otras intenciones.

El líder dice:

Cristo es el sol que nunca se pone, la verdadera luz que alumbra a cada persona. Invoquémoslo en alabanza:

℟. ¡Oh Señor, vida y salvacion nuestra!

Otro ministro dice:

Creador del universo, al darte gracias por el nuevo día que ahora empieza, te pedimos que el recuerdo de tu santa resurrección sea nuestro gozo durante este domingo. ℟.

This was the oath he swore to our father Abraham:
to set us free from the hands of our enemies,
free to worship him without fear,
holy and righteous in his sight
all the days of our life.

You, my child, shall be called the prophet of the Most High;
for you will go before the Lord to prepare his way,
to give his people knowledge of salvation
by the forgiveness of their sins.

In the tender compassion of our God
the dawn from on high shall break upon us,
to shine on those who dwell in darkness and the shadow of
   death,
and to guide our feet into the way of peace.

Glory to the Father, and to the Son, and to the Holy Spirit:
as it was in the beginning, is now, and will be for ever.
Amen.

> The antiphon may be repeated.

INTERCESSIONS

> 68   The intercessions follow the canticle. The leader first invites the assembly to pray, then another minister sings or recites the intentions.

> The proper intentions given in *The Liturgy of the Hours* may be used in place of the following, or other intentions may be added.

> The leader says:

Christ is the sun that never sets, the true light that shines on every person. Let us call out to him in praise:

℞. Lord, you are our life and our salvation.

> Another minister says:

Creator of the stars, we thank you for your gift, the first rays of the dawn, and we commemorate your resurrection. ℞.

Que tu Espíritu Santo nos enseñe a cumplir tu voluntad, y que tu sabiduría dirija hoy nuestras acciones. ℟.

Cada domingo concédenos la alegría de reunirnos como tu pueblo, alrededor de la mesa de tu Palabra [y de tu Cuerpo]. ℟.

Que sepamos contemplar las maravillas que tu generosidad nos concede, y vivamos durante todo el día en acción de gracias. ℟.

69 Si no se va a distribuir la sagrada comunión, la celebración continúa en el núm. 81.

RITO DE COMUNION

70 El líder va al lugar donde se reserva el sacramento, toma el recipiente o copón que contiene el Cuerpo del Señor, lo coloca en el altar y hace una genuflexión.

PADRENUESTRO

71 El líder invita a todes los presentes a cantar o decir el Padrenuestro con estas u otras palabras semejantes:

A **Fieles a la recomendación del Salvador
y siguiendo su divina enseñanza,
nos atrevemos a decir:**

B **Llenos de alegría por ser hijos de Dios,
digamos confiadamente
la oración que Cristo nos enseñó:**

C **El amor de Dios ha sido derramado
en nuestros corazones
con el Espíritu Santo que se nos ha dado;
digamos con fe y esperanza:**

D **Antes de participar en el banquete de la Eucaristía,
signo de reconciliación
y vínculo de unión fraterna,
oremos juntos como el Señor nos ha enseñado:**

May your Holy Spirit teach us to do your will today, and may your Wisdom guide us always. ℟.

Each Sunday give us the joy of gathering as your people, around the table of your Word [and your Body]. ℟.

From our hearts we thank you, for your countless blessings. ℟.

> 69   If holy communion is not to be distributed, the service continues at no. 81.

COMMUNION RITE

> 70   The leader goes to the place where the sacrament is reserved, takes the vessel or ciborium containing the body of the Lord, places it on the altar and genuflects.

LORD'S PRAYER

> 71   The leader invites all present to sing or say the Lord's Prayer in these or similar words:

A   **Let us pray with confidence to the Father in the words our Savior gave us:**

B   **Jesus taught us to call God our Father, and so we have the courage to say:**

C   **Let us ask our Father to forgive our sins and bring us to forgive those who sin against us.**

D   **Let us pray for the coming of the kingdom as Jesus taught us.**

El líder continúa, junto con la asamblea:

Padre nuestro, que estás en el cielo,
santificado sea tu Nombre;
venga a nosotros tu reino;
hágase tu voluntad en la tierra como en el cielo.
Danos hoy nuestro pan de cada día;
perdona nuestras ofensas,
como también nosotros perdonamos
a los que nos ofenden;
no nos dejes caer en la tentación,
y líbranos del mal.

EL SALUDO DE PAZ

72 El líder puede invitar a la asamblea a darse el saludo de paz con estas u otras palabras semejantes:

En el amor de Cristo, démonos unos a otros un saludo de paz.

Todos, según la costumbre del lugar, se dan la paz.

INVITACIÓN A COMULGAR

73 El líder hace genuflexión, toma el pan consagrado y, sosteniéndolo un poco elevado sobre el recipiente o copón, lo muestra al pueblo, diciendo:

Este es el Cordero de Dios,
que quita el pecado del mundo.
Dichosos los invitados a la cena del Señor.

Y, juntamente con el pueblo, añade:

Señor, no soy digno
de que entres en mi casa,
pero una palabra tuya
bastará para sanarme.

COMUNIÓN

74 El líder dice en secreto:

El Cuerpo de Cristo me guarde para la vida eterna.

The leader continues with the people:

Our Father, who art in heaven,
hallowed be thy name;
thy kingdom come;
thy will be done on earth as it is in heaven.
Give us this day our daily bread;
and forgive us our trespasses
as we forgive those who trespass against us;
and lead us not into temptation,
but deliver us from evil.

SIGN OF PEACE

72   The leader may invite the people to exchange the sign of peace in these or similar words:

In the love of Christ, let us offer one another a sign of peace.

All make an appropriate sign of peace, according to local custom.

INVITATION TO COMMUNION

73   The leader genuflects. Taking the host, the minister raises it slightly over the vessel or ciborium and, facing the people, says:

This is the Lamb of God
who takes away the sins of the world.
Happy are those who are called to his supper.

The communicants say:

Lord, I am not worthy to receive you
but only say the word and I shall be healed.

COMMUNION

74   The leader says quietly:

May the body of Christ bring me to everlasting life.

Y comulga reverentemente el Cuerpo de Cristo.

75   Después el líder (y los otros ministros especiales de la comunión) toma el recipiente o copón, se acerca a los que quieren comulgar y les presenta el pan consagrado, que sostiene un poco elevado, diciendo a cada uno de ellos:

El Cuerpo de Cristo.

El que va a comulgar responde Amén y comulga.

76   Durante la distribución de la comunión, se puede cantar un himno.

77   Acabada la comunión, el líder o un ministro especial de la comunión consume cualquier fragmento que quede o lo pone en el recipiente o copón y se lava las manos si lo juzga necesario. Si quedan hostias adicionales, el ministro o hace una genuflexión y las pone de nuevo en el tabernáculo o las pone otra vez en el recipiente o copón y lo devuelve a la iglesia de donde había traido la eucaristía para la distribución.

78   Se puede guardar unos momentos de silencio o cantar un salmo o cántico o una letanía de alabanza.

Oración después de la Comunión

79   El líder dice luego la Oración después de la Comunión apropiada del **Apéndice III** o una de las oraciones en el **Apéndice IV.** El líder primero invita a la asamblea a orar, diciendo:

Oremos.

Todos los presentes oran en silencio por un corto tiempo. Luego el líder dice la oración. Al final de la oración la asamblea responde **Amén**.

80   El servicio concluye con anuncios breves [la colecta de las ofrendas monetarias por parte de la asamblea], la bendición, y la despedida como en los núms. 83–86.

El Padrenuestro

81   Si no se distribuye la sagrada comunión, el líder invita a todos a rezar el Padrenuestro con estas u otras palabra semejantes:

A   **Fieles a la recomendación del Salvador
y siguiendo su divina enseñanza,
nos atrevemos a decir:**

The leader reverently consumes the body of Christ.

75   The leader (and other special ministers of holy communion) then takes the vessel or ciborium with the eucharist and goes to the communicants. The minister takes a host for each one, raises it slightly, and says:

The body of Christ.

The communicant answers Amen and receives communion.

76   During the distribution of communion, a hymn may be sung.

77   After communion the leader or a special minister of holy communion consumes any fragments which are found or puts them in the vessel or ciborium and then washes his or her hands if need be. If additional hosts remain, the minister either genuflects and puts them back into the tabernacle or else puts them back into the vessel or ciborium and returns it to the church from which he or she had obtained the eucharist for distribution.

78   A period of silence may now be observed, or a psalm, song of praise, or litany of praise may be sung.

PRAYER AFTER COMMUNION

79   The leader then says the proper Prayer after Communion from **Appendix III** or one of the prayers in **Appendix IV**. The leader first invites the assembly to pray, saying:

Let us pray.

All present pray in silence for a short time. Then the leader says the prayer. At the end of the prayer the assembly responds **Amen**.

80   The service concludes with the brief announcements [the collection of the monetary offerings of the assembly], the blessing, and the dismissal at nos. 83–86.

LORD'S PRAYER

81   If holy communion is not distributed, the leader invites all to pray the Lord's Prayer in these or similar words:

A   **Let us pray with confidence to the Father in the words our Savior gave us:**

B   **Llenos de alegría por ser hijos de Dios,
digamos confiadamente
la oración que Cristo nos enseñó:**

C   **El amor de Dios ha sido derramado
en nuestros corazones
con el Espíritu Santo que se nos ha dado;
digamos con fe y esperanza:**

> El líder continúa, junto con la asamblea:

**Padre nuestro, que estás en el cielo,
santificado sea tu Nombre;
venga a nosotros tu reino;
hágase tu voluntad en la tierra como en el cielo.
Danos hoy nuestro pan de cada día;
perdona nuestras ofensas,
como también nosotros perdonamos
a los que nos ofenden;
no nos dejes caer en la tentación,
y líbranos del mal.**

ORACIÓN CONCLUSIVA

> 82   El líder dice la Oración conclusiva. Se puede usar la Oración del Día (de *La Liturgia de las Horas*), que se da en el **Apéndice III**, o la siguiente oración:

**Padre amoroso,
escucha nuestras oraciones.
Ayúdanos a conocer tu voluntad
y a cumplirla con valor y fe.**

**Por nuestro Señor Jesucristo, tu Hijo,
que vive y reina contigo
en la unidad del Espíritu Santo y es Dios
por los siglos de los siglos.**

℟. Amén.

B   Jesus taught us to call God our Father, and so we have the courage to say:

C   Let us ask our Father to forgive our sins and bring us to forgive those who sin against us.

D   Let us pray for the coming of the kingdom as Jesus taught us.

> The leader continues with the people:

Our Father, who art in heaven,
hallowed be thy name;
thy kingdom come;
thy will be done on earth as it is in heaven.
Give us this day our daily bread;
and forgive us our trespasses
as we forgive those who trespass against us;
and lead us not into temptation,
but deliver us from evil.

CONCLUDING PRAYER

> 82   The leader says the Concluding Prayer. The prayer may be the Prayer of the Day (from *The Liturgy of the Hours*), given in **Appendix III**, or the following prayer may be used:

Father of love,
hear our prayers.
Help us to know your will
and to do it with courage and faith.

Grant this through our Lord Jesus Christ, your Son,
who lives and reigns with you and the Holy Spirit,
one God, for ever and ever.

℟. Amen.

RITO DE CONCLUSION

ANUNCIOS BREVES

83   Antes de despedir a la congregación se pueden hacer breves anuncios que afectan la vida y las actividades de la parroquia.

[COLECTA DE LAS OFRENDAS MONETARIAS POR PARTE DE LA ASAMBLEA]

84   Se pueden recoger las ofrendas de los fieles según las normas y las necesidades indicadas por el Ordinario local.

BENDICIÓN

85   Cuando el líder es diácono, dice:

El Señor esté con ustedes.

Todos responden:

Y con tu espíritu.

Bendice al pueblo usando la siguiente bendición. Puede también usar una de las bendiciones en el **Apéndice V**, o una de las bendiciones solemnes o de las oraciónes sobre el pueblo en el *Sacramentario*.

La bendición de Dios todopoderoso, Padre, Hijo, ✠ y Espíritu Santo descienda sobre ustedes.

Todos:

Amén.

Cuando el líder es laico/a, mientras se santigua dice:

El Señor nos bendiga, nos guarde de todo mal y nos lleve a la vida eterna.

Todos:

Amén.

CONCLUDING RITE

BRIEF ANNOUNCEMENTS

83   Brief announcements concerning parish life and activities may be made before the congregation is dismissed.

[COLLECTION OF THE MONETARY OFFERINGS OF THE ASSEMBLY]

84   The offerings of the faithful may be collected in accordance with the norms and the necessities indicated by the local Ordinary.

BLESSING

85   A leader who is a deacon says:

The Lord be with you.

All respond:

And also with you.

He blesses the people using the following blessing. He may also use one of the blessings in **Appendix V**, or one of the solemn blessings or prayers over the people in the *Sacramentary*.

**May almighty God bless you,
the Father, and the Son, ☩ and the Holy Spirit.**

All:

Amen.

A leader who is a layperson makes the sign of the cross on himself or herself and says:

**May the Lord bless us,
protect us from all evil
and bring us to everlasting life.**

All:

Amen.

DESPEDIDA

86   El líder luego añade:

Vayan en paz.

Todos:

Demos gracias a Dios.

DISMISSAL

86　The leader then adds:

Go in peace.

All:

Thanks be to God.

ORACION DE LA TARDE
[CON LA SAGRADA COMUNION]

EVENING PRAYER
[WITH HOLY COMMUNION]

ESQUEMA DEL RITO

RITOS INTRODUCTORIOS
    Introducción
    Himno

SALMODIA
    Antífona 1
    Salmo
    [Oración después del Salmo]
    Antífona 2
    Salmo
    [Oración después del Salmo]
    Antífona 3
    Cántico del Nuevo Testamento

LITURGIA DE LA PALABRA
    Primera Lectura
    Salmo Responsorial
    Segunda Lectura
    Aclamación del Evangelio
    Evangelio
    Homilía o Reflexión sobre las Lecturas
    Respuesta a la Palabra de Dios (Responsorio)
    [Despedida de los Catecúmenos]
    Cántico de Zacarías
    Preces

	O RITO DE COMUNION
Padrenuestro	Padrenuestro
	El Saludo de Paz
	Invitación a Comulgar
	Comunión
Oración Conclusiva	Oración después de la Comunión

RITO DE CONCLUSION
    Anuncios Breves
    [Colecta de las Ofrendas Monetarias por parte de la Asamblea]
    Bendición
    Despedida

OUTLINE OF THE RITE

INTRODUCTORY RITES
    Introduction
    Hymn

PSALMODY
    Antiphon 1
    Psalm
    [Psalm-prayer]
    Antiphon 2
    Psalm
    [Psalm-prayer]
    Antiphon 3
    New Testament Canticle

LITURGY OF THE WORD
    First Reading
    Responsorial Psalm
    Second Reading
    Gospel Acclamation
    Gospel
    Homily or Reflection on the Readings
    Response to the Word of God (Responsory)
    [Dismissal of Catechumens]
    Canticle of Zechariah
    Intercessions

	OR COMMUNION RITE
Lord's Prayer	Lord's Prayer
	Sign of Peace
	Invitation to Communion
	Communion
Concluding Prayer	Prayer after Communion

CONCLUDING RITE
    Brief Announcements
    [Collection of the Monetary Offerings of the Assembly]
    Blessing
    Dismissal

ORACION DE LA TARDE
[CON LA SAGRADA COMUNION]

87   Cuando la celebración dominical en la ausencia de un sacerdote toma la forma de la Oración de la Tarde de *La Liturgia de las Horas,* se puede usar lo siguiente como un texto común para todos los domingos. Sin embargo, cuando hay textos especiales para los domingos, solemnidades, y fiestas del Señor en *La Liturgia de las Horas*, se deben usar estos textos.

RITOS INTRODUCTORIOS

INTRODUCCIÓN

88   Cuando se ha reunido la asamblea, todos se ponen de pie mientras el líder, hace la señal de la cruz, canta o dice:

✛ **Dios mío, ven en mi auxilio.**

Todos responden:

Señor, date prisa en socorrerme.

Gloria al Padre, y al Hijo, y al Espíritu Santo.
Como era en el principio, ahora y siempre,
por los siglos de los siglos. Amén. (Aleluya.)

HIMNO

89   Se canta un himno apropiado. El siguiente himno es apropiado para los domingos en tiempo ordinario. En otros días se puede usar un himno apropiado al tiempo litúrgico o a la fiesta que se celebra.

Santo, santo, santo, Dios y Señor nuestro;
canta tus grandezas la hermosa creación;
junto con sus voces suba nuestro canto;
¡hosanna, hosanna, hosanna a nuestro Dios!

Santo, santo, santo, Dios y Señor nuestro;
hoy la Iglesia canta la obra de tu amor;
canten con nosotros ángeles y santos;
¡hosanna, hosanna, hosanna a nuestro Dios!

EVENING PRAYER
[WITH HOLY COMMUNION]

87 When the Sunday celebration in the absence of a priest takes the form of Evening Prayer from *The Liturgy of the Hours,* the following may be used as a common text for all Sundays. However, when special texts for Sundays, solemnities, and feasts of the Lord are contained in *The Liturgy of the Hours*, they may be used.

INTRODUCTORY RITES

INTRODUCTION

88 When the assembly has gathered, all stand while the leader, making the sign of the cross, sings or says:

✠ **God, come to my assistance.**

All respond:

Lord, make haste to help me.

Glory to the Father, and to the Son, and to the Holy Spirit: as it was in the beginning, is now, and will be for ever. Amen. (Alleluia.)

HYMN

89 A suitable hymn is sung. The following hymn is appropriate for the Sundays of Ordinary Time. On other days a hymn appropriate to the season or feast may be used.

**O radiant Light, O Sun divine
Of God the Father's deathless face,
O image of the Light sublime
That fills the heav'nly dwelling place.**

**O Son of God, the source of life,
Praise is your due by night and day.
Our happy lips must raise the strain
Of your esteemed and splendid name.**

**Lord Jesus Christ, as daylight fades,
As shine the lights of eventide,
We praise the Father with the Son,
The Spirit blest, and with them one.**

SALMODIA

90   La antífona propia es entonada por el cantor, el coro, o toda la asamblea antes de cada salmo. Todos repiten la antífona al final del salmo o después de cada estrofa. Todos pueden sentarse durante la salmodia.

El aleluya al final de la antífona se omite durante la Cuaresma.

Antífona 1   Desde Sión extenderá el Señor el poder de su cetro, y reinará eternamente, (aleluya).

Salmo 109 (110):1-5, 7

Oráculo del Señor a mi Señor:
"Siéntate a mi derecha,
y haré de tus enemigos
estrado de tus pies".

Desde Sión extenderá el Señor
el poder de tu cetro:
somete en la batalla a tus enemigos.

"Eres príncipe desde el día de tu nacimiento,
entre esplendores sagrados;
yo mismo te engendré, como rocío,
antes de la aurora".

El Señor lo ha jurado y no se arrepiente:
"Tú eres sacerdote eterno,
según el rito de Melquisedec".

El Señor a tu derecha, el día de su ira,
quebrantará a los reyes.

En su camino beberá del torrente,
por eso levantará la cabeza.

Gloria al Padre, y al Hijo, y al Espíritu Santo.
Como era en el principio, ahora y siempre,
por los siglos de los siglos. Amén.

ORACIÓN DESPUÉS DEL SALMO

91   Después de una breve pausa para orar en silencio, el líder puede ponerse de pie y decir:

PSALMODY

90 The proper antiphon is sung by the cantor, the choir, or the entire assembly before each psalm. The antiphon may be repeated by all at the end of the psalm or after each strophe. All may be seated during the psalmody.

The alleluia at the end of an antiphon is omitted during Lent.

Antiphon 1   **The Lord will stretch forth his mighty scepter from Zion, and he will reign for ever, (alleluia).**

Psalm 110:1-5, 7

The Lord's revelation to my Master:
"Sit on my right:
your foes I will put beneath your feet."

The Lord will wield from Zion
your scepter of power:
rule in the midst of all your foes.

A prince from the day of your birth
on the holy mountains;
from the womb before the dawn I begot you.

The Lord has sworn an oath he will not change.
"You are a priest for ever,
a priest like Melchizedek of old."

The Master standing at your right hand
will shatter kings in the day of his great wrath.

He shall drink from the stream by the wayside
and therefore he shall lift up his head.

Glory to the Father, and to the Son, and to the Holy Spirit:
as it was in the beginning, is now, and will be for ever.
Amen.

PSALM-PRAYER

91   After a brief pause for silent prayer, the leader may stand and say:

Padre Dios todopoderoso, danos la victoria, danos la paz. En nuestro Señor Jesucristo, Rey y Salvador, ya estamos sentados a tu diestra. Con alegría esperamos el poder alabarte en compañía de todos tus santos en nuestra patria celestial.

Se puede repetir la antífona.

Antífona 2   En presencia del Señor se estremece la tierra, (aleluya).

Salmo 113 (114)

Cuando Israel salió de Egipto,
los hijos de Jacob de un pueblo balbuciente,
Judá fue su santuario,
Israel fue su dominio.

El mar, al verlos, huyó,
el Jordán se echó atrás;
los montes saltaron como carneros;
las colinas, como corderos.

¿Qué te pasa, mar, que huyes,
y a ti, Jordán, que te echas atrás?
¿Y a ustedes, montes, que saltan como carneros;
colinas, que saltan como corderos?

En presencia del Señor se estremece la tierra,
en presencia del Dios de Jacob;
que transforma las peñas en estanques,
el pedernal en manantiales de agua.

Gloria al Padre, y al Hijo, y al Espíritu Santo.
Como era en el principio, ahora y siempre,
por los siglos de los siglos. Amén.

ORACIÓN DESPUÉS DEL SALMO

92   Después de una breve pausa para orar en silencio, el líder puede ponerse de pie y decir:

Father, we ask you to give us victory and peace. In Jesus Christ, our Lord and King, we are already seated at your right hand. We look forward to praising you in the fellowship of all your saints in our heavenly homeland.

The antiphon may be repeated.

Antiphon 2   The earth is shaken to its depths before the glory of your face, (alleluia).

Psalm 114

When Israel came forth from Egypt,
Jacob's son from an alien people,
Judah became the Lord's temple,
Israel became his kingdom.

The sea fled at the sight:
the Jordan turned back on its course,
the mountains leapt like rams
and the hills like yearling sheep.

Why was it, sea, that you fled,
that you turned back, Jordan, on your course?
Mountains, that you leapt like rams,
hills, like yearling sheep?

Tremble, O earth, before the Lord,
in the presence of the God of Jacob,
who turns the rock into a pool
and flint into a spring of water.

Glory to the Father, and to the Son, and to the Holy Spirit:
as it was in the beginning, is now, and will be for ever.
Amen.

PSALM-PRAYER

92   After a brief pause for silent prayer, the leader may stand and say:

Dios todopoderoso, misterio eterno de unidad y Trinidad, tú le otorgaste la vida al nuevo pueblo de Israel haciéndolo nacer del agua y del Espíritu, y lo constituiste una raza elegida, un reino de sacerdotes, una nación consagrada, un pueblo que escogiste para que fuera tuyo. Te pedimos nos concedas que todos aquellos a quienes has llamado a caminar en el esplendor de la luz nueva podamos rendirte servicio generoso y adoración sincera.

Se puede repetir la antífona.

Antífona 3   Reina el Señor, nuestro Dios, dueño de todo, aleluya.

Cf. Apocalipsis 19:1-7

Aleluya.
La salvación y la gloria y el poder son de nuestro Dios,
(℟. Aleluya.)
porque sus juicios son verdaderos y justos.
℟. Aleluya, (aleluya).

Aleluya.
Alabad al Señor, sus siervos todos,
(℟. Aleluya.)
los que le temen, pequeños y grandes.
℟. Aleluya, (aleluya).

Aleluya.
Porque reina el Señor, nuestro Dios, dueño de todo,
(℟. Aleluya.)
alegrémonos y gocemos y démosle gracias.
℟. Aleluya, (aleluya).

Aleluya.
Llegó la boda del Cordero,
(℟. Aleluya.)

Almighty God, ever-living mystery of unity and Trinity, you gave life to the new Israel by birth from water and the Spirit, and made it a chosen race, a royal priesthood, a people set apart as your eternal possession. May all those you have called to walk in the splendor of the new light render you fitting service and adoration.

The antiphon may be repeated.

Antiphon 3   All power is yours, Lord God, our mighty King, alleluia.

Cf. Revelation 19:1-7

Alleluia.
Salvation, glory, and power to our God:
(℟. Alleluia.)
his judgments are honest and true.
℟. Alleluia, (alleluia).

Alleluia.
Sing praise to our God, all you his servants,
(℟. Alleluia.)
all who worship him reverently, great and small.
℟. Alleluia, (alleluia).

Alleluia.
The Lord our all-powerful God is King;
(℟. Alleluia.)
let us rejoice, sing praise, and give him glory.
℟. Alleluia, (alleluia).

Alleluia.
The wedding feast of the Lamb has begun,
(℟. Alleluia.)

su esposa se ha embellecido.
℟. Aleluya, (aleluya).

Gloria al Padre, y al Hijo, y al Espíritu Santo.
Como era en el principio, ahora y siempre,
por los siglos de los siglos. Amén.

Se puede repetir la antífona.

Durante la Cuaresma se usa el siguiente cántico.

Antífona 3   Miren, estamos subiendo a Jerusalén y se va a
cumplir todo lo que está escrito acerca del Hijo
del hombre.

1 Pedro 2:21-24

Cristo padeció por nosotros,
dejándonos un ejemplo
para que sigamos sus huellas.

Él no cometió pecado
ni encontraron engaño en su boca;
cuando lo insultaban,
no devolvía el insulto.

En su pasión no profería amenazas;
al contrario,
se ponía en manos del que juzga justamente.

Cargado con nuestros pecados, subió al leño,
para que, muertos al pecado,
vivamos para la justicia.

Sus heridas nos han curado.

Gloria al Padre, y al Hijo, y al Espíritu Santo.
Como era en el principio, ahora y siempre,
por los siglos de los siglos. Amén.

Se puede repetir la antífona.

and his bride is prepared to welcome him.
℟. Alleluia, (alleluia).

Glory to the Father, and to the Son, and to the Holy Spirit:
as it was in the beginning, is now, and will be for ever.
Amen.

The antiphon may be repeated.

During Lent the following canticle is used.

Antiphon 3   We must now go up to Jerusalem where all that
has been written about the Son of Man will be
fulfilled.

1 Peter 2:21-24

Christ suffered for you,
and left you an example
to have you follow in his footsteps.

He did no wrong;
no deceit was found in his mouth.
When he was insulted,
he returned no insult.

When he was made to suffer,
he did not counter with threats.
Instead he delivered himself up
to the One who judges justly.

In his own body
he brought your sins to the cross,
so that all of us, dead to sin,
could live in accord with God's will.

By his wounds you were healed.

Glory to the Father, and to the Son, and to the Holy Spirit:
as it was in the beginning, is now, and will be for ever.
Amen.

The antiphon may be repeated.

LITURGIA DE LA PALABRA

93 Los domingos la Liturgia de la Palabra se celebra como en la Misa.

Las lecturas y el salmo aparecen en el *Leccionario para la Misa* para ese domingo en particular.

Antes de que se proclamen las lecturas, se puede ofrecer una breve introducción con el fin de estimular la atención de los que escuchan, poner las lecturas dentro de su contexto, y hacer ver las conexiones entre las lecturas.

PRIMERA LECTURA

94 Un/a lector/a proclama la primera lectura.

SALMO RESPONSORIAL

95 Después de la primera lectura, se canta el salmo asignado en el Leccionario. Si es necesario, se puede escoger otro salmo que esté en armonía con el texto de la primera lectura.

SEGUNDA LECTURA

96 Si se tienen tres lecturas, el/la lector/a proclama luego la segunda lectura.

ACLAMACIÓN DEL EVANGELIO

97 Se canta la aclamación del evangelio que se da en el Leccionario antes de proclamar el evangelio.

EVANGELIO

98 Un diácono proclama el evangelio de la manera normal. Sin embargo, una persona laica omite el saludo, "El Señor esté con ustedes", antes de leer el evangelio.

HOMILÍA O REFLEXIÓN SOBRE LAS LECTURAS

99 Un líder que es un diácono ofrece una homilía.

Cuando el líder es una persona laica que no ha sido delegada para predicar, el párroco puede preparar una homilía para que se lea durante la celebración.

En otros casos, cuando la persona laica ha sido delegada por el obispo para predicar, él o ella puede ofrecer a los presentes una breve explicación del texto bíblico, para que puedan comprender por la fe el significado de la celebración.

LITURGY OF THE WORD

93   On Sundays the Liturgy of the Word takes place as at Mass.

The readings and the psalm are those assigned in the *Lectionary for Mass* for that particular Sunday.

Before the readings are proclaimed, a brief introduction may be given in order to stimulate the attention of the listeners, to put the readings into context, and to point out connections between the readings.

FIRST READING

94   A reader proclaims the first reading.

RESPONSORIAL PSALM

95   After the first reading, the psalm assigned in the Lectionary is sung. If necessary, another psalm which is in harmony with the text of the first reading may be chosen.

SECOND READING

96   If there are to be three readings, a reader then proclaims the second reading.

GOSPEL ACCLAMATION

97   The gospel acclamation given in the Lectionary is sung before the proclamation of the gospel.

GOSPEL

98   A deacon proclaims the gospel in the usual manner. However, a layperson omits the greeting, "The Lord be with you," before reading the gospel.

HOMILY OR REFLECTION ON THE READINGS

99   A leader who is a deacon gives a homily.

When the leader is a layperson who has not been delegated to preach, the pastor may prepare a homily to be read during the celebration.

In other cases, when a layperson has been delegated to preach by the bishop, he or she may give those present a brief explanation of the biblical text, so that they may understand through faith the meaning of the celebration.

Después de la homilía hay un momento de silencio sagrado para reflexionar sobre la Palabra de Dios.

Respuesta a la Palabra de Dios (Responsorio)

100   Como una respuesta a la Palabra de Dios se puede cantar un canto responsorial o un responsorio corto como se da más abajo; sin embargo, el responsorio puede ser omitido. Pueden substituirse otros cantos que tengan el mismo propósito y carácter.

℣. **Bendito eres, Señor, en la bóveda del cielo.**
℟. Bendito eres, Señor, en la bóveda del cielo.

℣. **Digno de gloria y alabanza por los siglos.**
℟. En la bóveda del cielo.

℣. **Gloria al Padre, y al Hijo, y al Espíritu Santo.**
℟. Bendito eres, Señor, en la bóveda del cielo.

Despedida de los Catecúmenos

101   Si se va a distribuir la sagrada comunión y hay algunos catecúmenos presentes, se les puede despedir en este momento usando las opciones A o B; si tienen que quedarse para la conclusión de la Oración de la Tarde, se puede usar la opción C.

A   Para la despedida se puede usar la siguiente fórmula u otra parecida.

Catecúmenos, vayan en paz, y que el Señor los acompañe.

Catecúmenos:

Demos gracias a Dios.

B   Como otra fórmula opcional para despedir a los catecúmenos, el líder puede usar estas u otras palabras semejantes.

Mis queridos amigos, esta comunidad les envía ahora a reflexionar más profundamente sobre la palabra de Dios que han compartido con nosotros hoy. Pueden estar seguros de nuestro afecto, apoyo y oraciones por ustedes. Con gusto esperamos el día en que compartan plenamente de la Mesa del Señor.

After the homily there may be a period of sacred silence for reflection on the Word of God.

RESPONSE TO THE WORD OF GOD (RESPONSORY)

100   As a response to the Word of God a responsorial chant or short responsory, as given below, may be sung; however, the responsory may be omitted. Other chants with the same purpose and character may be substituted.

℣. **The whole creation proclaims the greatness of your glory.**
℟. The whole creation proclaims the greatness of your glory.

℣. **Eternal ages praise**
℟. the greatness of your glory.

℣. **Glory to the Father, and to the Son, and to the Holy Spirit.**
℟. The whole creation proclaims the greatness of your glory.

DISMISSAL OF CATECHUMENS

101   If holy communion is to be distributed and there are catechumens present, they may be dismissed at this point by use of option A or B; if they are to remain for the conclusion of Evening Prayer, option C may be used.

A   For the dismissal the following or similar words are used.

Catechumens, go in peace, and may the Lord remain with you always.

Catechumens:

Thanks be to God.

B   As an optional formulary for dismissing the catechumens, the minister may use these or similar words.

My dear friends, this community now sends you forth to reflect more deeply upon the Word of God which you have shared with us today. Be assured of our loving support and prayers for you. We look forward to the day when you will share fully in the Lord's Table.

C   Si los catecúmenos tienen que quedarse durante la distribucion de la sagrada comunión y la conclusión de la Oración de la Tarde, se les debe recordar que no pueden participar como lo hacen los bautizados. El líder les puede recordar esto con estas palabras u otras parecidas.

Aunque todavía no pueden ustedes participar de la sagrada comunión, quédense con nosotros como un signo de nuestra esperanza de que todos los hijos de Dios comerán y beberán con el Señor y trabajarán con su Espíritu para renovar la faz de la tierra.

CÁNTICO DE MARÍA

102   Todos se ponen de pie y cantan el siguiente cántico evangélico.

La siguiente antífona, la antífona propia del día, u otro texto apropiado, puede cantarse antes del cántico, primero por el cantor o el coro, y luego por la asamblea. Puede repetirse después de cada estrofa o al final del cántico.

Antífona   Se alegra mi espíritu en Dios, mi salvador.

Lucas 1:46-55

✠ **Proclama mi alma la grandeza del Señor,
se alegra mi espíritu en Dios, mi salvador;
porque ha mirado la humillación de su esclava.**

**Desde ahora me felicitarán todas las generaciones,
porque el Poderoso ha hecho obras grandes por mí:
su nombre es santo,
y su misericordia llega a sus fieles
de generación en generación.**

**Él hace proezas con su brazo:
dispersa a los soberbios de corazón,
derriba del trono a los poderosos
y enaltece a los humildes,
a los hambrientos los colma de bienes
y a los ricos los despide vacíos.**

C   If the catechumens are to remain for the distribution of holy communion and the conclusion of Evening Prayer, they should be reminded that they cannot partake as the baptized do. They may be reminded of this by the minister in these or similar words.

Although you cannot yet partake of holy communion, stay with us as a sign of our hope that all God's children will eat and drink with the Lord and work with the Holy Spirit to re-create the face of the earth.

CANTICLE OF MARY

102   All stand and sing the following gospel canticle.

The following antiphon, the antiphon proper to the day, or another suitable text, may be sung before the canticle, first by the cantor or the choir, and then by the people. It may be repeated after each strophe or at the end of the canticle.

Antiphon   My spirit rejoices in God my Savior.

Luke 1:46-55

✠ **My soul proclaims the greatness of the Lord,
my spirit rejoices in God my Savior
for he has looked with favor on his lowly servant.**

**From this day all generations will call me blessed:
the Almighty has done great things for me,
and holy is his Name.**

**He has mercy on those who fear him
in every generation.**

**He has shown the strength of his arm,
he has scattered the proud in their conceit.**

**He has cast down the mighty from their thrones,
and has lifted up the lowly.**

**He has filled the hungry with good things,
and the rich he has sent away empty.**

Auxilia a Israel, su siervo,
acordándose de la misericordia,
como lo había prometido a nuestros padres,
en favor de Abrahán y su descendencia por siempre.

Gloria al Padre, y al Hijo, y al Espíritu Santo.
Como era en el principio, ahora y siempre,
por los siglos de los siglos. Amén.

> Se puede repetir la antífona.

PRECES

> 103   Las preces siguen al cántico. El líder invita primero a la asamblea a orar, luego otro ministro canta o recita las intenciones.

> Se pueden usar las intenciones propias dadas en *La Liturgia de las Hora*s en lugar de las siguientes, o se pueden añadir otras intenciones.

> El líder dice:

Glorifiquemos a Dios, Padre, Hijo y Espíritu Santo, y supliquémosle, diciendo:

℞. Escucha a tu pueblo, Señor.

> Otro ministro dice:

Padre todopoderoso, haz que florezca en la tierra la justicia, y que tu pueblo se alegre en la paz. ℞.

Que todos los pueblos entren a formar parte de tu reino, y obtengan así la salvación. ℞.

Que los esposos cumplan tu voluntad, vivan en concordia, y sean siempre fieles a su mutuo amor. ℞.

Recompensa, Señor, a nuestros bienhechores, y concédeles la vida eterna. ℞.

Acoge con amor a los que han muerto víctimas del odio, de la violencia o de la guerra, y dales el descanso eterno. ℞.

> 104   Si no se va a distribuir la sagrada comunión, la celebración continúa en el núm. 116.

He has come to the help of his servant Israel
for he has remembered his promise of mercy,
the promise he made to our fathers,
to Abraham and his children for ever.

Glory to the Father, and to the Son, and to the Holy Spirit:
as it was in the beginning, is now, and will be for ever.
Amen.

> The antiphon may be repeated.

INTERCESSIONS

> 103   The intercessions follow the canticle. The leader first invites the assembly to pray, then another minister sings or recites the intentions.
>
> The proper intentions given in *The Liturgy of the Hours* may be used in place of the following, or other intentions may be added.
>
> The leader says:

We give glory to the one God Father, Son and Holy Spirit—
and in our weakness we pray:

℟. Lord, be with your people.

> Another minister says:

Holy Lord, Father all-powerful, let justice spring up on the earth; then your people will dwell in the beauty of peace. ℟.

Let every nation come into your kingdom, so that all peoples will be saved. ℟.

Let married couples live in your peace, and grow in mutual love. ℟.

Reward all who have done good to us, Lord, and grant them eternal life. ℟.

Look with compassion on victims of hatred and war, and grant them heavenly peace. ℟.

> 104   If holy communion is not to be distributed, the service continues at no. 116.

RITO DE COMUNION

105   El líder va al lugar donde se reserva el sacramento, toma el recipiente o copon que contiene el Cuerpo del Señor, lo coloca en el altar y hace una genuflexión.

PADRENUESTRO

106   El líder invita a todos los presentes a cantar o decir el Padrenuestro con estas u otras palabras semejantes:

A   **Fieles a la recomendación del Salvador**
y siguiendo su divina enseñanza,
nos atrevemos a decir:

B   **Llenos de alegría por ser hijos de Dios,**
digamos confiadamente
la oración que Cristo nos enseñó:

C   **El amor de Dios ha sido derramado**
en nuestros corazones
con el Espíritu Santo que se nos ha dado;
digamos con fe y esperanza:

D   **Antes de participar en el banquete de la Eucaristía,**
signo de reconciliación
y vínculo de unión fraterna,
oremos juntos como el Señor nos ha enseñado:

El líder continúa, junto con la asamblea:

Padre nuestro, que estás en el cielo,
santificado sea tu Nombre;
venga a nosotros tu reino;
hágase tu voluntad en la tierra como en el cielo.
Danos hoy nuestro pan de cada día;
perdona nuestras ofensas,
como también nosotros perdonamos
a los que nos ofenden;
no nos dejes caer en la tentación,
y líbranos del mal.

COMMUNION RITE

105   The leader goes to the place where the sacrament is reserved, takes the vessel or ciborium containing the body of the Lord, places it on the altar and genuflects.

LORD'S PRAYER

106   The leader invites all present to sing or say the Lord's Prayer in these or similar words:

A   **Let us pray with confidence to the Father in the words our Savior gave us:**

B   **Jesus taught us to call God our Father, and so we have the courage to say:**

C   **Let us ask our Father to forgive our sins and bring us to forgive those who sin against us.**

D   **Let us pray for the coming of the kingdom as Jesus taught us.**

The leader continues with the people:

**Our Father, who art in heaven,
hallowed be thy name;
thy kingdom come;
thy will be done on earth as it is in heaven.
Give us this day our daily bread;
and forgive us our trespasses
as we forgive those who trespass against us;
and lead us not into temptation,
but deliver us from evil.**

El Saludo de Paz

107   El líder puede invitar a la asamblea a darse el saludo de paz con estas u otras palabras semejantes:

En el amor de Cristo, démonos unos a otros un saludo de paz.

Todos, según la costumbre del lugar, se dan la paz.

Invitación a Comulgar

108   El líder hace genuflexión, toma el pan consagrado y, sosteniéndolo un poco elevado sobre el recipiente o copón, lo muestra al pueblo, diciendo:

**Este es el Cordero de Dios,
que quita el pecado del mundo.
Dichosos los invitados a la cena del Señor.**

Y, juntamente con el pueblo, añade:

Señor, no soy digno
de que entres en mi casa,
pero una palabra tuya
bastará para sanarme.

Comunión

109   El líder dice en secreto:

El Cuerpo de Cristo me guarde para la vida eterna.

Y comulga reverentemente el Cuerpo de Cristo.

110   Después el líder (y los otros ministros especiales de la comunión) toma el recipiente o copón, se acerca a los que quieren comulgar y les presenta el pan consagrado, que sostiene un poco elevado, diciendo a cada uno de ellos:

El Cuerpo de Cristo.

El que va a comulgar responde **Amén** y comulga.

111   Durante la distribución de la comunión, se puede cantar un himno.

112   Acabada la comunión, el líder o un ministro especial de la comunión consume cualquier fragmento que se encuentre o lo pone en el recipiente o copón y se lava las manos si lo juzga necesario. Si quedan hostias adicionales, el ministro o hace una genuflexión y las pone de nuevo en el tabernáculo o las pone otra vez en el recipiente o copón y lo regresa a la iglesia de donde había traído la eucaristía para la distribución.

SIGN OF PEACE

107   The leader may invite the people to exchange the sign of peace in these or similar words:

In the love of Christ, let us offer one another a sign of peace.

All make an appropriate sign of peace, according to local custom.

INVITATION TO COMMUNION

108   The leader genuflects. Taking the host, the minister raises it slightly over the vessel or ciborium and, facing the people, says:

**This is the Lamb of God
who takes away the sins of the world.
Happy are those who are called to his supper.**

The communicants say:

Lord, I am not worthy to receive you
but only say the word and I shall be healed.

COMMUNION

109   The leader says quietly:

May the body of Christ bring me to everlasting life.

The leader reverently consumes the body of Christ.

110   The leader (and other special ministers of holy communion) then takes the vessel or ciborium with the eucharist and goes to the communicants. The minister takes a host for each one, raises it slightly, and says:

The body of Christ.

The communicant answers **Amen** and receives communion.

111   During the distribution of communion, a hymn may be sung.

112   After communion the leader or a special minister of holy communion consumes any fragments which are found or puts them in the vessel or ciborium and then washes his or her hands if need be. If additional hosts remain, the minister either genuflects and puts them back into the tabernacle or else puts them back into the vessel or ciborium and returns it to the church from which he or she had obtained the eucharist for distribution.

113   Se puede guardar unos momentos de silencio o cantar un salmo o cántico o una letanía de alabanza.

Oración después de la Comunión

114   El líder dice luego la Oración después de la Comunión apropiada del **Apéndice III** o una de las oraciones en el **Apéndice IV**. El líder primero invita a la asamblea a orar, diciendo:

Oremos.

Todos los presentes oran en silencio por un corto tiempo. Luego el líder dice la oración. Al final de la oración la asamblea responde **Amén**.

115   El servicio concluye con anuncios breves [la colecta de las ofrendas monetarias por parte de la asamblea], la bendición, y la despedida como en los núms. 118–121.

El Padrenuestro

116   Si no se distribuye la sagrada comunión, el líder invita a todos a rezar el Padrenuestro con estas u otras palabras semejantes:

A   **Fieles a la recomendación del Salvador**
y siguiendo su divina enseñanza,
nos atrevemos a decir:

B   **Llenos de alegría por ser hijos de Dios,**
digamos confiadamente
la oración que Cristo nos enseñó:

C   **El amor de Dios ha sido derramado**
en nuestros corazones
con el Espíritu Santo que se nos ha dado;
digamos con fe y esperanza:

113   A period of silence may now be observed, or a psalm, song of praise, or litany of praise may be sung.

PRAYER AFTER COMMUNION

114   The leader then says the proper Prayer after Communion from **Appendix III** or one of the prayers in **Appendix IV**. The leader first invites the assembly to pray, saying:

Let us pray.

All present pray in silence for a short time. Then the leader says the prayer. At the end of the prayer the assembly responds **Amen**.

115   The service concludes with the brief announcements [the collection of the monetary offerings of the assembly], the blessing, and the dismissal at nos. 118–121.

LORD'S PRAYER

116   If holy communion is not distributed, the leader invites all to pray the Lord's Prayer in these or similar words:

A   **Let us pray with confidence to the Father in the words our Savior gave us:**

B   **Jesus taught us to call God our Father, and so we have the courage to say:**

C   **Let us ask our Father to forgive our sins and bring us to forgive those who sin against us.**

D   **Let us pray for the coming of the kingdom as Jesus taught us.**

El líder continúa, junto con la asamblea:

Padre nuestro, que estás en el cielo,
santificado sea tu Nombre;
venga a nosotros tu reino;
hágase tu voluntad en la tierra como en el cielo.
Danos hoy nuestro pan de cada día;
perdona nuestras ofensas,
como también nosotros perdonamos
a los que nos ofenden;
no nos dejes caer en la tentación,
y líbranos del mal.

ORACIÓN CONCLUSIVA

117 El líder dice la Oración conclusiva. Se puede usar la Oración del Día (de *La Liturgia de las Horas*), que se da en el **Apéndice III**, o la siguiente oración:

Señor,
guía el curso de los acontecimientos en el mundo
y da a tu Iglesia el gozo y la paz
de servirte en libertad.

Por nuestro Señor Jesucristo, tu Hijo,
que vive y reina contigo
en la unidad del Espíritu Santo y es Dios
por los siglos de los siglos.

℟. Amén.

RITO DE CONCLUSION

ANUNCIOS BREVES

118 Antes de despedir a la asamblea se pueden hacer breves anuncios que afectan la vida y las actividades de la parroquia.

[COLECTA DE LAS OFRENDAS MONETARIAS POR PARTE DE LA ASAMBLEA]

119 Después de las oraciones se pueden recoger las ofrendas de los fieles según las normas y las necesidades indicadas por el Ordinario local.

The leader continues with the people:

Our Father, who art in heaven,
hallowed be thy name;
thy kingdom come;
thy will be done on earth as it is in heaven.
Give us this day our daily bread;
and forgive us our trespasses
as we forgive those who trespass against us;
and lead us not into temptation,
but deliver us from evil.

CONCLUDING PRAYER

117 The leader says the Concluding Prayer. The prayer may be the Prayer of the Day (from *The Liturgy of the Hours*), given in **Appendix III**, or the following prayer may be used:

Lord,
guide the course of world events
and give your Church the joy and peace
of serving you in freedom.

We ask this through our Lord Jesus Christ, your Son,
who lives and reigns with you and the Holy Spirit,
one God, for ever and ever.

℟. Amen.

CONCLUDING RITE

BRIEF ANNOUNCEMENTS

118 Brief announcements concerning parish life and activities may be made before the congregation is dismissed.

[COLLECTION OF THE MONETARY OFFERINGS OF THE ASSEMBLY]

119 The offerings of the faithful may be collected in accordance with the norms and the necessities indicated by the local Ordinary.

BENDICIÓN

120 Un líder que es un diácono dice:

El Señor esté con ustedes.

Todos responden:

Y con tu espíritu.

Bendice al pueblo usando la siguiente bendición. Puede también usar una de las bendiciones en el **Apéndice V**, o una de las bendiciones solemnes o de las oraciones sobre el pueblo en el *Sacramentario*.

**La bendición de Dios todopoderoso,
Padre, Hijo, ✠ y Espíritu Santo
descienda sobre ustedes.**

Todos:

Amén.

Un líder que es una persona laica hace la señal de la cruz sobre sí mismo/a y dice:

**El Señor nos bendiga,
nos guarde de todo mal
y nos lleve a la vida eterna.**

Todos:

Amén.

DESPEDIDA

121 El líder luego añade:

Vayan en paz.

Todos:

Demos gracias a Dios.

BLESSING

120 A leader who is a deacon says:

The Lord be with you.

All respond:

And also with you.

He blesses the people using the following blessing. He may also use one of the blessings in **Appendix V**, or one of the solemn blessings or prayers over the people in the *Sacramentary*.

May almighty God bless you,
the Father, and the Son, ✠ and the Holy Spirit.

All:

Amen.

A leader who is a layperson makes the sign of the cross on himself or herself and says:

May the Lord bless us,
protect us from all evil
and bring us to everlasting life.

All:

Amen.

DISMISSAL

121 The leader then adds:

Go in peace.

All:

Thanks be to God.

CAPITULO II

CELEBRACION DE LA LITURGIA DE LA PALABRA

[CON LA SAGRADA COMUNION]

CHAPTER II

CELEBRATION OF THE LITURGY OF THE WORD

[WITH HOLY COMMUNION]

ESQUEMA DEL RITO

RITOS INICIALES
    Saludo
    Introducción
    Letanía en Alabanza de la Misericordia de Dios
    Oración Colecta

LITURGIA DE LA PALABRA
    Primera Lectura
    Salmo Responsorial
    Segunda Lectura
    Aclamación del Evangelio
    Evangelio
    Homilía o Reflexión sobre las Lecturas
    [Despedida de los Catecúmenos]
    Profesión de Fe
    Plegaria Universal
    Acción de Gracias

	RITO DE COMUNION
Padrenuestro	Padrenuestro
	El Saludo de Paz
	Invitación a Comulgar
	Comunión
	Oración después de la Comunión

O RITO DE CONCLUSION
    Anuncios Breves
    [Colecta de las Ofrendas Monetarias por parte de la Asamblea]
    Bendición
    Despedida

OUTLINE OF THE RITE

INTRODUCTORY RITES
> Greeting
> Introduction
> Litany in Praise of God's Mercy
> Opening Prayer

LITURGY OF THE WORD
> First Reading
> Responsorial Psalm
> Second Reading
> Gospel Acclamation
> Gospel
> Homily or Reflection on the Readings
> [Dismissal of Catechumens]
> Profession of Faith
> General Intercessions
> Act of Thanksgiving

Lord's Prayer	**OR COMMUNION RITE**
	Lord's Prayer
	Sign of Peace
	Invitation to Communion
	Communion
	Prayer after Communion

CONCLUDING RITE
> Brief Announcements
> [Collection of the Monetary Offerings of the Assembly]
> Blessing
> Dismissal

CELEBRACION DE LA LITURGIA DE LA PALABRA [CON LA SAGRADA COMUNION]

RITOS INICLALES

122 Cuando la asamblea se ha reunido, se puede cantar un himno apropiado. Después del canto, el líder dice:

En el nombre del Padre, y del Hijo, y del Espíritu Santo.

Todos hacen la señal de la cruz y responden:

Amén.

SALUDO

123 Si el líder es diácono, saluda a los presentes con las siguientes palabras u otras apropiadas, tomadas especialmente de la sagrada Escritura. La asamblea responde **Y con tu espíritu.**

A **La gracia de nuestro Señor Jesucristo,**
 el amor del Padre
 y la comunión del Espíritu Santo
 estén con todos ustedes.

B **La gracia y la paz de parte de Dios, nuestro Padre,**
 y de Jesucristo, el Señor,
 estén con todos ustedes.

C **El Señor esté con ustedes.**

D **El Señor, que dirige nuestros corazones**
 para que amemos a Dios,
 esté con todos ustedes.

E **La paz, la caridad y la fe,**
 de parte de Dios Padre,
 y de Jesucristo, el Señor,
 estén con todos ustedes.

F **El Dios de la esperanza,**
 que por la acción del Espíritu Santo
 nos colma con su alegría y con su paz,

CELEBRATION OF THE LITURGY OF THE WORD [WITH HOLY COMMUNION]

INTRODUCTORY RITES

122   When the assembly has gathered, a suitable song may be sung. After the singing, the leader says:

In the name of the Father, and of the Son, and of the Holy Spirit.

All make the sign of the cross and reply:

Amen.

GREETING

123   The leader who is a deacon then greets those present in the following or other suitable words, taken mainly from sacred Scripture.

A   **The grace of our Lord Jesus Christ and the love of God and the fellowship of the Holy Spirit be with you all.**

All respond:

And also with you.

B   **The grace and peace of God our Father and the Lord Jesus Christ be with you.**

All respond:

And also with you.

C   **The Lord be with you.**

All respond:

And also with you.

Any other customary form of greeting from Scripture may be used.

Si el líder es un/a laico/a saluda a los presentes con las siguientes palabras:

A **La gracia y paz de Dios nuestro Padre y de Jesucristo nuestro Señor estén con ustedes. Bendito sea Dios por siempre.**

Todos responden:

Bendito sea Dios por siempre.

B **Hermanas y hermanos,**
Dios nos invita a escuchar su Palabra
(y a compartir en el Cuerpo de Cristo).
Bendigámoslo por su bondad.
Bendito sea Dios por siempre.

Todos responden:

Bendito sea Dios por siempre.

INTRODUCCIÓN

124   El líder prepara a los presentes para la celebración usando estas palabras u otras parecidas:

Nos reunimos hoy a celebrar el Día del Señor. Nuestro párroco no puede estar con nosotros (o: está celebrando Misa en otro lugar). Unidos a nuestros hermanos y hermanas y con toda la Iglesia, vamos a escuchar ahora la Palabra de Dios y a unirnos en oración (y en la comunión eucarística).

LETANÍA EN ALABANZA DE LA MISERICORDIA DE DIOS

125   El líder continúa con la letanía en alabanza de la misericordia de Dios e invita a la asamblea a reconocerla con estas u otras palabras semejantes:

A **Mis hermanos y hermanas,**
al comenzar nuestra celebración
alabemos a nuestro Dios, porque él es misericordioso.

B **Al reunirnos como la familia de Dios,**
con confianza aclamamos el perdón del Padre,
porque Dios está lleno de bondad y compasión.

The leader who is a layperson greets those present in the following words:

A   **Grace and peace to you from God our Father and from the Lord Jesus Christ. Blessed be God for ever.**

All respond:

Blessed be God for ever.

B   **Sisters and brothers,**
God invites us to hear his Word
(and to share in the body of Christ).
Let us bless him for his goodness.
Blessed be God for ever.

All respond:

Blessed be God for ever.

INTRODUCTION

124   The leader prepares those present for the celebration using these or similar words:

We gather today to celebrate the Lord's Day. Our parish priest is unable to be with us (or: **is celebrating the Eucharist elsewhere today). One with our sisters and brothers and with the entire Church, let us now listen to God's Word and join in prayer (and in eucharistic communion).**

LITANY IN PRAISE OF GOD'S MERCY

125   The litany in praise of God's mercy follows. The leader invites the people to acknowledge the mercy of God in these or similar words:

A   **My brothers and sisters,**
as we begin our celebration,
let us praise our merciful God.

B   **Coming together as God's family,**
with confidence let us acclaim the Father's forgiveness,
for God is full of gentleness and compassion.

C **Para prepararnos a escuchar la Palabra sobre el amor de Dios en Cristo, reconozcamos que el Señor es fuente de perdón y fuerza.**

126 Después de una pausa para reflexionar en silencio se usa uno de los siguientes formularios.

Un ministro hace las siguientes invocaciones u otras parecidas:

A **Tiempo Ordinario**

Tú que has venido a buscar al que estaba perdido:
Señor, ten piedad.

Todos:

Señor, ten piedad.

Ministro:

Tú que has querido dar la vida en rescate por todos:
Cristo, ten piedad.

Todos:

Cristo, ten piedad.

Ministro:

Tú que reúnes a tus hijos dispersos:
Señor, ten piedad.

Todos:

Señor, ten piedad.

B **Tiempo Ordinario**

Tú que eres el camino que conduce al Padre:
Señor, ten piedad.

Todos:

Señor, ten piedad.

Ministro:

Tú que eres la verdad que ilumina los pueblos:
Cristo, ten piedad.

Todos:

Cristo, ten piedad.

C   **As we prepare to hear of God's love in Christ,**
let us acknowledge that the Lord is the source of
pardon and strength.

126   After a pause for silent reflection one of the following formularies is
used.

A minister makes the following or other invocations:

A   **Ordinary Time**

Lord Jesus, you came to seek out those who were lost:
Lord, have mercy.

All:

Lord, have mercy.

Minister:

You came to give your life for the sake of all:
Christ, have mercy.

All:

Christ, have mercy.

Minister:

You gather into one family your scattered children:
Lord, have mercy.

All:

Lord, have mercy.

B   **Ordinary Time**

Lord Jesus, you are the way that leads us to the Father:
Lord, have mercy.

All:

Lord, have mercy.

Minister:

Lord Jesus, you are the truth that enlightens your people:
Christ, have mercy.

All:

Christ, have mercy.

Ministro:

**Tú que eres la vida que renueva el mundo:
Señor, ten piedad.**

Todos:

Señor, ten piedad.

C   **Tiempo de Adviento**

**Tú que viniste al mundo para salvarnos:
Señor, ten piedad.**

Todos:

Señor, ten piedad.

Ministro:

**Tú que nos visitas continuamente con la gracia de tu Espíritu:
Cristo, ten piedad.**

Todos:

Cristo, ten piedad.

Ministro:

**Tú que vendrás un día a juzgar nuestras obras:
Señor, ten piedad.**

Todos:

Señor, ten piedad.

D   **Tiempo de Navidad**

**Tú eres el Rey de la paz y el Santo de Dios:
Señor, ten piedad.**

Todos:

Señor, ten piedad.

Ministro:

**Tú eres el Hijo de Dios y el Hijo de María:
Cristo, ten piedad.**

Minister:

**Lord Jesus, you are the life that renews the world:
Lord, have mercy.**

All:

Lord, have mercy.

C   Advent

**Lord Jesus, you came into the world for our salvation:
Lord, have mercy.**

All:

Lord, have mercy.

Minister:

**Lord Jesus, you continue to be with us by the grace of your
   Spirit:
Christ, have mercy.**

All:

Christ, have mercy.

Minister:

**Lord Jesus, you will come again in glory:
Lord, have mercy.**

All:

Lord, have mercy.

D   Christmas

**Lord Jesus, you are mighty God and prince of peace:
Lord, have mercy.**

All:

Lord, have mercy.

Minister:

**Lord Jesus, you are Son of God and Son of Mary:
Christ, have mercy.**

Todos:

Cristo, ten piedad.

Ministro:

**Tú eres el Verbo encarnado y el esplendor del Padre:
Señor, ten piedad.**

Todos:

Señor, ten piedad.

E   **Tiempo de Cuaresma**

**Tú que has venido a reconciliarnos los unos con los otros y
con el Padre:
Señor, ten piedad.**

Todos:

Señor, ten piedad.

Ministro:

**Tú que sanas las heridas del pecado y de la división:
Cristo, ten piedad.**

Todos:

Cristo, ten piedad.

Ministro:

**Tú que intercedes al Padre por nosotros:
Señor, ten piedad.**

Todos:

Señor, ten piedad.

F   **Cincuentena Pascual**

**Tú que nos has traído la salvación por tu misterio pascual:
Señor, ten piedad.**

Todos:

Señor, ten piedad.

All:

Christ, have mercy.

Minister:

**Lord Jesus, you are Word made flesh and splendor of the
  Father:**
Lord, have mercy.

All:

Lord, have mercy.

E   **Lent**

**Lord Jesus, you came to reconcile us to one another and to the
  Father:**
Lord, have mercy.

All:

Lord, have mercy.

Minister:

Lord Jesus, you heal the wounds of sin and division:
Christ, have mercy.

All:

Christ, have mercy.

Minister:

Lord Jesus, you intercede for us with your Father:
Lord, have mercy.

All:

Lord, have mercy.

F   **Easter**

You brought us to salvation by your paschal mystery:
Lord, have mercy.

All:

Lord, have mercy.

Ministro:

**Tú que nos renuevas con las maravillas de tu pasión:
Cristo, ten piedad.**

Todos:

Cristo, ten piedad.

Ministro:

**Tú que nos das tu cuerpo para hacernos uno con tu sacrificio
Pascual:
Señor, ten piedad.**

Todos:

Señor, ten piedad.

ORACIÓN COLECTA

127 Sigue la Oración colecta. La oración está tomada de la Oración del Día que se da en el **Apéndice III** para ese domingo, solemnidad, o fiesta del Señor.

El líder invita a la asamblea a orar, diciendo:

Oremos.

Todos los presentes oran en silencio por un breve tiempo.

Entonces el líder dice la oración. Al final de la oración la asamblea responde **Amén**.

LITURGIA DE LA PALABRA

128 Los domingos la Liturgia de la Palabra se celebra como en la Misa.

Las lecturas y el salmo son los que se han asignado en el *Leccionario para la Misa* para ese domingo particular.

Antes de que se proclamen las lecturas, se puede ofrecer una breve introducción con el fin de estimular la atención de los que escuchan, poner las lecturas dentro de su contexto, y hacer ver las conexiones entre las lecturas.

PRIMERA LECTURA

129 Un/a lector/a proclama la primera lectura.

Minister:

You renew us by the wonders of your passion:
Christ, have mercy.

All:

Christ, have mercy.

Minister:

You give us your body to make us one with your Easter sacrifice:
Lord, have mercy.

All:

Lord, have mercy.

OPENING PRAYER

127   The Opening Prayer follows. The prayer is taken from the Prayer of the Day given in **Appendix III** for the particular Sunday, solemnity, or feast of the Lord.

The leader invites the assembly to pray, saying:

Let us pray.

All present pray in silence for a short time.

Then the leader says the prayer. At the end of the prayer the assembly responds **Amen**.

LITURGY OF THE WORD

128   On Sundays the Liturgy of the Word takes place as at Mass.

The readings and the psalm are those assigned in the *Lectionary for Mass* for that particular Sunday.

Before the readings are proclaimed, a brief introduction may be given in order to stimulate the attention of the listeners, to put the readings into context, and to point out connections between the readings.

FIRST READING

129   A reader proclaims the first reading.

Salmo Responsorial

130   Después de la primera lectura, se canta el salmo asignado en el Leccionario. Si es necesario, se puede escoger otro salmo que esté en armonía con el texto de la primera lectura.

Segunda Lectura

131   Si se tienen tres lecturas, el/la lector/a proclama luego la segunda lectura.

Aclamación del Evngelio

132   Se canta la aclamación del evangelio que se da en el Leccionario antes de proclamar el evangelio.

Evangelio

133   Un diácono proclama el evangelio de la manera normal. Sin embargo, una persona laica omite el saludo, "El Señor esté con ustedes", antes de leer el evangelio.

Homilía o Reflexión sobre las Lecturas

134   Un líder que es un diácono ofrece una homilía.

Cuando el líder es una persona laica que no ha sido delegada para predicar, el párroco puede preparar una homilía para que se lea durante la celebración.

En otros casos, cuando la persona laica ha sido delegada por el obispo para predicar, él o ella puede ofrecer a los presentes una breve explicación del texto bíblico, para que puedan comprender por la fe el significado de la celebración.

Después de la homilía hay un momento de silencio sagrado para reflexionar sobre la Palabra de Dios.

Despedida de los Catecúmenos

135   Si hay algunos catecúmenos presentes, se les puede despedir en este momento usando las opciones A o B; si tienen que quedarse para la distribución de la sagrada comunión, se puede usar la opción C.

A   Para la despedida se puede usar la siguiente fórmula u otra parecida.

Catecúmenos, vayan en paz, y que el Señor los acompañe.

Catecúmenos:

Demos gracias a Dios.

RESPONSORIAL PSALM

130   After the first reading, the psalm assigned in the Lectionary is sung. If necessary, another psalm which is in harmony with the text of the first reading may be chosen.

SECOND READING

131   If there are to be three readings, a reader then proclaims the second reading.

GOSPEL ACCLAMATION

132   The gospel acclamation given in the Lectionary is sung before the proclamation of the gospel.

GOSPEL

133   A deacon proclaims the gospel in the usual manner. However, a layperson omits the greeting, "The Lord be with you," before reading the gospel.

HOMILY OR REFLECTION ON THE READINGS

134   A leader who is a deacon gives a homily.

When the leader is a layperson who has not been delegated to preach, the pastor may prepare a homily to be read during the celebration.

In other cases, when a layperson has been delegated to preach by the bishop, he or she may give those present a brief explanation of the biblical text, so that they may understand through faith the meaning of the celebration.

After the readings there may be a period of sacred silence for reflection on the Word of God.

DISMISSAL OF CATECHUMENS

135   If catechumens are present, they may be dismissed at this point by use of option A or B; if they are to remain for the distribution of holy communion, option C may be used.

A   For the dismissal the following or similar words are used.

Catechumens, go in peace, and may the Lord remain with you always.

Catechumens:

Thanks be to God.

B   Como otra fórmula opcional para despedir a los catecúmenos, el líder puede usar estas u otras palabras semejantes.

Mis queridos amigos, esta comunidad les envía ahora a reflexionar más profundamente sobre la palabra de Dios que han compartido con nosotros hoy. Pueden estar seguros de nuestro afecto, apoyo y oraciones por ustedes. Con gusto esperamos el día en que compartan plenamente de la Mesa del Señor.

C   Si los catecúmenos tienen que quedarse durante la distribución de la sagrada comunión y la conclusión de la Liturgia de la Palabra, se les debe recordar que no pueden participar como lo hacen los bautizados. El líder les puede recordar esto con estas palabras u otras parecidas.

Aunque todavía no pueden ustedes participar de la sagrada comunión, quédense con nosotros como un signo de nuestra esperanza de que todos los hijos de Dios comerán y beberán con el Señor y trabajarán con su Espíritu para renovar la faz de la tierra.

PROFESIÓN DE FE

136   Acabada la homilía, se hace la profesión de fe, recitando uno de los siguientes formularios:

A   **Símbolo Niceno-constantinopolitano**
Creo en un solo Dios,
   Padre todopoderoso, Creador del cielo y de la tierra,
   de todo lo visible y lo invisible.

Creo en un solo Señor, Jesucristo, Hijo único de Dios,
   nacido del Padre antes de todos los siglos:
   Dios de Dios, Luz de Luz,
   Dios verdadero de Dios verdadero,
   engendrado, no creado,
   de la misma naturaleza del Padre,
   por quien todo fue hecho;
   que por nosotros, los hombres,
   y por nuestra salvación bajó del cielo,

B   As an optional formulary for dismissing the catechumens, the minister may use these or similar words.

My dear friends, this community now sends you forth to reflect more deeply upon the Word of God which you have shared with us today. Be assured of our loving support and prayers for you. We look forward to the day when you will share fully in the Lord's Table.

C   If the catechumens are to remain for the distribution of holy communion and the conclusion of the liturgy, they should be reminded that they cannot partake as the baptized do. They may be reminded of this by the minister in these or similar words.

Although you cannot yet partake of holy communion, stay with us as a sign of our hope that all God's children will eat and drink with the Lord and work with the Holy Spirit to re-create the face of the earth.

PROFESSION OF FAITH

136   The profession of faith is recited using one of the following formula ries:

A   Nicene Creed

We believe in one God,
  the Father, the Almighty,
  maker of heaven and earth,
  of all that is seen and unseen.

We believe in one Lord, Jesus Christ,
  the only Son of God,
  eternally begotten of the Father,
  God from God, Light from Light,
  true God from true God,
  begotten, not made, one in Being with the Father.
  Through him all things were made.
  For us men and for our salvation
  he came down from heaven:

En las palabras que siguen, hasta se hizo hombre, todos se inclinan.

y por obra del Espíritu Santo
se encarno de María, la Virgen, y se hizo hombre;
y por nuestra causa fue crucificado
en tiempos de Poncio Pilato,
padeció y fue sepultado,
y resucitó al tercer día, según las Escrituras,
y subió al cielo, y está sentado a la derecha del Padre;
y de nuevo vendrá con gloria
para juzgar a vivos y muertos,
y su reino no tendrá fin.

Creo en el Espíritu Santo, Señor y dador de vida,
que procede del Padre y del Hijo,
que con el Padre y el Hijo
recibe una misma adoración y gloria,
y que habló por los profetas.

Creo en la Iglesia,
que es una, santa, católica y apostólica.
Confieso que hay un solo bautismo
para el perdón de los pecados.
Espero la resurrección de los muertos
y la vida del mundo futuro. Amén.

B Símbolo de Los Apóstoles

Creo en Dios, Padre todopoderoso,
Creador del cielo y de la tierra.

Creo en Jesucristo, su único Hijo, nuestro Señor,

En las palabras que siguen, hasta María Virgen, todos se inclinan.

que fue concebido por obra y gracia del Espíritu Santo,
nació de santa María Virgen,
padeció bajo el poder de Poncio Pilato,
fue crucificado, muerto y sepultado,
descendió a los infiernos,

[All bow during these two lines:]

by the power of the Holy Spirit
    he was born of the Virgin Mary, and became man.

For our sake he was crucified under Pontius Pilate;
    he suffered, died, and was buried.
    On the third day he rose again
      in fulfillment of the Scriptures;
    he ascended into heaven
      and is seated at the right hand of the Father.
He will come again in glory to judge the living and the
      dead,
    and his kingdom will have no end.

We believe in the Holy Spirit, the Lord, the giver of life,
    who proceeds from the Father and the Son.
    With the Father and the Son he is worshiped and glori-
      fied.
    He has spoken through the Prophets.
    We believe in one holy catholic and apostolic Church.
    We acknowledge one baptism for the forgiveness of sins.
    We look for the resurrection of the dead,
    and the life of the world to come. Amen.

B   Apostles' Creed

I believe in God, the Father almighty,
    creator of heaven and earth.

I believe in Jesus Christ, his only Son, our Lord.
    He was conceived by the power of the Holy Spirit
      and born of the Virgin Mary.
    He suffered under Pontius Pilate,
      was crucified, died, and was buried.
    He descended to the dead.

al tercer día resucitó de entre los muertos,
subió a los cielos
y está sentado a la derecha de Dios, Padre todopoderoso.
Desde allí ha de venir a juzgar a vivos y muertos.

Creo en el Espíritu Santo,
la santa Iglesia católica,
la comunión de los santos,
el perdón de los pecados,
la resurrección de la carne
y la vida eterna. Amén.

PLEGARIA UNIVERSAL

137 Se hace la oración de los fieles. El líder introduce y concluye la plegaria y un ministro asistente o uno de los presentes anuncia las intenciones.

De las peticiones que se dan en el Apéndice I se pueden usar aquellas que son más apropiadas para la ocasión o se pueden adaptar o componer otras invocaciones que sean apropiadas a las circunstancias de esa comunidad.

138 El líder introduce las intenciones generales con estas u otras palabras semejantes:

A Con fe y humildad presentemos nuestras necesidades al Dios de toda compasión.

B Con fe en las promesas de Dios, presentemos ahora nuestras necesidades y peticiones.

Las peticiones son proclamadas entonces por un ministro asistente.

139 El líder concluye las intercesiones con una de las siguientes oraciones o con otra que sea apropiada:

A Oh Dios,
que eres amor, refugio y fortaleza nuestra,
escucha las oraciones de tu Iglesia,
y concédenos hoy
lo que con fe te pedimos.

Por Cristo nuestro Señor.

On the third day he rose again.
He ascended into heaven,
    and is seated at the right hand of the Father.
He will come again to judge the living and the dead.

I believe in the Holy Spirit,
    the holy catholic Church,
    the communion of saints,
    the forgiveness of sins,
    the resurrection of the body,
    and the life everlasting. Amen.

GENERAL INTERCESSIONS

137   The general intercessions are then said. The leader introduces and concludes the intercessions and an assisting minister or one of those present announces the intentions.

From the petitions given in Appendix I those best suited to the occasion may be used or adapted, or other invocations that apply to the particular circumstances may be composed.

138   The leader introduces the general intercessions in these or similar words:

A   In faith and humility let us offer our needs to the God of compassion.

B   With faith in God's promises, let us now present our needs and petitions.

The petitions are then proclaimed by an assisting minister.

139   The leader concludes the intercessions with one of the following or another more suitable prayer:

A   God of love,
our refuge and our strength,
hear the prayers of your Church,
and grant us today
what we ask of you in faith.

We ask this through Christ our Lord.

Todos:

Amén.

B **Padré,**
a ti venimos con fe y amor
para alabar tu bondad
y reconocer nuestras necesidades.

Te suplicamos escuches nuestra oración
en nombre de Jesucristo, nuestro Señor.

Todos:

Amén.

Acción de Gracias

140 Después de la plegaria universal, el líder invita a la asamblea a dar gracias y todos alaban la gloria y la misericordia de Dios. Esto se puede hacer por medio de un salmo, un cántico, un himno, una letanía de alabanza, o una oración.

El líder y los fieles se ponen de pie y, de frente al altar, juntos cantan o recitan la acción de gracias usando uno de los siguientes formularios. Textos adicionales para dar gracias se encuentran en el **Apéndice II**.

El líder puede introducir la acción de gracias cantando o diciendo:

Demos gracias a nuestro Dios por su misericordia y su amor.

A   Salmo 99 (100)

Aclama al Señor, tierra entera,
sirvan al Señor con alegría,
entren en su presencia con vítores.

Sepan que el Señor es Dios:
que él nos hizo y somos suyos,
su pueblo y ovejas de su rebaño.

Entren por sus puertas con acción de gracias,
por sus atrios con himnos,
dándole gracias y bendiciendo su nombre:

>   All:

Amen.

B **Father,**
we come before you with faith and love
to praise your goodness
and to acknowledge our need.

We ask you to hear the prayers we make
in the name of Jesus the Lord.

>   All:

Amen.

ACT OF THANKSGIVING

> 140   After the general intercessions, the leader invites all to an act of thanksgiving, in which the faithful praise the glory and mercy of God. This can be done by use of a psalm, a canticle, a hymn, a litany of praise, or a prayer.
>
> The leader and the faithful stand and, facing the altar, together sing or recite the thanksgiving using one of the following forms. Additional acts of thanksgiving are given in **Appendix II**.
>
> The leader may introduce the act of thanksgiving by singing or saying:

Let us give thanks to our God for his mercy and love.

A   Psalm 100

Shout joyfully to the LORD, all you lands;
worship the LORD with cries of gladness;
come before God with joyful song.

Know that the LORD is God,
our maker to whom we belong,
whose people we are, God's well-tended flock.

Enter the temple gates with praise,
its courts with thanksgiving.
Give thanks to God, bless his name;

"El Señor es bueno,
su misericordia es eterna,
su fidelidad por todas las edades".

B   Salmo 112 (113)

Alaben, siervos del Señor,
alaben el nombre del Señor.
Bendito sea el nombre del Señor,
ahora y por siempre:
de la salida del sol hasta su ocaso,
alabado sea el nombre del Señor.

El Señor se eleva sobre todos los pueblos,
su gloria sobre los cielos.
¿Quién como el Señor, Dios nuestro,
que se eleva en su trono
y se abaja para mirar
al cielo y a la tierra?

Levanta del polvo al desvalido,
alza de la basura al pobre,
para sentarlo con los príncipes,
los príncipes de su pueblo;
a la estéril le da un puesto en la casa,
como madre feliz de hijos.

C   Salmo 117 (118):1-4, 19-29

Den gracias al Señor porque es bueno,
porque es eterna su misericordia.

Diga la casa de Israel:
eterna es su misericordia.
Diga la casa de Aarón:
eterna es su misericordia.
Digan los fieles del Señor:
eterna es su misericordia.

good indeed is the LORD,
Whose love endures forever,
whose faithfulness lasts through every age.

B   Psalm 113

Praise, you servants of the LORD,
praise the name of the LORD.
Blessed be the name of the LORD
both now and forever.
From the rising of the sun to its setting
let the name of the LORD be praised.

High above all nations is the LORD;
above the heavens God's glory.
Who is like the LORD,
our God enthroned on high,
looking down on heaven and earth?

The LORD raises the needy from the dust,
lifts the poor from the ash heap,
Seats them with princes,
the princes of the people,
Gives the childless wife a place,
the joyful mother of children.

C   Psalm 118:1-4, 19-29

Give thanks to the LORD, who is good,
whose love endures forever.

Let the house of Israel say:
God's love endures forever.
Let the house of Aaron say,
God's love endures forever.
Let those who fear the LORD say,
God's love endures forever.

Open the gates of victory;
I will enter and thank the LORD.
This is the LORD's own gate,

Ábranme las puertas del triunfo,
Y entraré para dar gracias al Señor.
Ésta es la puerta del Señor:
los vencedores entrarán por ella.
Te doy gracias porque me escuchaste
y fuiste mi salvación.

La piedra que desecharon los arquitectos
es ahora la piedra angular.
Es el Señor quien lo ha hecho,
ha sido un milagro patente.
Éste es el día en que actuó el Señor:
sea nuestra alegría y nuestro gozo.

Señor, danos la salvación;
Señor, danos prosperidad.
Bendito el que viene en nombre del Señor,
lo bendecimos desde la casa del Señor;
el Señor es Dios, él nos ilumina.

Ordenen una procesión con ramos
hasta los ángulos del altar.
Tú eres mi Dios, te doy gracias;
Dios mío, yo te ensalzo.
Den gracias al Señor porque es bueno,
porque es eterna su misericordia.

D   Salmo 135 (136):1-9, 13-14, 16-17, 21-26

Den gracias al Señor porque es bueno:
porque es eterna su misericordia.
Den gracias al Dios de los dioses:
porque es eterna su misericordia.
Den gracias al Señor de los señores:
porque es eterna su misericordia.

Sólo él hizo grandes maravillas:
porque es eterna su misericordia.

where the victors enter.
I thank you for you answered me;
you have been my savior.

The stone the builders rejected
has become the cornerstone.
By the LORD has this been done;
it is wonderful in our eyes.
This is the day the LORD has made;
let us rejoice in it and be glad.

LORD, grant salvation!
LORD, grant good fortune!
Blessed is he
who comes in the name of the LORD.
We bless you from the LORD's house.
The LORD is God and has given us light.

Join in procession with leafy branches
up to the horns of the altar.
You are my God, I give you thanks;
my God, I offer you praise.
Give thanks to the LORD, who is good,
whose love endures forever.

D   Psalm 136:1-9, 13-14, 16-17, 21-26

Praise the LORD, who is so good;
God's love endures forever;
Praise the God of gods;
God's love endures forever;
Praise the Lord of lords;
God's love endures forever;

Who alone has done great wonders,
God's love endures forever;
Who skillfully made the heavens,
Gods love endures forever;

Él hizo sabiamente los cielos:
porque es eterna su misericordia.
Él afianzó sobre las aguas la tierra:
porque es eterna su misericordia.

Él hizo lumbreras gigantes:
porque es eterna su misericordia.
El sol que gobierna el día:
porque es eterna su misericordia.
La luna que gobierna la noche:
porque es eterna su misericordia.

Él dividió en dos partes el mar Rojo:
porque es eterna su misericordia.
Y condujo por en medio a Israel:
porque es eterna su misericordia.
Guió por el desierto a su pueblo:
porque es eterna su misericordia.

Dio muerte a reyes poderosos:
porque es eterna su misericordia.
Les dio su tierra en heredad:
porque es eterna su misericordia.
En heredad a Israel su siervo:
porque es eterna su misericordia.

En nuestra humillación, se acordó de nosotros:
porque es eterna su misericordia.
Y nos libró de nuestros opresores:
porque es eterna su misericordia.
Él da alimento a todo viviente:
porque es eterna su misericordia.

Den gracias al Dios del cielo:
porque es eterna su misericordia.

Who spread the earth upon the waters,
God's love endures forever;

Who made the great lights,
God's love endures forever;
The sun to rule the day,
God's love endures forever;
The moon and stars to rule the night,
God's love endures forever;

Who split in two the Red Sea,
God's love endures forever;
And led Israel through it,
God's love endures forever;
Who led the people through the desert,
God's love endures forever;

Who struck down great kings,
God's love endures forever;
And made their lands a heritage,
God's love endures forever;
A heritage for Israel, God's servant,
God's love endures forever.

The LORD remembered us in our misery,
God's love endures forever;
Freed us from our foes,
God's love endures forever;
And gives food to all flesh,
God's love endures forever.

Praise the God of heaven,
God's love endures forever.

**Alaben al Señor en su templo,
alábenlo en su fuerte firmamento.
Alábenlo por sus obras magníficas,
alábenlo por su inmensa grandeza.**

**Alábenlo tocando trompetas,
alábenlo con arpas y cítaras.
Alábenlo con tambores y danzas,
alábenlo con trompas y flautas.**

**Alábenlo con platillos sonoros,
alábenlo con platillos vibrantes.
Todo ser que alienta alabe al Señor. (Aleluya.)**

141   Si no se va a distribuir la sagrada comunión, la celebración continúa en el núm. 153.

RITO DE COMUNION

142   El líder va al lugar donde se reserva el sacramento, toma el recipiente o copón que contiene el Cuerpo del Señor, lo coloca en el altar y hace una genuflexión.

PADRENUESTRO

143   El líder invita a todos los presentes a cantar o decir el Padrenuestro con estas u otras palabras semejantes:

A   **Fieles a la recomendación del Salvador
y siguiendo su divina enseñanza,
nos atrevemos a decir:**

B   **Llenos de alegría por ser hijos de Dios,
digamos confiadamente
la oración que Cristo nos enseñó:**

C   **El amor de Dios ha sido derramado
en nuestros corazones
con el Espíritu Santo que se nos ha dado;
digamos con fe y esperanza:**

Praise God in his holy sanctuary;
give praise in the mighty dome of heaven.
Give praise for his mighty deeds,
praise him for his great majesty.

Give praise with blasts upon the horn,
praise him with harp and lyre.
Give praise with tambourines and dance,
praise him with flutes and strings.

Give praise with crashing cymbals,
praise him with sounding cymbals.
Let everything that has breath
give praise to the LORD! (Alleluia!)

141 If holy communion is not to be distributed, the service continues at no. 153.

COMMUNION RITE

142 The leader goes to the place where the sacrament is reserved, takes the vessel or ciborium containing the body of the Lord, places it on the altar and genuflects.

LORD'S PRAYER

143 The leader invites all present to sing or say the Lord's Prayer in these or similar words:

A **Let us pray with confidence to the Father in the words our Savior gave us:**

B **Jesus taught us to call God our Father, and so we have the courage to say:**

C **Let us ask our Father to forgive our sins and bring us to forgive those who sin against us.**

D   Antes de participar en el banquete de la Eucaristía,
    signo de reconciliación
    y vínculo de union fraterna,
    oremos juntos como el Señor nos ha enseñado:

> El líder continúa, junto con la asamblea:

**Padre nuestro, que estás en el cielo,
santificado sea tu Nombre;
venga a nosotros tu reino;
hágase tu voluntad en la tierra como en el cielo.
Danos hoy nuestro pan de cada día;
perdona nuestras ofensas,
como también nosotros perdonamos
a los que nos ofenden;
no nos dejes caer en la tentación,
y líbranos del mal.**

EL SALUDO DE PAZ

> 144   El líder puede invitar a la asamblea a darse el saludo de paz con estas u otras palabras semejantes:

En el amor de Cristo, demonos unos a otros un saludo de paz.

> Todos, según la costumbre del lugar, se dan la paz.

INVITACIÓN A COMULGAR

> 145   El líder hace genuflexión, toma el pan consagrado y, sosteniéndolo un poco elevado sobre el recipiente o copón, lo muestra al pueblo, diciendo:

**Éste es el Cordero de Dios,
que quita el pecado del mundo.
Dichosos los invitados a la cena del Señor.**

> Y, juntamente con el pueblo, añade:

Señor, no soy digno
de que entres en mi casa,
pero una palabra tuya
bastará para sanarme.

D **Let us pray for the coming of the kingdom as Jesus taught us.**

The leader continues with the people:

Our Father, who art in heaven,
hallowed be thy name;
thy kingdom come;
thy will be done on earth as it is in heaven.
Give us this day our daily bread;
and forgive us our trespasses
as we forgive those who trespass against us;
and lead us not into temptation,
but deliver us from evil.

Sign of Peace

144   The leader may invite the people to exchange the sign of peace in these or similar words:

In the love of Christ, let us offer one another a sign of peace.

All make an appropriate sign of peace, according to local custom.

Invitation to Communion

145   The leader genuflects. Taking the host, the minister raises it slightly over the vessel or ciborium and, facing the people, says:

This is the Lamb of God
who takes away the sins of the world.
Happy are those who are called to his supper.

The communicants say:

Lord, I am not worthy to receive you
but only say the word and I shall be healed.

Comunión

146 El líder dice en secreto:

El Cuerpo de Cristo me guarde para la vida eterna.

Y comulga reverentemente el Cuerpo de Cristo.

147 Después el líder (y los otros ministros especiales de la comunión) toma el recipiente o copón, se acerca a los que quieren comulgar y les presenta el pan consagrado, que sostiene un poco elevado, diciendo a cada uno de ellos:

El Cuerpo de Cristo.

El que va a comulgar responde **Amén** y comulga.

148 Durante la distribución de la comunión, se puede cantar un himno.

149 Acabada la comunión, el líder o un ministro extraordinario de la comunión consume cualquier fragmento que se encuentre o lo pone en el recipiente o copón y se lava las manos si lo juzga necesario. Si quedan hostias adicionales, el ministro o hace una genuflexión y las pone de nuevo en el tabernáculo o las pone otra vez en el recipiente o copón y lo regresa a la iglesia de donde había traído la eucaristía para la distribución.

150 Se puede guardar unos momentos de silencio o cantar un salmo o cántico o una letanía de alabanza.

Oración después de la Comunión

151 El líder dice luego la Oración después de la Comunión apropiada del **Apéndice III** o una de las oraciones en el **Apéndice IV**. El líder primero invita a la asamblea a orar, diciendo:

Oremos.

Todos los presentes oran en silencio por un corto tiempo. Luego el líder dice la oración. Al final de la oración la asamblea responde **Amén**.

152 El servicio concluye con anuncios breves [la colecta de las ofrendas monetarias por parte de la asamblea], la bendición, y la despedida como en los núm. 154–157.

El Padrenuestro

153 Si no se distribuye la sagrada comunión, el líder invita a todos a rezar el Padrenuestro con estas u otras palabras semejantes:

COMMUNION

146　The leader says quietly:

May the body of Christ bring me to everlasting life.

The leader reverently consumes the body of Christ.

147　The leader (and other special ministers of holy communion) then takes the vessel or ciborium with the eucharist and goes to the communicants. The minister takes a host for each one, raises it slightly and says:

The body of Christ.

The communicant answers **Amen** and receives communion.

148　During the distribution of communion, a hymn may be sung.

149　After communion the leader or a special minister of holy communion consumes any fragments which are found or puts them in the vessel or ciborium and then washes his or her hands if need be. If additional hosts remain, the minister either genuflects and puts them back into the tabernacle or else puts them back into the vessel or ciborium and returns it to the church from which he or she had obtained the eucharist for distribution.

150　A period of silence may now be observed, or a psalm, song of praise, or litany of praise may be sung.

PRAYER AFTER COMMUNION

151　The leader then says the proper Prayer after Communion from **Appendix III** or one of the prayers in **Appendix IV**. The leader first invites the assembly to pray, saying:

Let us pray.

All present pray in silence for a short time. Then the leader says the prayer. At the end of the prayer the assembly responds **Amen**.

152　The service concludes with the brief announcements [the collection of the monetary offerings of the assembly], the blessing, and the dismissal at nos. 154–157.

LORD'S PRAYER

153　If holy communion is not distributed, the leader invites all to pray the Lord's Prayer in these or similar words:

A   Fieles a la recomendación del Salvador
     y siguiendo su divina enseñanza,
     nos atrevemos a decir:

B   Llenos de alegría por ser hijos de Dios,
     digamos confiadamente
     la oración que Cristo nos enseñó:

C   El amor de Dios ha sido derramado
     en nuestros corazones
     con el Espíritu Santo que se nos ha dado;
     digamos con fe y esperanza:

> El líder continúa, junto con la asamblea:

Padre nuestro, que estás en el cielo,
santificado sea tu Nombre;
venga a nosotros tu reino;
hágase tu voluntad en la tierra como en el cielo.
Danos hoy nuestro pan de cada día;
perdona nuestras ofensas,
como también nosotros perdonamos
a los que nos ofenden;
no nos dejes caer en la tentación,
y líbranos del mal.

RITO DE CONCLUSION

ANUNCIOS BREVES

154   Antes de despedir a la asamblea se pueden hacer breves anuncios que afectan la vida y las actividades de la parroquia.

[COLECTA DE LAS OFRENDAS MONETARIAS POR PARTE DE LA ASAMBLEA]

155   Después de las oraciones se pueden recoger las ofrendas de los fieles según las normas y las necesidades indicadas por el Ordinario local.

A   Let us pray with confidence to the Father in the words our Savior gave us:

B   Jesus taught us to call God our Father, and so we have the courage to say:

C   Let us ask our Father to forgive our sins and bring us to forgive those who sin against us.

D   Let us pray for the coming of the kingdom as Jesus taught us.

> The leader continues with the people:

Our Father, who art in heaven,
hallowed be thy name;
thy kingdom come;
thy will be done on earth as it is in heaven.
Give us this day our daily bread;
and forgive us our trespasses
as we forgive those who trespass against us;
and lead us not into temptation,
but deliver us from evil.

CONCLUDING RITE

BRIEF ANNOUNCEMENTS

> 154   Brief announcements concerning parish life and activities may be made before the congregation is dismissed.

[COLLECTION OF THE MONETARY OFFERINGS OF THE ASSEMBLY]

> 155   The offerings of the faithful may be collected in accordance with the norms and the necessities indicated by the local Ordinary.

BENDICIÓN

156   Un líder que es diácono dice:

El Señor esté con ustedes.

Todos responden:

Y con tu espíritu.

Bendice al pueblo usando la siguiente bendición. Puede también usar una de las bendiciones en el **Apendice V**, o una de las bendiciones solemnes o de las oraciones sobre el pueblo en el *Sacramentario*.

La bendición de Dios todopoderoso, Padre, Hijo, ✠ y Espíritu Santo descienda sobre ustedes.

Todos:

Amén.

Un líder que es una persona laica hace la señal de la cruz sobre sí mismo/a y dice:

El Señor nos bendiga, nos guarde de todo mal y nos lleve a la vida eterna.

Todos:

Amén.

DESPEDIDA

157   El líder luego añade:

Vayan en paz.

Todos:

Demos gracias a Dios.

158   Si se desea, un himno puede concluir la celebración.

BLESSING

156   A leader who is a deacon says:

The Lord be with you.

All respond:

And also with you.

He blesses the people using the following blessing. He may also use one of the blessings in **Appendix V**, or one of the solemn blessings or prayers over the people in the *Sacramentary*.

**May almighty God bless you,
the Father, and the Son, ☩ and the Holy Spirit.**

All:

Amen.

A leader who is a layperson makes the sign of the cross on himself or herself and says:

**May the Lord bless us,
protect us from all evil
and bring us to everlasting life.**

All:

Amen.

DISMISSAL

157   The leader then adds:

Go in the peace of Christ.

All:

Thanks be to God.

158   If desired, a song may conclude the celebration.

APENDICE I

PLEGARIA UNIVERSAL

APPENDIX I

GENERAL INTERCESSIONS

PLEGARIA UNIVERSAL

159 Se pueden escoger las intercesiones apropiadas de las que se ofrecen aquí, o se pueden componer otras intenciones semejantes. Por lo general debe ofrecerse por lo menos una petición de cada una de las siguientes categorías:

a) por la Iglesia;
b) por la vida y la salvación del mundo;
c) por los que están afligidos por varias necesidades;
d) por la comunidad local.

A Por la Iglesia

1. **Por N., nuestro Papa, N., nuestro obispo, N., nuestro párroco, y todos los ministros de la Iglesia de Cristo, para que el Espíritu Santo les fortalezca al predicar la buena nueva de salvación, roguemos al Señor.**

2. **Por la Iglesia de Jesucristo, heredera en la esperanza de la vida eterna; para que podamos estar siempre vigilantes y sobrios mientras esperamos el día del Señor, roguemos al Señor.**

3. **Para que todos los que somos miembros de la Iglesia perseveremos en la sabiduría revelada por Cristo, roguemos al Señor.**

4. **Por todos los líderes de la Iglesia de Cristo, para que sean dignos ejemplos que otros puedan imitar, roguemos al Señor.**

5. **Por todos los miembros de la Iglesia de Jesucristo, para que permanezcamos siempre dispuestos a escuchar la Palabra de Dios y tengamos fuerza para cumplirla, roguemos al Señor.**

6. **Por todos los que forman la Iglesia de Jesucristo, para que puedan ser una verdadera casa de oración, roguemos al Señor.**

7. **Para que cada parroquia de nuestra diócesis sea un signo vivo de la presencia de Cristo en el mundo, roguemos al Señor.**

GENERAL INTERCESSIONS

159 Appropriate intercessions may be chosen from those given below, or other similar intentions may be composed. As a rule at least one petition should be offered from each of the following categories:

a) for the Church;
b) for the life and salvation of the world;
c) for those weighed down by various needs;
d) for the local community.

A   For the Church

1. For N., our Pope, N., our bishop, N., our pastor, and all ministers of Christ's Church, that they may be strengthened by the Holy Spirit in their preaching the good news of salvation, let us pray to the Lord.

2. For the Church of Jesus Christ, heirs in hope of eternal life; that we may forever be awake and sober as we await the day of the Lord, let us pray to the Lord.

3. That all who are members of the Church may hold fast to the wisdom revealed by Christ, let us pray to the Lord.

4. For all the leaders of Christ's Church, that they may be worthy examples for others to imitate, let us pray to the Lord.

5. For all who make up the Church of Jesus Christ, that we may always remain open to hearing the Word of God and have the strength to keep it, let us pray to the Lord.

6. For all who make up the Church of Jesus Christ, that we may be a true house of prayer, let us pray to the Lord.

7. That each parish of our diocese may be a living sign of the presence of Christ in the world, let us pray to the Lord.

B Por la Vida y Salvación del Mundo

1. Por nuestros líderes locales, estatales, y nacionales, para que su ejemplo inspire a muchos jóvenes a dedicar su vida al servicio público, roguemos al Señor.

2. Para que Dios bendiga a los oficiales públicos con los dones de sabiduría y comprensión y en atender las necesidades de su pueblo, roguemos al Señor.

3. Por la paz del mundo, para que todos los líderes estén conscientes del hambre de justicia y reconciliación entre su pueblo, roguemos al Señor.

4. Para que las leyes civiles reflejen los valores cristianos y eviten la opresión de los débiles, roguemos al Señor.

5. Por la paz, la justicia, y la esperanza en nuestro mundo, roguemos al Señor.

C Por los Afligidos con Varias Necesidades

1. Por los que viven donde hay guerra, para que puedan ver tanto el término de la violencia como la verdadera reconciliación en sus patrias, roguemos al Señor.

2. Para que los que sufren sientan el amor y cariño de Cristo por medio de la generosidad de los cristianos, roguemos al Señor.

3. Para que los que viven en tinieblas, los que nuestro mundo mantiene marginados, reciban la ayuda que necesitan y vean afirmada su dignidad humana, roguemos al Señor.

4. Para que el Evangelio de paz y justicia prevalezca en los corazones de todos los que usan la violencia, roguemos al Señor.

5. Por todos los hombres y mujeres que sufren soledad, rechazo, y persecución porque se esfuerzan en extender la paz y la comprensión en nuestro mundo, roguemos al Señor.

B   For the Life and Salvation of the World

1. For our local, state, and national leaders, that their example may inspire young people to devote their lives to public service, let us pray to the Lord.

2. That public officials may be blessed with the gifts of wisdom and understanding in serving the needs of their people, let us pray to the Lord.

3. For peace throughout the world, that all leaders may be open to the hungers of their people for justice and reconciliation, let us pray to the Lord.

4. That public policy may reflect Christian values and avoid oppression of the weak, let us pray to the Lord.

5. For peace, justice and hope in our world, let us pray to the Lord.

C   For Those Weighed Down by Various Needs

1. For those who live in war-torn lands, that they may witness the cessation of violence and true reconciliation in their lands, let us pray to the Lord.

2. That those who suffer in any way may experience the love and concern of Christ through the generosity of Christ's disciples, let us pray to the Lord.

3. That those who live in darkness and are shunned as outcasts in today's world may receive assistance in their needs and affirmation of their human dignity, let us pray to the Lord.

4. That the Gospel of peace and justice may prevail in the hearts of all who resort to violence, let us pray to the Lord.

5. For all men and women who risk loneliness, rejection, and even persecution in their efforts to spread peace and understanding in our world, let us pray to the Lord.

6. Por todos los que viven en pobreza y con hambre, y en tantas otras condiciones que rebajan su dignidad humana, roguemos al Señor.

7. Por todos los que sufren enfermedad y debilidad, hambre y sed, falta de hogar y de empleo; para que el amor de Dios dé remedio a sus necesidades, roguemos al Señor.

D   Por la Comunidad Local

1. Por los fieles difuntos, para que gocen de la plenitud del Reino de Dios, roguemos al Señor.

2. Para que a imitación de María, nuestra Madre, mostremos admiración y respeto por el don de la vida humana, roguemos al Señor.

3. Por los que en esté día se encuentran al borde de la muerte, para que reciban la recompensa de sus obras, roguemos al Señor.

4. Por nuestros muertos, para que llevados a la gloria de Dios, vivan eternamente en el reino celestial, roguemos al Señor.

5. Por los enfermos e impedidos, especialmente N. y N.; para que su paciencia en el sufrimiento nos revele a todos la presencia de Dios como fuente de su fortaleza, roguemos al Señor.

6. Por las vocaciones sacerdotales, especialmente en nuestra diócesis, para que haya suficientes sacerdotes que ejerzan su ministerio en todas nuestras parroquias y comunidades, roguemos al Señor.

7. Por vocaciones al presbiterado y al diaconado, para que en nuestras comunidades Dios llame a ministros de la Palabra y de los sacramentos, roguemos al Señor.

6. For all who live in poverty and hunger, and other conditions which are degrading to their human dignity, let us pray to the Lord.

7. For those who suffer from sickness and disease, hunger and thirst, homelessness and unemployment; that they may receive a loving response to their needs, let us pray to the Lord.

D   For the Local Community

1. For the faithful departed, that they may come to the full blessedness of God's Kingdom, let us pray to the Lord.

2. That in imitation of Mary, our Mother, we may evidence awe and wonder for the gift of human life, let us pray to the Lord.

3. For those who are near death today, that they may receive the reward of their labors, let us pray to the Lord.

4. That those who have died may be brought to the glory of God's heavenly kingdom, let us pray to the Lord.

5. For the sick and infirm, especially N. and N.; that their patient suffering may show forth the presence of God as the source of their strength, let us pray to the Lord.

6. For vocations to the priesthood, especially for our diocese, that there be sufficient priests to serve all our parishes and communities, let us pray to the Lord.

7. For vocations to the priesthood and diaconate, that God may call forth from our communities ministers of the Word and sacraments for our diocese, let us pray to the Lord.

APENDICE II

ACCION DE GRACIAS

APPENDIX II

ACTS OF THANKSGIVING

ACCION DE GRACIAS

160 Las siguientes formas de dar gracias se pueden usar además de las que se dan en el núm 140.

I. SALMOS

A SALMO 135 (136)

Den gracias al Señor porque es bueno:
porque es eterna su misericordia.
Den gracias al Dios de los dioses:
porque es eterna su misericordia.
Den gracias al Señor de los señores:
porque es eterna su misericordia.

Sólo él hizo grandes maravillas:
porque es eterna su misericordia.
Él hizo sabiamente los cielos:
porque es eterna su misericordia.
Él afianzó sobre las aguas la tierra:
porque es eterna su misericordia.

Él hizo lumbreras gigantes:
porque es eterna su misericordia.
El sol que gobierna el día:
porque es eterna su misericordia.
La luna que gobierna la noche:
porque es eterna su misericordia.

Él hirió a Egipto en sus primogénitos:
porque es eterna su misericordia.
Y sacó a Israel de aquel país:
porque es eterna su misericordia.
Con mano poderosa y brazo extendido:
porque es eterna su misericordia.

Él dividió en dos partes el mar Rojo:
porque es eterna su misericordia.
Y condujo por en medio a Israel:
porque es eterna su misericordia.

ACTS OF THANKSGIVING

160   The following acts of thanksgiving may be used in addition to those in no. 140.

I. PSALMS OF THANKSGIVING

A   PSALM 136

Praise the LORD, who is so good;
God's love endures forever;
Praise the God of gods;
God's love endures forever;
Praise the Lord of lords;
God's love endures forever;

Who alone has done great wonders,
God's love endures forever;
Who skillfully made the heavens,
God's love endures forever;
Who spread the earth upon the waters,
God's love endures forever;

Who made the great lights,
God's love endures forever;
The sun to rule the day,
God's love endures forever;
The moon and stars to rule the night,
God's love endures forever;

Who struck down the firstborn of Egypt,
God's love endures forever;
And led Israel from their midst,
God's love endures forever;
With mighty hand and outstretched arm,
God's love endures forever;

Who split in two the Red Sea,
God's love endures forever;
And led Israel through it,
God's love endures forever;

Arrojó en el mar Rojo al Faraón:
porque es eterna su misericordia.

Guió por el desierto a su pueblo:
porque es eterna su misericordia.
Él hirió a reyes famosos:
porque es eterna su misericordia.
Dio muerte a reyes poderosos:
porque es eterna su misericordia.

A Sijón, rey de los amorreos:
porque es eterna su misericordia.
Y a Hog, rey de Basán:
porque es eterna su misericordia.

Les dio su tierra en heredad:
porque es eterna su misericordia.
En heredad a Israel su siervo:
porque es eterna su misericordia.

En nuestra humillación, se acordó de nosotros:
porque es eterna su misericordia.
Y nos libró de nuestros opresores:
porque es eterna su misericordia.

Él da alimento a todo viviente:
porque es eterna su misericordia.
Den gracias al Dios del cielo:
porque es eterna su misericordia.

B SALMO 146 (147)

Alaben al Señor, que la música es buena;
nuestro Dios merece una alabanza armoniosa.

El Señor reconstruye Jerusalén,
reúne a los deportados de Israel;
él sana los corazones destrozados,
venda sus heridas.

But swept Pharaoh and his army into the Red Sea,
God's love endures forever;

Who led the people through the desert,
God's love endures forever;
Who struck down great kings,
God's love endures forever;
Slew powerful kings,
God's love endures forever;

Sihon, king of the Amorites,
God's love endures forever;
Og, king of Bashan,
God's love endures forever;

And made their lands a heritage,
God's love endures forever;
A heritage for Israel, God's servant,
God's love endures forever.

The LORD remembered us in our misery,
God's love endures forever;
Freed us from our foes,
God's love endures forever;

And gives food to all flesh,
God's love endures forever.

Praise the God of heaven,
God's love endures forever.

B   PSALM 147

How good to celebrate our God in song;
how sweet to give fitting praise.

The LORD rebuilds Jerusalem,
gathers the dispersed of Israel,
Heals the brokenhearted,
binds up their wounds,

Cuenta el número de las estrellas,
a cada una la llama por su nombre.

Nuestro Señor es grande y poderoso,
su sabiduría no tiene medida.
El Señor sostiene a los humildes,
humilla hasta el polvo a los malvados.

Entonen la acción de gracias al Señor,
toquen la cítara para nuestro Dios,
que cubre el cielo de nubes,
preparando la lluvia para la tierra;

que hace brotar hierba en los montes,
para los que sirven al hombre;
que da su alimento al ganado
y a las crías de cuervo que graznan.

No aprecia el vigor de los caballos,
no estima los jarretes del hombre:
el Señor aprecia a sus fieles,
que confían en su misericordia.

II. CANTICOS

A   CÁNTICO DE CRÓNICAS   1 Crónicas 29:10-13

Bendito eres, Señor,
Dios de nuestro padre Israel,
por los siglos de los siglos.

Tuyos son, Señor, la grandeza y el poder,
la gloria, el esplendor, la majestad,
porque tuyo es cuanto hay en cielo y tierra,
tú eres rey y soberano de todo.

De ti viene la riqueza y la gloria,
tú eres Señor del universo,
en tu mano está el poder y la fuerza,
tú engrandeces y confortas a todos.

Numbers all the stars,
calls each of them by name.

Great is our Lord, vast in power,
with wisdom beyond measure.
The LORD sustains the poor,
but casts the wicked to the ground.

Sing to the LORD with thanksgiving;
with the lyre celebrate our God,
Who covers the heavens with clouds,
provides rain for the earth,

makes grass sprout on the mountains,
Who gives animals their food
and ravens what they cry for.

God takes no delight in the strength of horses,
no pleasure in the runner's stride.
Rather the LORD takes pleasure in the devout,
those who await God's faithful care.

II. CANTICLES

A CANTICLE OF CHRONICLES   1 Chronicles 29:10-13

Blessed may you be, O LORD,
God of Israel our father,
from eternity to eternity.
Yours, O LORD, are grandeur and power,
majesty, splendor, and glory.

For all in heaven and on earth is yours;
yours, O LORD, is the sovereignty;
you are exalted as head over all.

Riches and honor are from you,
and you have dominion over all.
In your hand are power and might;
it is yours to give grandeur and strength to all.

Por eso, Dios nuestro,
nosotros te damos gracias,
alabando tu nombre glorioso.

B   CÁNTICO DE JUDIT   Judit 16:2-3a, 15-19

¡Alaben a mi Dios con tambores,
eleven cantos al Señor con cítaras,
ofrézeanle los acordes de un salmo de alabanza,
ensalcen e invoquen su nombre!

Cantaré a mi Dios un cántico nuevo:
Señor, tú eres grande y glorioso,
admirable en tu fuerza, invencible.

Que te sirva toda la creación,
porque tú lo mandaste, y existió;
enviaste tu aliento, y la construiste,
nada puede resistir a tu voz.

Sacudirán las olas los cimientos de los montes,
las peñas en tu presencia se derretirán como cera,
pero tú serás propicio a tus fieles.

C   CÁNTICO DE DANIEL   Daniel 3:57-88, 56

Criaturas todas del Señor, bendigan al Señor;
ensálcenlo con himnos por los siglos.
Ángeles del Señor, bendigan al Señor;
cielos, bendigan al Señor.
Aguas del espacio, bendigan al Señor;
ejércitos del Señor, bendigan al Señor.
Sol y luna, bendigan al Señor;
astros del cielo, bendigan al Señor.

Lluvia y rocío, bendigan al Señor;
vientos todos, bendigan al Señor.
Fuego y calor, bendigan al Señor;
fríos y heladas, bendigan al Señor.
Rocíos y nevadas, bendigan al Señor;

Therefore, our God, we give you thanks
and we praise the majesty of your name.

B   CANTICLE OF JUDITH   Judith 16:1, 13-15

Strike up the instruments,
a song to my God with timbrels,
chant to the LORD with cymbals;
Sing to him a new song,
exalt and acclaim his name.

A new hymn I will sing to my God.
O LORD, great are you and glorious,
wonderful in power and unsurpassable.
Let your every creature serve you;
for you spoke, and they were made,
you sent forth your spirit, and they were created;
no one can resist your word.

The mountains to their bases, and the seas, are shaken;
the rocks, like wax, melt before your glance.
But to those who fear you,
you are very merciful.

C   CANTICLE OF DANIEL   Daniel 3:57-88, 56

Bless the Lord, all you works of the Lord.
Praise and exalt him above all forever.
Angels of the Lord, bless the Lord.
You heavens, bless the Lord.
All you waters above the heavens, bless the Lord.
All you hosts of the Lord, bless the Lord.
Sun and moon, bless the Lord.
Stars of heaven, bless the Lord.

Every shower and dew, bless the Lord.
All you winds, bless the Lord.
Fire and heat, bless the Lord.
Cold and chill, bless the Lord.
Dew and rain, bless the Lord.

témpanos y hielos, bendigan al Señor.
Escarchas y nieves, bendigan al Señor;
noche y día, bendigan al Señor.
Luz y tinieblas, bendigan al Señor;
rayos y nubes, bendigan al Señor.

Bendiga la tierra al Señor,
ensálcelo con himnos por los siglos.
Montes y cumbres, bendigan al Señor;
cuanto germina en la tierra, bendiga al Señor.
Manantiales, bendigan al Señor;
mares y ríos, bendigan al Señor.
Cetáceos y peces, bendigan al Señor;
aves del cielo, bendigan al Señor.
Fieras y ganados, bendigan al Señor;
ensálcenlo con himnos por los siglos.

Hijos de los hombres, bendigan al Señor;
bendiga Israel al Señor.
Sacerdotes del Señor, bendigan al Señor;
siervos del Señor, bendigan al Señor.
Almas y espíritus justos, bendigan al Señor;
santos y humildes de corazón, bendigan al Señor.
Ananías, Azarías y Misael, bendigan al Señor,
ensálcenlo con himnos por los siglos.

Bendigamos al Padre y al Hijo con el Espíritu Santo,
ensalcémoslo con himnos por los siglos.
Bendito el Señor en la bóveda del cielo,
alabado y glorioso y ensalzado por los siglos.

D CÁNTICO DE MARÍA   Lucas 1:46-55

Proclama mi alma la grandeza del Señor,
se alegra mi espíritu en Dios, mi salvador;
porque ha mirado la humillación de su esclava.

Frost and chill, bless the Lord.
Ice and snow, bless the Lord.
Nights and days, bless the Lord.
Light and darkness, bless the Lord.
Lightnings and clouds, bless the Lord.

Let the earth bless the Lord.
Praise and exalt him above all for ever.
Mountains and hills, bless the Lord.
Everything growing from the earth, bless the Lord.
You springs, bless the Lord.
Seas and rivers, bless the Lord.
You dolphins and all water creatures, bless the Lord.
All you birds of the air, bless the Lord.
All you beasts, wild and tame, bless the Lord.
You sons of men, bless the Lord.

O Israel, bless the Lord.
Praise and exalt him above all for ever.
Priests of the Lord, bless the Lord.
Servants of the Lord, bless the Lord.
Spirits and souls of the just, bless the Lord.
Holy men of humble heart, bless the Lord.
Hananiah, Azariah, Mishael, bless the Lord.
Praise and exalt him above all forever.

Let us bless the Father, and the Son, and the Holy Spirit.
Let us praise and exalt him above all forever.
Blessed are you, Lord, in the firmament of heaven.
Praiseworthy and glorious and exalted above all forever.

D   CANTICLE OF MARY   Luke 1:46-55

My soul proclaims the greatness of the Lord,
my spirit rejoices in God my Savior
for he has looked with favor on his lowly servant.

Desde ahora me felicitarán todas las generaciones,
porque el Poderoso ha hecho obras grandes por mí:
su nombre es santo,
y su misericordia llega a sus fieles
de generación en generación.

Él hace proezas con su brazo:
dispersa a los soberbios de corazón,
derriba del trono a los poderosos
y enaltece a los humildes,
a los hambrientos los colma de bienes
y a los ricos los despide vacíos.

Auxilia a Israel, su siervo,
acordándose de la misericordia,
como lo había prometido a nuestros padres,
en favor de Abrahán y su descendencia por siempre.

E   CÁNTICO DEL APOCALIPSIS   Apocalipsis 4:11; 5:9, 10, 12

Eres digno, Señor, Dios nuestro,
de recibir la gloria, el honor y el poder,
porque tú has creado el universo;
porque por tu voluntad lo que no existía fue creado.

Eres digno de tomar el libro y abrir sus sellos,
porque fuiste degollado
y con tu sangre compraste para Dios
hombres de toda raza, lengua, pueblo y nación.

Y has hecho de ellos para nuestro Dios
un reino de sacerdotes,
y reinan sobre la tierra.

Digno es el Cordero degollado
de recibir el poder, la riqueza, la sabiduría,
la fuerza, el honor, la gloria y la alabanza.

From this day all generations will call me blessed:
the Almighty has done great things for me,
and holy is his Name.

He has mercy on those who fear him
in every generation.

He has shown the strength of his arm,
he has scattered the proud in their conceit.

He has cast down the mighty from their thrones,
and has lifted up the lowly.

He has filled the hungry with good things,
and the rich he has sent away empty.

He has come to the help of his servant Israel
for he has remembered his promise of mercy,
the promise he made to our fathers,
to Abraham and his children for ever.

E   CANTICLE OF REVELATION   Revelation 4:11; 5:9, 10, 12

Worthy are you, Lord our God,
to receive glory and honor and power,
for you created all things;
because of your will they came to be and were created.

Worthy are you to receive the scroll
and to break open its seals,
for you were slain and with your blood
you purchased for God
those from every tribe and tongue,
people and nation.

You made them a kingdom
and priests for our God,
and they will reign on earth.

Worthy is the Lamb that was slain
to receive power and riches, wisdom and strength,
honor and glory and blessing.

F   Cántico del Apocalipsis   Apocalipsis 11:17-18; 12:10b-12a

Gracias te damos, Señor Dios omnipotente,
el que eres y el que eras,
porque has asumido el gran poder
y comenzaste a reinar.

Se encolerizaron las gentes,
llegó tu cólera,
y el tiempo de que sean juzgados los muertos,
y de dar el galardón a tus siervos, los profetas,
y a los santos y a los que temen tu nombre,
y a los pequeños y a los grandes.

Ahora se estableció la salud y el poderío,
y el reinado de nuestro Dios,
y la potestad de su Cristo;
porque fue precipitado
el acusador de nuestros hermanos,
el que los acusaba ante nuestro Dios día y noche.

Ellos le vencieron en virtud de la sangre del Cordero
y por la palabra del testimonio que dieron,
y no amaron tanto su vida que temieran la muerte.
Por esto, estén alegres, cielos,
y los que moran en sus tiendas.

G   Cántico del Apocalipsis   Cf. Apocalipsis 19:1-7

Aleluya.
La salvación y la gloria y el poder son de nuestro Dios,
(℟. Aleluya.)
porque sus juicios son verdaderos y justos.
℟. Aleluya, (aleluya).

Aleluya.
Alabad al Señor, sus siervos todos,
(℟. Aleluya.)
los que le temen, pequeños y grandes.
℟. Aleluya, (aleluya).

F   CANTICLE OF REVELATION   Revelation 11:17-18; 12:10b-12a

We give thanks to you, Lord God almighty,
who are and who were.
For you have assumed your great power
and have established your reign.

The nations raged,
but your wrath has come,
and the time for the dead to be judged,
and to recompense your servants, the prophets,
and the holy ones and those who fear your name,
the small and the great alike.

Now have salvation and power come,
and the kingdom of our God
and the authority of his Anointed.
For the accuser of our brothers is cast out,
who accuses them before our God day and night.

They conquered him by the blood of the Lamb
and by the word of their testimony;
love for life did not deter them from death.
Therefore, rejoice, you heavens,
and you who dwell in them.

G   CANTICLE OF REVELATION   Cf. Revelation 19:1-7

Alleluia.
Salvation, glory, and might belong to our God,
(℟. Alleluia.)
for true and just are his judgments.
℟. Alleluia, (alleluia).

Alleluia.
Praise our God, all you his servants,
(℟. Alleluia.)
and you who revere him, small and great.
℟. Alleluia, (alleluia).

Aleluya.
Porque reina el Señor, nuestro Dios, dueño de todo,
(℟. Aleluya.)
alegrémonos y gocemos y démosle gracias.
℟. Aleluya, (aleluya).

Aleluya.
Llegó la boda del Cordero,
(℟. Aleluya.)
su esposa se ha embellecido.
℟. Aleluya, (aleluya).

H   Cántico de Efesios   Efesios 1:3-10

Bendito sea Dios,
Padre de nuestro Señor Jesucristo,
que nos ha bendecido en la persona de Cristo
con toda clase de bienes espirituales y celestiales.

℟. Gloria y alabanza a ti, nuestro Dios,
    te alabamos, te damos gracias.

Él nos eligió en la persona de Cristo,
antes de crear el mundo,
para que fuésemos santos
e irreprochables ante él por el amor.

℟. Gloria y alabanza a ti, nuestro Dios,
    te alabamos, te damos gracias.

Él nos ha destinado en la persona de Cristo,
por pura iniciativa suya,
a ser sus hijos,
para que la gloria de su gracia,
que tan generosamente nos ha concedido
en su querido Hijo,
redunde en alabanza suya.

℟. Gloria y alabanza a ti, nuestro Dios,
    te alabamos, te damos gracias.

Alleluia.
The Lord has established his reign, our God, the almighty.
(℟. Alleluia.)
Let us rejoice and be glad and give him glory.
℟. Alleluia, (alleluia).

Alleluia.
The wedding day of the Lamb has come,
(℟. Alleluia.)
his bride has made herself ready.
℟. Alleluia, (alleluia).

H   CANTICLE OF EPHESIANS   Ephesians 1:3-10

Blessed be the God and Father
of our Lord Jesus Christ,
who has blessed us in Christ
with every spiritual blessing in the heavens.

℟. Glory and praise to you, O God,
    we worship you, we give you thanks.

God chose us in him,
before the foundation of the world,
to be holy
and without blemish before him.

℟. Glory and praise to you, O God,
    we worship you, we give you thanks.

In love he destined us
for adoption to himself through Jesus Christ,
in accord with the favor of his will,
for the praise of the glory of his grace
that he granted us in the beloved.

℟. Glory and praise to you, O God,
    we worship you, we give you thanks.

Por este Hijo, por su sangre,
hemos recibido la redención,
el perdón de los pecados.
El tesoro de su gracia, sabiduría y prudencia
ha sido un derroche para con nosotros,
dándonos a conocer el misterio de su voluntad.

℟. Gloria y alabanza a ti, nuestro Dios,
   te alabamos, te damos gracias.

Éste es el plan
que había proyectado realizar por Cristo
cuando llegase el momento culminante:
recapitular en Cristo todas las cosas
del cielo y de la tierra.

℟. Gloria y alabanza a ti, nuestro Dios,
   te alabamos, te damos gracias.

III. HIMNOS

A   GLORIA

Gloria a Dios en el cielo,
   y en la tierra paz a los hombres
   que ama el Señor.
Por tu inmensa gloria
   te alabamos, te bendecimos,
   te adoramos, te glorificamos,
   te damos gracias,
   Señor Dios, Rey celestial,
   Dios Padre todopoderoso.
   Señor, Hijo único, Jesucristo.
Señor Dios, Cordero de Dios,
   Hijo del Padre;
   tú que quitas el pecado del mundo,
   ten piedad de nosotros;
   tú que quitas el pecado del mundo,
   atiende nuestra súplica;

In him we have redemption by his blood,
the forgiveness of transgressions,
in accord with the riches of his grace
that he lavished upon us.

℞. Glory and praise to you, O God,
　　we worship you, we give you thanks.

In all wisdom and insight,
he has made known to us the mystery of his will
in accord with his favor
that he set forth in him.

℞. Glory and praise to you, O God,
　　we worship you, we give you thanks.

A plan for the fullness of times,
to sum up all things in Christ,
in heaven and on earth.

℞. Glory and praise to you, O Lord.

III. HYMNS

A　Gloria

Glory to God in the highest,
and peace to his people on earth.
Lord God, heavenly King,
almighty God and Father,
　　we worship you, we give you thanks,
　　we praise you for your glory.

Lord Jesus Christ, only Son of the Father,
Lord God, Lamb of God,
you take away the sins of the world:
　　have mercy on us;
you are seated at the right hand of the Father:
　　receive our prayer.

tú que estás sentado a la derecha del Padre,
ten piedad de nosotros;
porque sólo tú eres Santo,
sólo tú Señor,
solo tú Altísimo, Jesucristo,
con el Espíritu Santo
en la gloria de Dios Padre.
Amén.

B TE DEUM

A ti, oh Dios, te alabamos, a ti, Señor, te reconocemos.
A ti, eterno Padre, te venera toda la creación.

Los ángeles todos, los cielos y todas las potestades te honran.
Los querubines y serafines te cantan sin cesar:

Santo, Santo, Santo es el Señor, Dios del universo.
Los cielos y la tierra están llenos de la majestad de tu gloria.

A ti te ensalza el glorioso coro de los apóstoles,
la multitud admirable de los profetas,
el blanco ejército de los mártires.

A ti la Iglesia santa, extendida por toda la tierra,
te proclama:

Padre de inmensa majestad,
Hijo único y verdadero, digno de adoración,
Espíritu Santo, Defensor.

Tú eres el Rey de la gloria, Cristo.
Tú eres el Hijo único del Padre.

Tú, para liberar al hombre,
aceptaste la condición humana
sin desdeñar el seno de la Virgen.

For you alone are the Holy One,
you alone are the Lord,
you alone are the Most High,
  Jesus Christ,
  with the Holy Spirit,
  in the glory of God the Father. Amen.

B   Te Deum

You are God: we praise you;
You are the Lord: we acclaim you;
You are the eternal Father:
All creation worships you.

To you all angels, all the powers of heaven,
Cherubim and Seraphim, sing in endless praise:
  Holy, holy, holy Lord, God of power and might,
  heaven and earth are full of your glory.

The glorious company of apostles praise you.
The noble fellowship of prophets praise you.
The white-robed army of martyrs praise you.

Throughout the world the holy Church acclaims you:
  Father, of majesty unbounded,
  your true and only Son, worthy of all worship,
  and the Holy Spirit, advocate and guide.

You, Christ, are the king of glory,
the eternal Son of the Father.

When you became man to set us free
you did not spurn the Virgin's womb.

Tú, rotas las cadenas de la muerte,
abriste a los creyentes el reino del cielo.

Tú te sientas a la derecha de Dios
en la gloria del Padre.
Creemos que un día has de venir como juez.

Te rogamos, pues, que vengas en ayuda de tus siervos,
a quienes redimiste con tu preciosa sangre.
Haz que en la gloria eterna nos asociemos a tus santos.

C   HIMNO DE GRACIAS

1. Gracias por el amor del cielo.
   Gracias por el inmenso mar.
   Gracias por el cantar del bosque.
   Aleluya.

2. Gracias por el amor del mundo.
   Gracias por la felicidad.
   Gracias por todos mis hermanos.
   Aleluya.

3. Gracias por este nuevo día.
   Gracias por nuestra juventud.
   Gracias por la amistad de todos.
   Aleluya.

4. Gracias por toda la hermosura.
   Gracias por nuestra gran unión.
   Gracias por todas las bondades.
   Aleluya.

5. Gracias por tu venida al mundo.
   Gracias por el inmenso mar.
   Gracias por el cantar del bosque.
   Aleluya.

You overcame the sting of death,
and opened the kingdom of heaven to all believers.

You are seated at God's right hand in glory.
We believe that you will come, and be our judge.

Come then, Lord, and help your people,
bought with the price of your own blood,
and bring us with your saints
to glory everlasting.

C   HYMN FROM THE DIDACHE

Father, we thank thee, who hast planted
Thy holy Name within our hearts.
Knowledge and faith and life immortal
Jesus, thy Son, to us imparts.
Thou, Lord, didst make all for thy pleasure,
Didst give us food for all our days,
Giving in Christ the Bread eternal;
Thine is the power, be thine the praise.

Watch o'er thy Church, O Lord, in mercy,
Save it from evil, guard it still,
Perfect it in thy love, unite it,
Cleansed and conformed unto thy will.
As grain, once scattered on the hillsides,
Was in this broken bread made one,
So from all lands thy Church be gathered
Into thy kingdom by thy Son.

Music: Louis Bourgeois, 1543
Text: Didache, c. 110
Translator: F. Bland Tucker, 1940, alt.

IV. LETANÍA

Señor, ten piedad	Señor, ten piedad
Cristo, ten piedad	Cristo, ten piedad
Señor, ten piedad	Señor, ten piedad
Jesucristo, el Altísimo	¡Gloria a Ti, Señor!
Jesucristo, el Santo	¡Gloria a Ti, Señor!
Jesucristo, Verbo de Dios	¡Gloria a Ti, Señor!
Jesucristo, hijo único del Padre	¡Gloria a Ti, Señor!
Jesucristo, hijo de María	¡Gloria a Ti, Señor!
Jesucristo, crucificado por nosotros	¡Gloria a Ti, Señor!
Jesucristo, resucitado de entre los muertos	¡Gloria a Ti, Señor!
Jesucristo, reinando en la gloria	¡Gloria a Ti, Señor!
Jesucristo, que vendrás en gloria	¡Gloria a Ti, Señor!
Jesucristo, nuestro Señor	¡Gloria a Ti, Señor!
Jesucristo, nuestra esperanza	¡Gloria a Ti, Señor!
Jesucristo, nuestra paz	¡Gloria a Ti, Señor!
Jesucristo, nuestro Salvador	¡Gloria a Ti, Señor!
Jesucristo, nuestra salvación	¡Gloria a Ti, Señor!
Jesucristo, nuestra resurrección	¡Gloria a Ti, Señor!
Jesucristo, juez de todos	¡Gloria a Ti, Señor!
Jesucristo, Señor de la Iglesia	¡Gloria a Ti, Señor!
Jesucristo, Señor de la creación	¡Gloria a Ti, Señor!
Jesucristo, amante de todos	¡Gloria a Ti, Señor!
Jesucristo, vida del mundo	¡Gloria a Ti, Señor!
Jesucristo, libertad de los presos	¡Gloria a Ti, Señor!
Jesucristo, consuelo de los afligidos	¡Gloria a Ti, Señor!
Jesucristo, dador del Espíritu	¡Gloria a Ti, Señor!
Jesucristo, dador de todo buen don	¡Gloria a Ti, Señor!
Jesucristo, fuente de nueva vida	¡Gloria a Ti, Señor!
Jesucristo, Señor de la vida	¡Gloria a Ti, Señor!
Jesucristo, sumo y eterno sacerdote	¡Gloria a Ti, Señor!
Jesucristo, sacerdote y víctima	¡Gloria a Ti, Señor!
Jesucristo, pastor verdadero	¡Gloria a Ti, Señor!
Jesucristo, luz verdadera	¡Gloria a Ti, Señor!

IV. LITANY

Lord, have mercy
Christ, have mercy
Lord, have mercy

Lord, have mercy
Christ, have mercy
Lord, have mercy

Jesus, the Most High
Jesus, the holy One
Jesus, Word of God
Jesus, only Son of the Father
Jesus, Son of Mary
Jesus, crucified for us
Jesus, risen from the dead
Jesus, reigning in glory
Jesus, coming in glory

Glory and praise to you!
Glory and praise to you!
Glory and praise to you!
Glory and praise to you!
Glory and praise to you!
Glory and praise to you!
Glory and praise to you!
Glory and praise to you!
Glory and praise to you!

Jesus, our Lord
Jesus, our hope
Jesus, our peace
Jesus, our Savior
Jesus, our salvation
Jesus, our resurrection

Glory and praise to you!
Glory and praise to you!
Glory and praise to you!
Glory and praise to you!
Glory and praise to you!
Glory and praise to you!

Jesus, Judge of all
Jesus, Lord of the Church
Jesus, Lord of creation
Jesus, Lover of all
Jesus, life of the world
Jesus, freedom for the
    imprisoned
Jesus, joy of the sorrowing
Jesus, giver of the Spirit
Jesus, giver of good gifts
Jesus, source of new life
Jesus, Lord of life
Jesus, eternal high priest
Jesus, priest and victim
Jesus, true Shepherd
Jesus, true Light

Glory and praise to you!
Glory and praise to you!
Glory and praise to you!
Glory and praise to you!
Glory and praise to you!

Glory and praise to you!
Glory and praise to you!
Glory and praise to you!
Glory and praise to you!
Glory and praise to you!
Glory and praise to you!
Glory and praise to you!
Glory and praise to you!
Glory and praise to you!
Glory and praise to you!

Jesucristo, pan del cielo	¡Gloria a Ti, Señor!
Jesucristo, pan vivo	¡Gloria a Ti, Señor!
Jesucristo, pan eucarístico	¡Gloria a Ti, Señor!
Jesucristo, pan que da la vida	¡Gloria a Ti, Señor!
Jesucristo, maná santo	¡Gloria a Ti, Señor!
Jesucristo, nueva alianza	¡Gloria a Ti, Señor!
Jesucristo, alimento para la vida eterna	¡Gloria a Ti, Señor!
Jesucristo, alimento para nuestra jornada	¡Gloria a Ti, Señor!
Jesucristo, banquete santo	¡Gloria a Ti, Señor!
Jesucristo, sacrificio verdadero	¡Gloria a Ti, Señor!
Jesucristo, sacrificio perfecto	¡Gloria a Ti, Señor!
Jesucristo, sacrificio eterno	¡Gloria a Ti, Señor!
Jesucristo, víctima divina	¡Gloria a Ti, Señor!
Jesucristo, mediador de la nueva alianza	¡Gloria a Ti, Señor!
Jesucristo, misterio del altar	¡Gloria a Ti, Señor!
Jesucristo, misterio de fe	¡Gloria a Ti, Señor!
Jesucristo, medicina para la inmortalidad	¡Gloria a Ti, Señor!
Jesucristo, promesa de la gloria eterna	¡Gloria a Ti, Señor!
Jesucristo, Cordero de Dios, que quitas el pecado del mundo	ten piedad de nosotros
Jesucristo, Liberador de nuestras culpas, que quitas el pecado del mundo	ten piedad de nosotros
Jesucristo, Redentor del mundo, que quitas el pecado del mundo	ten piedad de nosotros
Cristo, óyenos	Cristo, óyenos
Cristo, escúchanos	Cristo, escúchanos

Jesus, bread of heaven	Glory and praise to you!
Jesus, bread of life	Glory and praise to you!
Jesus, bread of thanksgiving	Glory and praise to you!
Jesus, life-giving bread	Glory and praise to you!
Jesus, holy manna	Glory and praise to you!
Jesus, new covenant	Glory and praise to you!
Jesus, food for everlasting life	Glory and praise to you!
Jesus, food for our journey	Glory and praise to you!
Jesus, holy banquet	Glory and praise to you!
Jesus, true sacrifice	Glory and praise to you!
Jesus, perfect sacrifice	Glory and praise to you!
Jesus, eternal sacrifice	Glory and praise to you!
Jesus, divine Victim	Glory and praise to you!
Jesus, Mediator of the new covenant	Glory and praise to you!
Jesus, mystery of the altar	Glory and praise to you!
Jesus, mystery of faith	Glory and praise to you!
Jesus, medicine of immortality	Glory and praise to you!
Jesus, pledge of eternal glory	Glory and praise to you!

Jesus, Lamb of God,
you take away the sins of the world: have mercy on us

Jesus, Bearer of our sins,
you take away the sins of the world: have mercy on us

Jesus, Redeemer of the world,
you take away the sins of the world: have mercy on us

Christ, hear us	Christ, hear us
Christ, graciously hear us	Christ, graciously hear us
Lord Jesus, hear our prayer	Lord Jesus, hear our prayer

V. ORACIONES DE GRATITUD

El líder puede introducir cada oración cantando o diciendo:

Demos gracias a Dios, porque Dios es bueno.

Todos responden:

Porque es eterna su misericordia.

ADVIENTO

A   **Bendito seas, Padre nuestro,**
fuente de toda bondad:
Tú nos has rescatado del poder de la muerte;
Tú nos invitas a que te busquemos para que te encontremos.
Te damos gracias, oh Dios nuestro.

℟.   Gloria a ti, gloria y alabanza, ahora y por siempre.

Bendito seas por tu Palabra viva,
tu Hijo, nuestro Señor Jesucristo:
en él Tú has cumplido las promesas
hechas por los antiguos profetas.
Su venida nos muestra que eres siempre fiel.
Te damos gracias, oh Dios nuestro.

℟.   Gloria a ti, gloria y alabanza, ahora y por siempre.

Bendito seas por tu Espíritu vivificador,
nuestro consuelo y nuestro guía:
El Espíritu que renueva toda la tierra
y fortalece nuestra esperanza
mientras aguardamos la gloriosa venida
de nuestro Salvador, Jesucristo.
Te damos gracias, oh Dios nuestro.

℟.   Gloria a ti, gloria y alabanza, ahora y por siempre.

Bendito seas, Padre, Hijo, y Espíritu Santo:
a ti toda alabanza, honor, y gloria
por los siglos de los siglos.

℟.   Amén.

V. PRAYERS OF THANKSGIVING

The leader may introduce each prayer by singing or saying:

Give thanks to the Lord, for God is good.

All respond:

God's mercy endures for ever.

ADVENT

A **Blessed are you, God our Father,**
source of all that is good:
You rescued us from the power of death;
you invite us to seek and find you.
We give you thanks, O God.

 ℟. Glory to you, glory and praise, now and for all ages.

Blessed are you for your living Word,
your Son, our Lord Jesus Christ:
in him you have accomplished the promises
made through the prophets of old.
His coming taught us that you are faithful for ever.
We give you thanks, O God.

 ℟. Glory to you, glory and praise, now and for all ages.

Blessed are you for your life-giving Spirit,
our consoler and our guide:
The Spirit who makes all things new
and strengthens us as we await in joyful hope
the coming of our Savior, Jesus Christ.
We give you thanks, O God.

 ℟. Glory to you, glory and praise, now and for all ages.

Blessed are you, Father, Son, and Holy Spirit:
to you be praise, honor, and glory,
for ever and ever.

 ℟. Amen.

B   **Dios y Señor nuestro, te damos gracias por Jesucristo, tu Hijo, que vino a nuestro mundo en humildad y pobreza.**

> ℟. Gloria a Dios en el cielo,
> y en la tierra paz a los hombres que ama el Señor.

Jesús es el anunciado por todos los profetas;
Jesús, el esperado por la Virgen María con mucho amor;
Jesús, el proclamado por Juan Bautista
como el que viene en nombre del Señor,
Jesús, el que se ha revelado a sí mismo en medio de nosotros.

> ℟. Gloria a Dios en el cielo,
> y en la tierra paz a los hombres que ama el Señor.

El Espíritu de Jesus nos ayuda a estar atentos
a todo lo que prepara la venida de tu reino;
el Espíritu nos imparte el gozo
de entrar en el misterio de la Navidad.

> ℟. Gloria a Dios en el cielo,
> y en la tierra paz a los hombres que ama el Señor.

Alabanza, gloria, y honor al Padre, al Hijo,
y al Espíritu Santo por los siglos de los siglos.

> ℟. Amén.

C   **Señor Dios nuestro, que amas a todos, te bendecimos:**
Tú que tanto amaste al mundo
nos diste a tu Hijo único para nuestra salvación.
Señor Dios, te alabamos.

> ℟. Gloria a ti, Señor.
> Te adoramos, te damos gracias.

B   **Lord God,**
we give you thanks for Jesus Christ, your Son,
who came into our world in humility and poverty.

℟. Glory to God in the highest,
and peace to God's people on earth.

Jesus is the One that all the prophets have announced;
the One that the Virgin Mary awaited with love;
the One whose coming John the Baptist proclaimed,
and who revealed himself in our midst.

℟. Glory to God in the highest,
and peace to God's people on earth.

The Spirit of Jesus makes us attentive
to everything that prepares for the coming of your kingdom;
the Spirit gives us the joy
of entering into the mystery of Christmas.

℟. Glory to God in the highest,
and peace to God's people on earth.

Praise, glory, and honor to the Father, Son,
and Holy Spirit,
for ever and ever.

℟. Amen.

C   **Lord our God, lover of all, we bless you:**
you so loved the world
that you gave us your only Son for our salvation.
Lord God, we praise you.

℟. Glory and praise to you, O God,
we worship you, we give you thanks.

Señor Dios nuestro, que nos amas a todos, te bendecimos:
por el poder del Espíritu Santo,
tu Hijo nació de María Virgen.
Se hizo uno de nosotros y vivió entre nosotros,
para que por El pudiéramos llegar a ser
sus hermanas y hermanos. Señor Dios, te alabamos.

℟. Gloria a ti, Señor.
   Te adoramos, te damos gracias.

Señor Dios nuestro, que nos amas a todos, te bendecimos:
por medio de tu Espíritu nos haces ver a Jesús,
que viene en tu nombre, en la eucaristía que compartimos.
Señor Dios, te alabamos.

℟. Gloria a ti, Señor.
   Te adoramos, te damos gracias.

Señor Dios nuestro, que nos amas a todos, te bendecimos:
Padre, Hijo, y Espíritu Santo,
por los siglos de los siglos.

℟. Amén.

Cuaresma

D   Gloria a ti, Señor.
    Tú nos has creado de una manera admirable
    y nos has renovado aún más admirablemente.
    Tú nunca abandonas a los pecadores;
    Tú los buscas con grande amor.

℟. Qué maravillosas son tus obras, Señor!

Gloria a ti, Señor.
Tú has enviado a tu Hijo al mundo:

Lord our God, lover of all, we bless you:
by the power of the Holy Spirit,
your Son was born of the Virgin Mary.
He became one of us and lived in our midst,
that through him we might become his sisters and brothers.
Lord God, we praise you.

℞. Glory and praise to you, O God,
　　we worship you, we give you thanks.

Lord our God, lover of all, we bless you:
through your Spirit you enable us to see Jesus,
who comes in your name, in the eucharist we share.
Lord God, we praise you.

℞. Glory and praise to you, O God,
　　we worship you, we give you thanks.

Lord our God, lover of all, we bless you:
Father, Son, and Holy Spirit,
for ever and ever.

℞. Amen.

LENT

D　Glory to you, O Lord.
You created us in a marvelous fashion
and renew us in a still more wondrous way.
You never abandon sinners;
you seek them out with your love.

℞. Wonderful are your works, O Lord.

Glory to you, O Lord.
You sent your Son into the world:

por su cruz, El destruyó el pecado y la muerte;
por su resurrección, El nos dio nueva vida,
una vida que nunca termina, una abundancia de gozo.

℟. ¡Qué maravillosas son tus obras, Señor!

Gloria a ti, Señor.
Sin cesar tú nos renuevas
por medio de los sacramentos de salvación;
nos libras de la esclavitud del pecado,
y nos haces nuevamente en la imagen de tu Hijo.

℟. ¡Qué maravillosas son tus obras, Señor!

Te glorificamos, Padre, por las maravillas de tu misericordia,
y te alabamos unidos a toda la Iglesia:
a ti todo honor y toda gloria, por Cristo,
en el Espíritu Santo, ahora y por siempre.

℟. Amén.

E   Bendito seas, oh Dios y Padre nuestro:
tu paciencia es inagotable y tu amor sin medida;
tú nos das momentos propicios
y nos concedes días de salvación.
Grande eres, oh Señor y Dios nuestro.

℟. Bendito sea Dios, ahora y por siempre. Amén.

Bendito seas, oh Jesús, Hijo del Dios vivo:
Tú has sido fiel hasta la muerte de cruz;
Tú recibes con gran bondad al pecador arrepentido
y le perdonas sus pecados.
Santo eres, Jesucristo, Señor nuestro.

℟. Bendito sea Dios, ahora y por siempre. Amén.

Bendito seas, oh Espíritu Santo,
Amor que ahuyenta de nuestro corazón todo temor:
Tú nos fortaleces ante la tentación

by his passion, he destroyed sin and death;
by his rising, he gave us new life,
a life never ending, an abundance of joy.

℟. Wonderful are your works, O Lord.

**Glory to you, O Lord.
You renew us without ceasing
through the sacraments of salvation;
from the bondage of sin you free us,
in the image of your Son you remake us.**

℟. Wonderful are your works, O Lord.

**We glorify you, O God, for the marvels of your mercy,
and we praise you with the whole Church:
to you be glory and honor, through Christ,
and in the Holy Spirit, now and for ever.**

℟. Amen.

E   **Blessed are you, God and Father:
your patience is untiring, and your love is without fault;
you offer us favorable times,
and give us days of salvation.
Great are you, O Lord our God.**

℟. Blessed are you, O God, now and for all ages.

**Blessed are you, Jesus Christ, Son of the living God:
you are faithful even to the cross;
you welcome the repentant with kindness
and pardon their sins.
Holy are you, Lord Jesus Christ.**

℟. Blessed are you, O God, now and for all ages.

**Blessed are you, Holy Spirit,
the love who remove all fear from our hearts:
you strengthen us in temptation**

y nos brindas vida nueva.
Fuerte eres, oh Espíritu del Señor.

℟. Bendito sea Dios, ahora y por siempre. Amén.

Grande eres, oh Dios;
Santo eres, oh Dios;
Fuerte eres, oh Dios,
ahora y por siempre. Amén.

℟. Bendito sea Dios, ahora y por siempre. Amén.

PASCUA

F **Te alabamos, oh Dios, y te bendecimos,**
te damos gracias, Padre, por este gran día
en el que has dado la victoria a tu Hijo,
nuestro resplandeciente Señor Jesucristo.
Te alabamos, oh Dios, nuestro Salvador.

℟. Te damos gracias, oh Dios.
Tu amor es infinito. ¡Aleluya, aleluya!

Te alabamos, oh Dios, y te bendecimos,
Señor de la vida y de la muerte,
porque no abandonaste a tu Hijo a la corrupción,
sino que lo resucitaste a nueva vida.
Te alabamos, oh Dios, nuestro Salvador.

℟. Te damos gracias, oh Dios.
Tu amor es infinito. ¡Aleluya, aleluya!

Te alabamos, oh Dios, y te bendecimos,
porque resucitaste a tu Hijo
para que pasáramos de la muerte a la vida
en las aguas del bautismo.
Te alabamos, oh Dios, nuestro Salvador.

℟. Te damos gracias, oh Dios.
Tu amor es infinito. ¡Aleluya, aleluya!

and give new life.
Strong are you, O Spirit of the Lord.

℟. Blessed are you, O God, now and for all ages.

Great are you, O God;
holy are you, O God;
strong are you, O God,
now and for all ages.

℟. Blessed are you, O God, now and for all ages.

EASTER

F　**We praise you, O God, and we bless you,**
we give you thanks, Father, for this great day
on which you have given victory to your Son,
our resplendent Lord Jesus Christ.
Praise to you, O God our Savior.

℟. We give you thanks, O God,
your love is everlasting. Alleluia, alleluia!

We praise you, O God, and we bless you,
master of life and of death,
for you did not abandon your Son to the tomb,
but raised him to new life.
Praise to you, O God our Savior.

℟. We give you thanks, O God,
your love is everlasting. Alleluia, alleluia!

We praise you, O God, and we bless you,
for you raised up your Son
that we too might pass from death to life
through the waters of baptism.
Praise to you, O God our Savior.

℟. We give you thanks, O God,
your love is everlasting. Alleluia, alleluia!

Te alabamos, oh Dios, y te bendecimos:
Padre, Hijo, y Espíritu Santo,
ahora y por siempre.

℟. Amén.

TIEMPO ORDINARIO

G   Te damos gracias, Señor Dios,
al contemplar las maravillas de tu creación
que nos invitan a celebrar tus obras.

℟. Padre nuestro, te damos gracias, te alabamos por tu bondad.

Te damos gracias
por el agua que da vida a la tierra,
por el ritmo de los tiempos y las estaciones.

℟. Padre nuestro, te damos gracias, te alabamos por tu bondad.

Te damos gracias por la semilla que se siembra,
muere y crece nuevamente,
anunciándonos el misterio de la muerte y resurrección.

℟. Padre nuestro, te damos gracias, te alabamos por tu bondad.

Te damos gracias por el trabajo humano,
por el que la tierra produce fruto
ahora convertido por Jesucristo en ofrenda nueva.

℟. Padre nuestro, te damos gracias, te alabamos por tu bondad.

Te damos gracias
por la victoria sobre el pecado del mundo
y por los obstáculos vencidos.

℟. Padre nuestro, te damos gracias, te alabamos por tu bondad.

We praise you, O God, and we bless you:
Father, Son, and Holy Spirit,
now and for all ages.

℞. Amen.

ORDINARY TIME

G   Lord God,
we contemplate the marvels of your creation
that invite us to celebrate your deeds,
and we give you thanks.

℞. Father, we thank you, we praise you for your goodness.

For the water that gives life to the earth,
for the rhythms of time and seasons,
we give you thanks.

℞. Father, we thank you, we praise you for your goodness.

For the grain that is planted,
which dies and grows again,
announcing to us the mystery of death and resurrection,
we give you thanks.

℞. Father, we thank you, we praise you for your goodness.

For the work of human hands,
through which the earth bears fruit
and becomes a new offering in Jesus Christ,
we give you thanks.

℞. Father, we thank you, we praise you for your goodness.

For victories over sin in our world
and for obstacles surmounted,
we give you thanks.

℞. Father, we thank you, we praise you for your goodness.

Te damos gracias
por la creación que clama por la perfección en Cristo
y que anhela su venida.

℟. Padre nuestro, te damos gracias, te alabamos por tu bondad.

Te damos gracias, oh Dios:
Padre, Hijo, y Espíritu Santo,
y alabamos tu santo nombre
por los siglos de los siglos.

℟. Amén.

H   Tú eres nuestra alegría, Señor Dios nuestro.
De ti recibimos el aliento
para cantar el nuevo himno de los bautizados.

℟. Te alabamos, oh Dios, ahora y por siempre.

Reunidos en tu nombre,
en comunión con el Espíritu Santo,
te damos gracias porque nos has hecho miembros de tu
   Iglesia.

℟. Te alabamos, oh Dios, ahora y por siempre.

Alzamos nuestras voces en este mundo
para proclamar la Buena Nueva de tu amor:
Cristo vive, Ha resucitado.

℟. Te alabamos, oh Dios, ahora y por siempre.

Llenos del Espíritu Santo,
sentimos el fuego de tu amor en nuestros corazones.
¡Gloria a ti, oh Dios, para quien nada es imposible!
A ti la gloria, por tu Hijo, en tu Espíritu,
ahora y por siempre.

℟. Amén.

For creation that groans for perfection in Christ
and longs for his coming,
we give you thanks.

℟. Father, we thank you, we praise you for your goodness.

We give you thanks, O God:
Father, Son, and Holy Spirit,
and we praise your holy name
for ever and ever.

℟. Amen.

H You are our joy, Lord our God.
From you we receive the breath that we need
to sing the new song of the baptized.

℟. Praise and thanks to you, our God, now and for all ages.

Gathered together in your name,
in communion with the Holy Spirit,
we give you thanks that you have made us
members of your Church.

℟. Praise and thanks to you, our God, now and for all ages.

We raise our voices in the world
to proclaim the Good News of your love:
Christ is living,
he is risen.

℟. Praise and thanks to you, our God, now and for all ages.

With hearts filled with the Holy Spirit,
we feel the fire of your love within us.
Glory to you, God, who stop at nothing!
Glory to you, through your Son, in your Spirit,
now and for ever.

℟. Amen.

I   **Padre,**
    te damos gracias por tu santo Nombre
    que nos has concedido que viva en nuestros corazones,
    y por la fe y vida que has plantado en nuestro ser,
    por medio de Jesús, tu humilde siervo.

    ℟. Gloria a ti, oh Dios, gloria y alabanza por siempre.

    Señor, Tú eres
    quien ha creado el universo para la gloria de tu Nombre.
    Tú eres, quien nos ha dado el alimento
    a fin de que podamos expresarte nuestra gratitud.
    Pero también nos favoreces con un alimento espiritual
    para que podamos vivir contigo,
    por medio de Jesús tu humilde siervo.

    ℟. Gloria a ti, oh Dios, gloria y alabanza por siempre.

    Acuérdate de tu Iglesia, Señor.
    Presérvala de todo mal y hazla perfecta en tu amor.
    Así como este pan fraccionado se ha unido para ser uno,
    concede que tu Espíritu
    reúna en tu Reino a la Iglesia
    de todos los confines de la tierra
    por medio de Jesús, tu humilde siervo.

    ℟. Gloria a ti, oh Dios, gloria y alabanza por siempre.

Fiestas de la Virgen María

J   **Con la Virgen María y en su honor,**
    te damos gracias, Señor Dios nuestro.

    ℟. Bendito seas, Señor.

    Bendito eres, Señor Dios nuestro,
    por haber escogido a María para ser la madre de tu Hijo.
    Al confiarle a ella esta misión
    honraste a nuestra raza.

    ℟. Bendito seas, Señor.

I   **Father,**
    we give you thanks for your holy Name
    that you have caused to live in our hearts,
    and for the faith and life that you put into us,
    through Jesus your humble servant.

    ℟. Glory to you, O God, glory and praise for ever.

    Lord, it is you,
    who created the universe for the glory of your Name,
    it is you, who have given us food
    that we might give you thanks.
    But you grace us with a spiritual food
    in order that we might live with you,
    through Jesus your humble servant.

    ℟. Glory to you, O God, glory and praise for ever.

    Remember your Church, O Lord,
    preserve it from all evil
    and make it perfect in your love.
    As this broken bread has been gathered to become one,
    may your Spirit gather the Church
    from the ends of the earth
    into your Kingdom,
    through Jesus your humble servant.

    ℟. Glory to you, O God, glory and praise for ever.

FEASTS OF THE VIRGIN MARY

J   **With the Virgin Mary, and in her honor,**
    we give thanks to the Lord our God.

    ℟. Blessed are you, O Lord.

    Blessed are you, Lord our God,
    for having chosen Mary to be the mother of your Son.
    By confiding this mission to her
    you gave honor to our race.

    ℟. Blessed are you, O Lord.

**Bendito eres, Señor Dios nuestro,
por confiarnos a María como nuestra madre
y por darnos a Jesús como nuestro Salvador.**

℟. Bendito seas, Señor.

**Bendito eres, Señor Dios nuestro,
por haber hecho que María entrara en la plenitud de tu gloria.
Con Jesús, su Hijo, "el primogénito de entre los muertos",
ella es la primera en recibir lo que tienes preparado
para todos nosotros.**

℟. Bendito seas, Señor.

**Alabanza, gloria, honor y gratitud a nuestro Dios:
Padre, Hijo, y Espíritu Santo,
por los siglos de los siglos.**

℟. Amén.

Blessed are you, Lord our God,
for entrusting us to Mary as our mother
and for giving us Jesus as our Savior.

℟. Blessed are you, O Lord.

Blessed are you, Lord our God,
for having made Mary enter into the fullness of your glory.
With Jesus, her Son, "the first born from the dead,"
she is the first to receive what you prepared
for us all.

℟. Blessed are you, O Lord.

Praise, glory, honor, and thanksgiving to our God:
Father, Son, and Holy Spirit,
for ever and ever.

℟. Amen.

APENDICE III

ORACIONES DEL DIA Y ORACIONES DESPUES DE LA COMUNION PARA LOS DOMINGOS, SOLEMNIDADES, Y FIESTAS DEL SEÑOR

APPENDIX III

PRAYERS OF THE DAY AND PRAYERS AFTER COMMUNION FOR SUNDAYS, SOLEMNITIES, AND FEASTS OF THE LORD

ORACIONES DEL DIA Y ORACIONES DESPUES DE LA COMUNION PARA LOS DOMINGOS, SOLEMNIDADES, Y FIESTAS DEL SEÑOR

161   Las siguientes Oraciones del Día y Oraciones después de la Comunión, están tomadas del Sacramentario, para utilizarlas los domingos, las solemnidades, y las fiestas del Señor como se indica en las tres formas de la celebración dominical.

PRIMER DOMINGO DE ADVIENTO

ORACIÓN DEL DÍA

Oremos.

Todos oran en silencio durante unos momentos.

**Señor, despierta en nosotros el deseo
de prepararnos a la venida de Cristo
con la práctica de las obras de misericordia
para que, puestos a su derecha el día del juicio,
podamos entrar al Reino de los cielos.**

**Por nuestro Señor Jesucristo, tu Hijo,
que vive y reina contigo
en la unidad del Espíritu Santo y es Dios
por los siglos de los siglos.**

ORACIÓN DESPUÉS DE LA COMUNIÓN

Oremos.

Todos oran en silencio durante unos momentos, a no ser que este silencio ya se haya hecho antes.

**Por nuestra participación en esta Eucaristía,
enséñanos, Señor,
a no fijar nuestro corazón en las cosas pasajeras,
sino en los bienes eternos.**

Por Jesucristo, nuestro Señor.

PRAYERS OF THE DAY AND PRAYERS AFTER COMMUNION FOR SUNDAYS, SOLEMNITIES, AND FEASTS OF THE LORD

161   The following Prayers of the Day and Prayers after Communion, taken from the Sacramentary, are for use on Sundays, solemnities and feasts of the Lord as indicated in the various forms of the Sunday celebration.

FIRST SUNDAY OF ADVENT

PRAYER OF THE DAY

Let us pray
[that we may take Christ's coming seriously]

> Pause for silent prayer.

All-powerful God,
increase our strength of will for doing good
that Christ may find an eager welcome at his coming
and call us to his side in the kingdom of heaven,
where he lives and reigns with you and the Holy Spirit,
one God, for ever and ever.

PRAYER AFTER COMMUNION

Let us pray.

> Pause for silent prayer, if this has not preceded.

Father,
may our communion
teach us to love heaven.
May its promise and hope
guide our way on earth.

We ask this through Christ our Lord.

SEGUNDO DOMINGO DE ADVIENTO

ORACIÓN DEL DÍA

Oremos.

Todos oran en silencio durante unos momentos.

**Que nuestras responsabilidades terrenas
no nos impidan, Señor,
prepararnos a la venida de tu Hijo,
y que la sabiduría que viene del cielo,
nos disponga a recibirlo
y a participar de su propia vida.**

**Por nuestro Señor Jesucristo, tu Hijo,
que vive y reina contigo
en la unidad del Espíritu Santo y es Dios
por los siglos de los siglos.**

ORACIÓN DESPUÉS DE LA COMUNIÓN

Oremos.

Todos oran en silencio durante unos momentos, a no ser que este silencio ya
se haya hecho antes.

**Como fruto de nuestra participación
en este sacramento de vida eterna,
enséñanos, Señor,
a no apegarnos a las cosas terrenales
y a estimar las del cielo.**

Por Jesucristo, nuestro Señor.

SECOND SUNDAY OF ADVENT

**Let us pray
[that nothing may hinder us from receiving Christ with joy]**

Pause for silent prayer.

**God of power and mercy,
open our hearts in welcome.
Remove the things that hinder us
from receiving Christ with joy,
so that we may share his wisdom
and become one with him
when he comes in glory,
for he lives and reigns with you and the Holy Spirit,
one God, for ever and ever.**

PRAYER AFTER COMMUNION

Let us pray.

Pause for silent prayer, if this has not preceded.

**Father,
you give us food from heaven.
By our sharing in this mystery,
teach us to judge wisely the things of earth
and to love the things of heaven.**

Grant this through Christ our Lord.

TERCER DOMINGO DE ADVIENTO

ORACIÓN DEL DÍA

Oremos.

Todos oran en silencio durante unos momentos.

**Mira, Señor, a tu pueblo
que espera con fe la fiesta del nacimiento de tu Hijo,
y concédele celebrar el gran misterio de nuestra salvación
con un corazón nuevo e inmensa alegría.**

**Por nuestro Señor Jesucristo, tu Hijo,
que vive y reina contigo
en la unidad del Espíritu Santo y es Dios
por los siglos de los siglos.**

ORACIÓN DESPUÉS DE LA COMUNIÓN

Oremos.

Todos oran en silencio durante unos momentos, a no ser que este silencio ya se haya hecho antes.

**Que esta Eucaristía
nos purifique, Señor, de toda mancha
y nos prepare así
a celebrar dignamente la Navidad ya próxima.**

Por Jesucristo, nuestro Señor.

THIRD SUNDAY OF ADVENT

Let us pray
[that God will fill us with joy at the coming of Christ]

Pause for silent prayer.

Lord God,
may we, your people,
who look forward to the birthday of Christ
experience the joy of salvation
and celebrate that feast with love and thanksgiving.

We ask this through our Lord Jesus Christ, your Son,
who lives and reigns with you and the Holy Spirit,
one God, for ever and ever.

PRAYER AFTER COMMUNION

Let us pray.

Pause for silent prayer, if this has not preceded.

God of mercy,
may this eucharist bring us your divine help,
free us from our sins,
and prepare us for the birthday of our Savior,
who is Lord for ever and ever.

CUARTO DOMINGO DE ADVIENTO

Oremos.

Todos oran en silencio durante unos momentos.

**Derrama, Señor, tu gracia sobre nosotros,
que por el anuncio del ángel hemos conocido
la encarnación de tu Hijo,
para que lleguemos, por su pasión y su cruz,
a la gloria de la resurrección.**

**Por nuestro Señor Jesucristo, tu Hijo,
que vive y reina contigo
en la unidad del Espíritu Santo y es Dios
por los siglos de los siglos.**

Oración después de la Comunión

Oremos.

Todos oran en silencio durante unos momentos, a no ser que este silencio ya se haya hecho antes.

**Tú que nos has dado en este sacramento
la prenda de nuestra salvación,
concédenos, Padre todopoderoso,
prepararnos cada día con mayor fervor
para celebrar dignamente el nacimiento de tu Hijo,
que vive y reina por los siglos de los siglos.**

FOURTH SUNDAY OF ADVENT

PRAYER OF THE DAY

Let us pray
[as Advent draws to a close, that Christ will truly come into
our hearts]

Pause for silent prayer.

Lord,
fill our hearts with your love,
and as you revealed to us by an angel
the coming of your Son as man,
so lead us through his suffering and death
to the glory of his resurrection,
for he lives and reigns with you and the Holy Spirit,
one God, for ever and ever.

PRAYER AFTER COMMUNION

Let us pray.

Pause for silent prayer, if this has not preceded.

Lord,
in this sacrament
we receive the promise of salvation;
as Christmas draws near
make us grow in faith and love
to celebrate the coming of Christ our Savior,
who is Lord for ever and ever.

LA NATIVIDAD DEL SEÑOR

ORACIÓN DEL DÍA

Oremos.

Todos oran en silencio durante unos momentos.

**Dios nuestro,
que de modo admirable creaste al hombre
a tu imagen y semejanza, y de modo más admirable
lo elevaste con el nacimiento de tu Hijo,
concédenos participar de la vida divina de aquél
que ha querido participar de nuestra humanidad.**

**Por nuestro Señor Jesucristo, tu Hijo,
que vive y reina contigo
en la unidad del Espíritu Santo y es Dios
por los siglos de los siglos.**

ORACIÓN DESPUÉS DE LA COMUNIÓN

Oremos.

Todos oran en silencio durante unos momentos, a no ser que este silencio ya
se haya hecho antes.

**Concédenos, Dios misericordioso,
que el salvador del mundo, que hoy nos ha nacido
para comunicarnos su vida divina,
nos dé también el don de su inmortalidad.**

El cual vive y reina por los siglos de los siglos.

BIRTH OF THE LORD (CHRISTMAS)

PRAYER OF THE DAY

Let us pray
[for the glory promised by the birth of Christ]

Pause for silent prayer.

Lord God,
we praise you for creating man,
and still more for restoring him in Christ.
Your Son shared our weakness:
may we share his glory,
for he lives and reigns with you and the Holy Spirit,
one God, for ever and ever.

PRAYER AFTER COMMUNION

Let us pray.

Pause for silent prayer, if this has not preceded.

Father,
the child born today is the Savior of the world.
He made us your children.
May he welcome us into your kingdom
where he lives and reigns with you for ever and ever.

LA SAGRADA FAMILIA

Oración del Día

Oremos.

Todos oran en silencio durante unos momentos.

**Señor y Dios nuestro,
tú que nos has dado en la Sagrada Familia de tu Hijo,
el modelo perfecto para nuestras familias,
concédenos practicar sus virtudes domésticas
y estar unidos por los lazos de tu amor,
para que podamos ir a gozar con ella eternamente
de la alegría de tu casa.**

**Por nuestro Señor Jesucristo, tu Hijo,
que vive y reina contigo
en la unidad del Espíritu Santo y es Dios
por los siglos de los siglos.**

Oración después de la Comunión

Oremos.

Todos oran en silencio durante unos momentos, a no ser que este silencio ya
se haya hecho antes.

**Padre lleno de amor,
concede a los que acabamos de alimentarnos
con este sacramento celestial,
imitar siempre los ejemplos de la Sagrada Familia,
para que, después de las pruebas de esta vida,
podamos gozar eternamente con ellos en el cielo.**

Por Jesucristo, nuestro Señor.

HOLY FAMILY

PRAYER OF THE DAY

Let us pray
[for peace in our families]

Pause for silent prayer.

Father,
help us to live as the holy family,
united in respect and love.
Bring us to the joy and peace of your eternal home.

Grant this through our Lord Jesus Christ, your Son,
who lives and reigns with you and the Holy Spirit,
one God, for ever and ever.

PRAYER AFTER COMMUNION

Let us pray.

Pause for silent prayer, if this has not preceded.

Eternal Father,
we want to live as Jesus, Mary, and Joseph,
in peace with you and one another.
May this communion strengthen us
to face the troubles of life.

Grant this through Christ our Lord.

SANTA MARIA, MADRE DE DIOS

ORACIÓN DEL DÍA

Oremos.

Todos oran en silencio durante unos momentos.

**Señor Dios, que por la fecunda virginidad de María
diste al género humano e1 don de la salvación eterna,
concédenos gozar de la intercesión de aquélla
por quien recibimos al autor de la vida,
Jesucristo, Señor nuestro,
que vive y reina contigo
en la unidad del Espíritu Santo y es Dios
por los siglos de los siglos.**

ORACIÓN DESPUÉS DE LA COMUNIÓN

Oremos.

Todos oran en silencio durante unos momentos, a no ser que este silencio ya se haya hecho antes.

**Señor, que estos sacramentos celestiales
que hemos recibido con alegría,
sean fuente de vida eterna para nosotros,
que nos gloriamos de proclamar a la siempre Virgen María
como Madre de tu Hijo y Madre de la Iglesia.**

Por Jesucristo, nuestro Señor.

MARY, MOTHER OF GOD

PRAYER OF THE DAY

Let us pray
  **[that Mary, the mother of the Lord, will help us by her
    prayers]**

Pause for silent prayer.

**God our Father,
may we always profit by the prayers
of the Virgin Mother Mary,
for you bring us life and salvation
through Jesus Christ her Son
who lives and reigns with you and the Holy Spirit,
one God, for ever and ever.**

PRAYER AFTER COMMUNION

Let us pray.

Pause for silent prayer, if this has not preceded.

**Father,
as we proclaim the Virgin Mary
to be the mother of Christ and the mother of the Church,
may our communion with her Son
bring us to salvation.**

We ask this through Christ our Lord.

LA EPIFANIA DEL SEÑOR

ORACIÓN DEL DÍA

Oremos.

Todos oran en silencio durante unos momentos.

**Señor, Dios nuestro, que por medio de una estrella,
diste a conocer en este día, a todos los pueblos
el nacimiento de tu Hijo,
concede a los que ya te conocemos por la fe,
llegar a contemplar, cara a cara,
la hermosura de tu inmensa gloria.**

**Por nuestro Señor Jesucristo, tu Hijo,
que vive y reina contigo
en la unidad del Espíritu Santo y es Dios
por los siglos de los siglos.**

ORACIÓN DESPUÉS DE LA COMUNIÓN

Oremos.

Todos oran en silencio durante unos momentos, a no ser que este silencio ya
se haya hecho antes.

**Que tu luz, Señor, nos guíe y nos acompañe siempre
y para que comprendamos cada día más
este sacramento en el que hemos participado
y podamos recibirlo con mayor amor.**

Por Jesucristo, nuestro Señor.

EPIPHANY OF THE LORD

PRAYER OF THE DAY

Let us pray
[that we will be guided by the light of faith]

> Pause for silent prayer.

Father,
you revealed your Son to the nations
by the guidance of a star.
Lead us to your glory in heaven
by the light of faith.

We ask this through our Lord Jesus Christ, your Son,
who lives and reigns with you and the Holy Spirit,
one God, for ever and ever.

PRAYER AFTER COMMUNION

Let us pray.

> Pause for silent prayer, if this has not preceded.

Father,
guide us with your light.
Help us to recognize Christ in this eucharist
and welcome him with love
for he is Lord for ever and ever.

EL BAUTISMO DEL SEÑOR

Oremos.

Todos oran en silencio durante unos momentos.

**Dios todopoderoso y eterno,
que proclamaste solemnemente
que Cristo era tu Hijo amado
cuando fue bautizado en el Jordán
y descendió el Espíritu Santo sobre él,
concede a tus hijos adoptivos, renacidos del agua y del
Espíritu,
perseverar siempre fieles en el cumplimiento de tu voluntad.**

**Por nuestro Señor Jesucristo, tu Hijo,
que vive y reina contigo
en la unidad del Espíritu Santo y es Dios
por los siglos de los siglos.**

ORACIÓN DESPUÉS DE LA COMUNIÓN

Oremos.

Todos oran en silencio durante unos momentos, a no ser que este silencio ya
se haya hecho antes.

**A cuantos hemos participado
del Cuerpo y la Sangre de tu Hijo,
concédenos, Señor, escuchar con fe su palabra,
para que así podamos llamarnos hijos tuyos y serlo de verdad.**

Por Jesucristo, nuestro Señor.

BAPTISM OF THE LORD

PRAYER OF THE DAY

Let us pray
[that we will be faithful to our baptism]

Pause for silent prayer.

Almighty, eternal God,
when the Spirit descended upon Jesus
at his baptism in the Jordan,
you revealed him as your own beloved Son.
Keep us, your children born of water and the Spirit,
faithful to our calling.

We ask this through our Lord Jesus Christ, your Son,
who lives and reigns with you and the Holy Spirit,
one God, for ever and ever.

Or:

Father,
your only Son revealed himself to us by becoming man.
May we who share his humanity
come to share his divinity,
for he lives and reigns with you and the Holy Spirit,
one God, for ever and ever.

PRAYER AFTER COMMUNION

Let us pray.

Pause for silent prayer, if this has not preceded.

Lord,
you feed us with bread from heaven.
May we hear your Son with faith
and become your children in name and in fact.

We ask this in the name of Jesus the Lord.

PRIMER DOMINGO DE CUARESMA

Oración del Día

Oremos.

Todos oran en silencio durante unos momentos.

**Concédenos, Dios todopoderoso,
que las prácticas anuales
propias de la Cuaresma
nos ayuden a progresar
en el conocimiento de Cristo
y a llevar una vida más cristiana.**

**Por nuestro Señor Jesucristo, tu Hijo,
que vive y reina contigo
en la unidad del Espíritu Santo y es Dios
por los siglos de los siglos.**

Oración después de la Comunión

Oremos.

Todos oran en silencio durante unos momentos, a no ser que este silencio ya se haya hecho antes.

**Que este pan celestial
alimente, Señor, en nosotros la fe,
aumente la esperanza, refuerce la caridad,
y nos enseñe a sentir hambre de Cristo,
que es el pan vivo y verdadero,
y a vivir de toda palabra que proceda de tu boca.**

Por Jesucristo, nuestro Señor.

FIRST SUNDAY OF LENT

PRAYER OF THE DAY

Let us pray
[that this Lent will help us reproduce in our lives the self-
sacrificing love of Christ]

Pause for silent prayer.

Father,
through our observance of Lent,
help us to understand the meaning
of your Son's death and resurrection,
and teach us to reflect it in our lives.

Grant this through our Lord Jesus Christ, your Son,
who lives and reigns with you and the Holy Spirit,
one God, for ever and ever.

PRAYER AFTER COMMUNION

Let us pray.

Pause for silent prayer, if this has not preceded.

Father,
you increase our faith and hope,
you deepen our love in this communion.
Help us to live by your words
and to seek Christ, our bread of life,
who is Lord for ever and ever.

SEGUNDO DOMINGO DE CUARESMA

Oración del Día

Oremos.

Todos oran en silencio durante unos momentos.

Señor, Padre santo,
que nos mandaste escuchar a tu amado Hijo,
alimenta nuestra fe con tu palabra
y purifica los ojos de nuestro espíritu,
para que podamos alegrarnos
en la contemplación de tu gloria.

Por nuestro Señor Jesucristo, tu Hijo,
que vive y reina contigo
en la unidad del Espíritu Santo y es Dios
por los siglos de los siglos.

Oración después de la Comunión

Oremos.

Todos oran en silencio durante unos momentos, a no ser que este silencio ya se haya hecho antes.

Te damos gracias, Señor,
porque al darnos en este sacramento
el Cuerpo glorioso de tu Hijo,
nos permites participar ya, desde este mundo,
de los bienes eternos de tu Reino.

Por Jesucristo, nuestro Señor.

SECOND SUNDAY OF LENT

PRAYER OF THE DAY

Let us pray
[for the grace to respond to the Word of God]

Pause for silent prayer.

God our Father,
help us to hear your Son.
Enlighten us with your word,
that we may find the way to your glory.

We ask this through our Lord Jesus Christ, your Son,
who lives and reigns with you and the Holy Spirit,
one God, for ever and ever.

PRAYER AFTER COMMUNION

Let us pray.

Pause for silent prayer, if this has not preceded.

Lord,
we give thanks for these holy mysteries
which bring to us here on earth
a share in the life to come,
through Christ our Lord.

TERCER DOMINGO DE CUARESMA

ORACIÓN DEL DÍA

Oremos.

Todos oran en silencio durante unos momentos.

**Dios misericordioso, fuente de toda bondad,
que nos has propuesto como remedio del pecado
el ayuno, la oración y las obras de misericordia,
mira con piedad
a quienes reconocemos nuestras miserias
y estamos agobiados por nuestras culpas,
y reconfórtanos con tu amor.**

**Por nuestro Señor Jesucristo, tu Hijo,
que vive y reina contigo
en la unidad del Espíritu Santo y es Dios
por los siglos de los siglos.**

ORACIÓN DESPUÉS DE LA COMUNIÓN

Oremos.

Todos oran en silencio durante unos momentos, a no ser que este silencio ya se haya hecho antes.

**Tú que nos has alimentado, ya desde esta vida,
con el pan del cielo, prenda de nuestra salvación,
concédenos, Señor,
manifestar en todos nuestros actos el misterio de tu Eucaristía.**

Por Jesucristo, nuestro Señor.

THIRD SUNDAY OF LENT

PRAYER OF THE DAY

> **Let us pray**
> **[for confidence in the love of God and the strength to over-**
> **come all our weakness]**
>
> Pause for silent prayer.
>
> **Father,**
> **you have taught us to overcome our sins**
> **by prayer, fasting and works of mercy.**
> **When we are discouraged by our weakness,**
> **give us confidence in your love.**
>
> **We ask this through our Lord Jesus Christ, your Son,**
> **who lives and reigns with you and the Holy Spirit,**
> **one God, for ever and ever.**

PRAYER AFTER COMMUNION

> **Let us pray.**
>
> Pause for silent prayer, if this has not preceded.
>
> **Lord,**
> **in sharing this sacrament**
> **may we receive your forgiveness**
> **and be brought together in unity and peace.**
>
> **We ask this through Christ our Lord.**

CUARTO DOMINGO DE CUARESMA

Oremos.

Todos oran en silencio durante unos momentos.

**Dios nuestro,
que has reconciliado contigo
a la humanidad entera
por medio de tu Hijo,
concede al pueblo cristiano
prepararse con fe viva y entrega generosa
a celebrar las fiestas de la Pascua.**

**Por nuestro Señor Jesucristo, tu Hijo,
que vive y reina contigo
en la unidad del Espíritu Santo y es Dios
por los siglos de los siglos.**

ORACIÓN DESPUÉS DE LA COMUNIÓN

Oremos.

Todos oran en silencio durante unos momentos, a no ser que este silencio ya
se haya hecho antes.

**Dios nuestro,
luz que alumbra a todos
que vienen a este mundo,
ilumina nuestros corazones
con el resplandor de tu gracia,
para que nuestros pensamientos te sean agradables
y te amemos con toda sinceridad.**

Por Jesucristo, nuestro Señor.

FOURTH SUNDAY OF LENT

PRAYER OF THE DAY

Let us pray
[for a greater faith and love]

Pause for silent prayer.

Father of peace,
we are joyful in your Word,
your Son Jesus Christ,
who reconciles us to you.
Let us hasten toward Easter
with the eagerness of faith and love.

We ask this through our Lord Jesus Christ, your Son,
who lives and reigns with you and the Holy Spirit,
one God, for ever and ever.

PRAYER AFTER COMMUNION

Let us pray.

Pause for silent prayer, if this has not preceded.

Father,
you enlighten all who come into the world.
Fill our hearts with the light of your gospel,
that our thoughts may please you,
and our love be sincere.

Grant this through Christ our Lord.

QUINTO DOMINGO DE CUARESMA

Oración del Día

Oremos.

Todos oran en silencio durante unos momentos.

**Ven, Señor, en nuestra ayuda,
para que podamos vivir y actuar siempre
con aquel amor que impulsó a tu Hijo
a entregarse por nosotros.**

**Por nuestro Señor Jesucristo, tu Hijo,
que vive y reina contigo
en la unidad del Espíritu Santo y es Dios
por los siglos de los siglos.**

Oración después de la Comunión

Oremos.

Todos oran en silencio durante unos momentos, a no ser que este silencio ya se haya hecho antes.

**Concédenos, Dios todopoderoso,
a cuantos participamos
del Cuerpo y la Sangre de tu Hijo,
vivir siempre como miembros suyos.**

Por Jesucristo, nuestro Señor.

FIFTH SUNDAY OF LENT

Let us pray
[for the courage to follow Christ]

Pause for silent prayer.

Father,
help us to be like Christ your Son,
who loved the world and died for our salvation.
Inspire us by his love,
guide us by his example,
who lives and reigns with you and the Holy Spirit,
one God, for ever and ever.

PRAYER AFTER COMMUNION

Let us pray.

Pause for silent prayer, if this has not preceded.

Almighty Father,
by this sacrifice
may we always remain one with your Son, Jesus Christ,
whose body and blood we share,
for he is Lord for ever and ever.

DOMINGO DE RAMOS
"De la pasión del Señor"

Oremos.

Todos oran en silencio durante unos momentos.

Dios todopoderoso y eterno,
que has querido entregarnos como ejemplo de humildad
a Cristo, nuestro salvador,
hecho hombre y clavado en una cruz,
concédenos vivir según las enseñanzas de su pasión,
para participar con él, un día,
de su gloriosa resurrección.

Por nuestro Señor Jesucristo, tu Hijo,
que vive y reina contigo
en la unidad del Espíritu Santo y es Dios
por los siglos de los siglos.

Oración después de la Comunión

Oremos.

Todos oran en silencio durante unos momentos, a no ser que este silencio ya
se haya hecho antes.

Tú que nos has alimentado con esta Eucaristía,
y por medio de la muerte de tu Hijo
nos das la esperanza de alcanzar
lo que la fe nos promete,
concédenos, Señor, llegar,
por medio de su resurrección,
a la meta de nuestras esperanzas.

Por Jesucristo, nuestro Señor.

PASSION (PALM) SUNDAY

Let us pray
[for a closer union with Christ during this holy season]

Pause for silent prayer.

Almighty, ever-living God,
you have given the human race Jesus Christ our Savior
as a model of humility.
He fulfilled your will
by becoming man and giving his life on the cross.
Help us to bear witness to you
by following his example of suffering
and make us worthy to share in his resurrection.

We ask this through our Lord Jesus Christ, your Son,
who lives and reigns with you and the Holy Spirit,
one God, for ever and ever.

Let us pray.

Pause for silent prayer, if this has not preceded.

Lord,
you have satisfied our hunger with this eucharistic food.
The death of your Son gives us hope and strengthens our
faith.
May his resurrection give us perseverance
and lead us to salvation.

We ask this through Christ our Lord.

DOMINGO DE PASCUA
DE LA RESURRECCION DEL SEÑOR

ORACIÓN DEL DÍA

Oremos.

Todos oran en silencio durante unos momentos.

**Dios nuestro,
que en esta día nos has abierto las puertas de la vida eterna
por medio de tu Hijo, vencedor de la muerte,
concede a quienes celebramos hoy la Pascua de Resurrección,
resucitar también a una nueva vida,
renovados por la gracia del Espíritu Santo.**

**Por nuestro Señor Jesucristo, tu Hijo,
que vive y reina contigo
en la unidad del Espíritu Santo y es Dios
por los siglos de los siglos.**

ORACIÓN DESPUÉS DE LA COMUNIÓN

Oremos.

Todos oran en silencio durante unos momentos, a no ser que este silencio ya
se haya hecho antes.

**Señor, protege siempre a tu Iglesia con amor paterno,
para que, renovada ya por los sacramentos de Pascua,
pueda llegar a la gloria de la resurrección.**

Por Jesucristo, nuestro Señor.

EASTER SUNDAY

Let us pray
[that the risen Christ will raise us up and renew our lives]

Pause for silent prayer.

God our Father,
by raising Christ your Son
you conquered the power of death
and opened for us the way to eternal life.
Let our celebration today
raise us up and renew our lives
by the Spirit that is within us.

Grant this through our Lord Jesus Christ, your Son,
who lives and reigns with you and the Holy Spirit,
one God, for ever and ever.

PRAYER AFTER COMMUNION

Let us pray.

Pause for silent prayer, if this has not preceded.

Father of love,
watch over your Church
and bring us to the glory of the resurrection
promised by this Easter sacrament.

We ask this in the name of Jesus the Lord.

SEGUNDO DOMINGO DE PASCUA

ORACIÓN DEL DÍA

Oremos.

Todos oran en silencio durante unos momentos.

**Dios de eterna misericordia, que reavivas la fe de tu pueblo
con la celebración anual de las fiestas pascuales,
aumenta en nosotros tu gracia,
para que comprendamos a fondo la inestimable riqueza
del bautismo que nos ha purificado,
del Espíritu que nos ha dado una vida nueva
y de la Sangre que nos ha redimido.**

**Por nuestro Señor Jesucristo, tu Hijo,
que vive y reina contigo
en la unidad del Espíritu Santo y es Dios
por los siglos de los siglos.**

ORACIÓN DESPUÉS DE LA COMUNIÓN

Oremos.

Todos oran en silencio durante unos momentos, a no ser que este silencio ya
se haya hecho antes.

**Concédenos, Dios todopoderoso,
que la gracia recibida en este sacramento
nos impulse siempre a servirte mejor.**

Por Jesucristo, nuestro Señor.

SECOND SUNDAY OF EASTER

PRAYER OF THE DAY

Let us pray
[for a deeper awareness of our Christian baptism]

Pause for silent prayer.

God of mercy,
you wash away our sins in water,
you give us new birth in the Spirit,
and redeem us in the blood of Christ.
As we celebrate Christ's resurrection
increase our awareness of these blessings,
and renew your gift of life within us.

We ask this through our Lord Jesus Christ, your Son,
who lives and reigns with you and the Holy Spirit,
one God, for ever and ever.

PRAYER AFTER COMMUNION

Let us pray.

Pause for silent prayer, if this has not preceded.

Almighty God,
may the Easter sacraments we have received
live forever in our minds and hearts.

We ask this through Christ our Lord.

TERCER DOMINGO DE PASCUA

ORACIÓN DEL DÍA

Oremos.

Todos oran en silencio durante unos momentos.

**Señor, tú que nos has renovado en el espíritu
al devolvernos la dignidad de hijos tuyos,
concédenos aguardar, llenos de júbilo y esperanza,
el día glorioso de la resurrección.**

**Por nuestro Señor Jesucristo, tu Hijo,
que vive y reina contigo
en la unidad del Espíritu Santo y es Dios
por los siglos de los siglos.**

ORACIÓN DESPUÉS DE LA COMUNIÓN

Oremos.

Todos oran en silencio durante unos momentos, a no ser que este silencio ya
se haya hecho antes.

**Mira, Señor, con bondad a estos hijos tuyos
que has renovado por medio de los sacramentos,
y condúcelos al gozo eterno de la resurrección.**

Por Jesucristo, nuestro Señor.

THIRD SUNDAY OF EASTER

Let us pray
   **[that Christ will give us a share in the glory of his unending
      life]**

   Pause for silent prayer.

**God our Father,
may we look forward with hope to our resurrection,
for you have made us your sons and daughters,
and restored the joy of our youth.**

**We ask this through our Lord Jesus Christ, your Son,
who lives and reigns with you and the Holy Spirit,
one God, for ever and ever.**

PRAYER AFTER COMMUNION

Let us pray.

   Pause for silent prayer, if this has not preceded.

**Lord,
look on your people with kindness
and by these Easter mysteries
bring us to the glory of the resurrection.**

We ask this in the name of Jesus the Lord.

CUARTO DOMINGO DE PASCUA

ORACIÓN DEL DÍA

Oremos.

Todos oran en silencio durante unos momentos.

Dios omnipotente y misericordioso,
guíanos a la felicidad eterna de tu Reino,
a fin de que el pequeño rebaño de tu Hijo
pueda llegar seguro
a donde ya está su Pastor, resucitado,
que vive y reina contigo
en la unidad del Espíritu Santo y es Dios
por los siglos de los siglos.

ORACIÓN DESPUÉS DE LA COMUNIÓN

Oremos.

Todos oran en silencio durante unos momentos, a no ser que este silencio ya
se haya hecho antes.

Vela, Señor, con solicitud, por las ovejas
que rescataste con la Sangre preciosa de tu Hijo,
para que puedan alcanzar, un día,
la felicidad eterna de tu Reino.

Por Jesucristo, nuestro Señor.

FOURTH SUNDAY OF EASTER

PRAYER OF THE DAY

Let us pray
  [that Christ our shepherd will lead us through the difficulties of this life]

Pause for silent prayer.

Almighty and ever-living God,
give us new strength
from the courage of Christ our shepherd,
and lead us to join the saints in heaven,
where he lives and reigns with you and the Holy Spirit,
one God, for ever and ever.

PRAYER AFTER COMMUNION

Let us pray.

Pause for silent prayer, if this has not preceded.

Father, eternal shepherd,
watch over the flock redeemed by the blood of Christ
and lead us to the promised land.

Grant this through Christ our Lord.

QUINTO DOMINGO DE PASCUA

ORACIÓN DEL DÍA

Oremos.

Todos oran en silencio durante unos momentos.

**Señor, tú que te has dignado redimirnos
y has querido hacernos hijos tuyos,
míranos siempre con amor de Padre
y haz que cuantos creemos en Cristo
obtengamos la verdadera libertad y la herencia eterna.**

**Por nuestro Señor Jesucristo, tu Hijo,
que vive y reina contigo
en la unidad del Espíritu Santo y es Dios
por los siglos de los siglos.**

ORACIÓN DESPUÉS DE LA COMUNIÓN

Oremos.

Todos oran en silencio durante unos momentos, a no ser que este silencio ya se haya hecho antes.

**Señor, tú que nos has concedido participar
en esta Eucaristía,
míranos con bondad
y ayúdanos a vencer nuestra fragilidad humana,
para poder nvir como hijos tuyos.**

Por Jesucristo, nuestro Señor.

FIFTH SUNDAY OF EASTER

PRAYER OF THE DAY

Let us pray
[that we may enjoy true freedom]

Pause for silent prayer.

God our Father,
look upon us with love.
You redeem us and make us your children in Christ.
Give us true freedom
and bring us to the inheritance you promised.

We ask this through our Lord Jesus Christ, your Son,
who lives and reigns with you and the Holy Spirit,
one God, for ever and ever.

PRAYER AFTER COMMUNION

Let us pray.

Pause for silent prayer, if this has not preceded.

Merciful Father,
may these mysteries give us new purpose
and bring us to a new life in you.

Grant this through Christ our Lord.

SEXTO DOMINGO DE PASCUA

ORACIÓN DEL DÍA

Oremos.

Todos oran en silencio durante unos momentos.

**Concédenos, Dios todopoderoso,
continuar celebrando con amor y alegría
la victoria de Cristo resucitado,
y que el misterio de su pascua
transforme nuestra vida y se manifieste en nuestras obras.**

**Por nuestro Señor Jesucristo, tu Hijo,
que vive y reina contigo
en la unidad del Espíritu Santo y es Dios
por los siglos de los siglos.**

ORACIÓN DESPUÉS DE LA COMUNIÓN

Oremos.

Todos oran en silencio durante unos momentos, a no ser que este silencio ya se haya hecho antes.

**Dios todopoderoso y eterno,
que, en Cristo resucitado,
nos has hecho renacer a la vida eterna,
haz que este misterio pascual
en el que acabamos de participar
por medio de la Eucaristía,
dé en nosotros abundantes frutos de salvación.**

Por Jesucristo, nuestro Señor.

SIXTH SUNDAY OF EASTER

Let us pray
[that we may practice in our lives the faith we profess]

Pause for silent prayer.

Ever-living God,
help us to celebrate our joy
in the resurrection of the Lord
and to express in our lives
the love we celebrate.

Grant this through our Lord Jesus Christ, your Son,
who lives and reigns with you and the Holy Spirit,
one God, for ever and ever.

Let us pray.

Pause for silent prayer, if this has not preceded.

Almighty and ever-living Lord,
you restored us to life
by raising Christ from death.
Strengthen us by this Easter sacrament;
may we feel its saving power in our daily life.

We ask this through Christ our Lord.

LA ASCENSION DEL SEÑOR

Oración del Día

Oremos.

Todos oran en silencio durante unos momentos.

**Llena, Señor, nuestro corazón de gratitud y de alegría
por la gloriosa ascensión de tu Hijo,
ya que su triunfo es también nuestra victoria,
pues a donde llegó él, nuestra cabeza,
tenemos la esperanza cierta de llegar nosotros,
que somos su cuerpo.**

**Por nuestro Señor Jesucristo, tu Hijo,
que vive y reina contigo
en la unidad del Espíritu Santo y es Dios
por los siglos de los siglos.**

Oración después de la Comunión

Oremos.

Todos oran en silencio durante unos momentos, a no ser que este silencio ya
se haya hecho antes.

**Dios todopoderoso,
que ya desde este mundo nos haces participar
de tu vida divina,
aviva en nosotros el deseo de la patria eterna,
donde nos aguarda Cristo, Hijo tuyo y hermano nuestro.**

Él, que vive y reina por los siglos de los siglos.

ASCENSION OF THE LORD

Let us pray
[that the risen Christ will lead us to eternal life]

Pause for silent prayer.

**God our Father,
make us joyful in the ascension of your Son Jesus Christ.
May we follow him into the new creation,
for his ascension is our glory and our hope.**

**We ask this through our Lord Jesus Christ, your Son,
who lives and reigns with you and the Holy Spirit,
one God, for ever and ever.**

PRAYER AFTER COMMUNION

Let us pray.

Pause for silent prayer, if this has not preceded.

**Father,
in this eucharist
we touch the divine life you give to the world.
Help us to follow Christ with love
to eternal life where he is Lord for ever and ever.**

SEPTIMO DOMINGO DE PASCUA

Oremos.

Todos oran en silencio durante unos momentos.

**Concede, Señor,
a quienes creemos firmemente que nuestro Salvador
comparte ya tu gloria,
sentir que él está también con nosotros,
según su promesa,
hasta el fin de los tiempos.**

**Por nuestro Señor Jesucristo, tu Hijo,
que vive y reina contigo
en la unidad del Espíritu Santo y es Dios
por los siglos de los siglos.**

ORACIÓN DESPUÉS DE LA COMUNIÓN

Oremos.

Todos oran en silencio durante unos momentos, a no ser que este silencio ya
se haya hecho antes.

**Escúchanos, Señor,
y haz que nuestra comunión con Cristo glorificado
nos afiance en la esperanza
de que toda la Iglesia alcanzará, un día,
la gloria del Señor resucitado,
que vive y reina por los siglos de los siglos.**

SEVENTH SUNDAY OF EASTER

PRAYER OF THE DAY

Let us pray
[that we may recognize the presence of Christ in our midst]

Pause for silent prayer.

Father,
help us keep in mind that Christ our Savior
lives with you in glory
and promised to remain with us until the end of time.

We ask this through our Lord Jesus Christ, your Son,
who lives and reigns with you and the Holy Spirit,
one God, for ever and ever.

PRAYER AFTER COMMUNION

Let us pray.

Pause for silent prayer, if this has not preceded.

God our Savior,
hear us,
and through this holy mystery give us hope
that the glory you have given Christ
will be given to the Church, his body,
for he is Lord for ever and ever.

DOMINGO DE PENTECOSTES

ORACIÓN DEL DÍA

Oremos.

Todos oran en silencio durante unos momentos.

**Dios nuestro,
que por el misterio de Pentecostés
santificas a tu Iglesia extendida por todas las naciones,
concede al mundo entero
los dones del Espíritu Santo
y continúa realizando entre los fieles
la unidad y el amor
de la primitiva Iglesia.**

**Por nuestro Señor Jesucristo, tu Hijo,
que vive y reina contigo
en la unidad del Espíritu Santo y es Dios
por los siglos de los siglos.**

ORACIÓN DESPUÉS DE LA COMUNIÓN

Oremos.

Todos oran en silencio durante unos momentos, a no ser que este silencio ya se haya hecho antes.

**Señor, tú que nos concedes
participar de la vida divina
por medio de tus sacramentos,
conserva en nosotros el don de tu amor
y la presencia viva del Espíritu Santo,
para que esta comunión
nos ayude a obtener nuestra salvación eterna.**

Por Jesucristo, nuestro Señor.

PENTECOST

PRAYER OF THE DAY

Let us pray
[that the Spirit will work through our lives to bring Christ
to the world]

Pause for silent prayer.

God our Father,
let the Spirit you sent on your Church
to begin the teaching of the gospel
continue to work in the world
through the hearts of all who believe.

We ask this through our Lord Jesus Christ, your Son,
who lives and reigns with you and the Holy Spirit,
one God, for ever and ever.

PRAYER AFTER COMMUNION

Let us pray.

Pause for silent prayer, if this has not preceded.

Father,
may the food we receive in the eucharist
help our eternal redemption.
Keep within us the vigor of your Spirit
and protect the gifts you have given to your Church.

We ask this in the name of Jesus the Lord.

LA SANTISIMA TRINIDAD
Domingo después de Pentecostés

ORACIÓN DEL DÍA

Oremos.

Todos oran en silencio durante unos momentos.

**Dios Padre, que al enviar al mundo
al Verbo de verdad y al Espíritu de santidad,
revelaste a los hombres tu misterio admirable,
concédenos que al profesar la fe verdadera,
reconozcamos la gloria de la eterna Trinidad
y adoremos la unidad de su majestad omnipotente.**

**Por nuestro Señor Jesucristo, tu Hijo,
que vive y reina contigo
en la unidad del Espíritu Santo y es Dios
por los siglos de los siglos.**

ORACIÓN DESPUÉS DE LA COMUNIÓN

Oremos.

Todos oran en silencio durante unos momentos, a no ser que este silencio ya se haya hecho antes.

**Que la recepción de este sacramento
y nuestra profesión de fe
en la Trinidad santa y eterna,
y en su unidad indivisible,
nos aprovechen, Señor, Dios nuestro,
para la salvación del cuerpo y el alma.**

Por Jesucristo, nuestro Señor.

TRINITY SUNDAY

Sunday after Pentecost

PRAYER OF THE DAY

> **Let us pray**
> **[to the one God, Father, Son and Spirit, that our lives may**
> **bear witness to our faith]**
>
> Pause for silent prayer.
>
> **Father,**
> **you sent your Word to bring us truth**
> **and your Spirit to make us holy.**
> **Through them we come to know the mystery of your life.**
> **Help us to worship you, one God in three Persons,**
> **by proclaiming and living our faith in you.**
>
> **Grant this through our Lord Jesus Christ, your Son,**
> **who lives and reigns with you and the Holy Spirit,**
> **one God, for ever and ever.**

PRAYER AFTER COMMUNION

> **Let us pray.**
>
> Pause for silent prayer, if this has not preceded.
>
> **Lord God,**
> **we worship you, a Trinity of Persons, one eternal God.**
> **May our faith and the sacrament we receive**
> **bring us health of mind and body.**
>
> **We ask this through Christ our Lord.**

EL CUERPO Y LA SANGRE DE CRISTO

ORACIÓN DEL DÍA

Oremos.

Todos oran en silencio durante unos momentos.

**Señor nuestro Jesucristo, que en este sacramento admirable
nos dejaste el memorial de tu pasión,
concédenos venerar de tal modo
los sagrados misterios de tu Cuerpo y de tu Sangre,
que experimentemos constantemente en nosotros
el fruto de tu redención.**

**Tú que vives y reinas con el Padre
en la unidad del Espíritu Santo y eres Dios
por los siglos de los siglos.**

ORACIÓN DESPUÉS DE LA COMUNIÓN

Oremos.

Todos oran en silencio durante unos momentos, a no ser que este silencio ya
se haya hecho antes.

**Concédenos, Señor, disfrutar eternamente
del gozo de tu divinidad que ahora pregustamos,
en la comunión de tu Cuerpo y de tu Sangre.**

Tú que vives y reinas por los siglos de los siglos.

BODY AND BLOOD OF CHRIST

Let us pray
[to the Lord who gives himself in the eucharist, that this
   sacrament may bring us salvation and peace]

Pause for silent prayer.

**Lord Jesus Christ,
you gave us the eucharist
as the memorial of your suffering and death.
May our worship of this sacrament of your body and blood
help us to experience the salvation you won for us
and the peace of the kingdom
where you live with the Father and the Holy Spirit,
one God, for ever and ever.**

PRAYER AFTER COMMUNION

Let us pray.

Pause for silent prayer, if this has not preceded.

**Lord Jesus Christ,
you give us your body and blood in the eucharist
as a sign that even now we share your life.
May we come to possess it completely in the kingdom
where you live for ever and ever.**

SEGUNDO DOMINGO ORDINARIO

ORACIÓN DEL DÍA

Oremos.

Todos oran en silencio durante unos momentos.

**Dios todopoderoso y eterno,
que con amor gobiernas los cielos y la tierra,
escucha paternalmente las súplicas de tu pueblo
y haz que los días de nuestra vida transcurran en tu paz.**

**Por nuestro Señor Jesucristo, tu Hijo,
que vive y reina contigo
en la unidad del Espíritu Santo y es Dios
por los siglos de los siglos.**

ORACIÓN DESPUÉS DE LA COMUNIÓN

Oremos.

Todos oran en silencio durante unos momentos, a no ser que este silencio ya se haya hecho antes.

**Infúndenos, Señor, el espíritu de tu caridad
para que, alimentados del mismo pan del cielo,
permanezcamos siempre unidos por el mismo amor.**

Por Jesucristo, nuestro Señor.

SECOND SUNDAY IN ORDINARY TIME

PRAYER OF THE DAY

Let us pray
[to our Father for the gift of peace]

Pause for silent prayer.

Father of heaven and earth,
hear our prayers,
and show us the way to peace in the world.

Grant this through our Lord Jesus Christ, your Son,
who lives and reigns with you and the Holy Spirit,
one God, for ever and ever.

PRAYER AFTER COMMUNION

Let us pray.

Pause for silent prayer, if this has not preceded.

Lord,
you have nourished us with bread from heaven.
Fill us with your Spirit,
and make us one in peace and love.

We ask this through Christ our Lord.

TERCER DOMINGO ORDINARIO

ORACIÓN DEL DÍA

Oremos.

> Todos oran en silencio durante unos momentos.

**Dios eterno y todopoderoso,
conduce nuestra vida por el camino de tus mandamientos
para que, unidos a tu Hijo amado,
podamos producir frutos abundantes.**

**Por nuestro Señor Jesucristo, tu Hijo,
que vive y reina contigo
en la unidad del Espíritu Santo y es Dios
por los siglos de los siglos.**

ORACIÓN DESPUÉS DE LA COMUNIÓN

Oremos.

> Todos oran en silencio durante unos momentos, a no ser que este silencio ya
> se haya hecho antes.

**Te damos gracias, Señor,
por habernos alimentado
con el Cuerpo y la Sangre de tu Hijo
y te pedimos que este don tuyo
sea para nosotros fuente inagotable de vida.**

Por Jesucristo, nuestro Señor.

THIRD SUNDAY IN ORDINARY TIME

PRAYER OF THE DAY

Let us pray
[for unity and peace]

Pause for silent prayer.

All-powerful and ever-living God,
direct your love that is within us,
that our efforts in the name of your Son
may bring mankind to unity and peace.

We ask this through our Lord Jesus Christ, your Son,
who lives and reigns with you and the Holy Spirit,
one God, for ever and ever.

PRAYER AFTER COMMUNION

Let us pray.

Pause for silent prayer, if this has not preceded.

God, all-powerful Father,
may the new life you give us increase our love
and keep us in the joy of your kingdom.

We ask this in the name of Jesus the Lord.

CUARTO DOMINGO ORDINARIO

Oración del Día

Oremos.

Todos oran en silencio durante unos momentos.

**Concédenos, Señor, Dios nuestro,
amarte con todo el corazón
y, con el mismo amor,
amar a nuestros prójimos.**

**Por nuestro Señor Jesucristo, tu Hijo,
que vive y reina contigo
en la unidad del Espíritu Santo y es Dios
por los siglos de los siglos.**

Oración después de la Comunión

Oremos.

Todos oran en silencio durante unos momentos, a no ser que este silencio ya se haya hecho antes.

**Que el sacramento del Cuerpo y la Sangre de tu Hijo
que acabamos de recibir,
nos ayude, Señor,
a vivir más profundamente nuestra fe.**

Por Jesucristo, nuestro Señor.

FOURTH SUNDAY IN ORDINARY TIME

Let us pray
[for a greater love of God and of our fellow men]

Pause for silent prayer.

Lord our God,
help us to love you with all our hearts
and to love all men as you love them.

Grant this through our Lord Jesus Christ, your Son,
who lives and reigns with you and the Holy Spirit,
one God, for ever and ever.

PRAYER AFTER COMMUNION

Let us pray.

Pause for silent prayer, if this has not preceded.

Lord,
you invigorate us with this help to our salvation.
By the eucharist give the true faith continued growth
throughout the world.

We ask this in the name of Jesus the Lord.

QUINTO DOMINGO ORDINARIO

ORACIÓN DEL DÍA

Oremos.

Todos oran en silencio durante unos momentos.

**Señor, que tu amor incansable
cuide y proteja siempre a estos hijos tuyos,
que han puesto en tu gracia
toda su esperanza.
Por nuestro Señor Jesucristo, tu Hijo,
que vive y reina contigo
en la unidad del Espíritu Santo y es Dios
por los siglos de los siglos.**

ORACIÓN DESPUÉS DE LA COMUNIÓN

Oremos.

Todos oran en silencio durante unos momentos, a no ser que este silencio ya se haya hecho antes.

**Señor, tú que has querido hacernos participar
de un mismo pan y de un mismo cáliz,
concédenos vivir de tal manera unidos en Cristo,
que nuestro trabajo sea eficaz para la salvación del mundo.**

Por Jesucristo, nuestro Señor.

FIFTH SUNDAY IN ORDINARY TIME

Let us pray
[that God will watch over us and protect us]

Pause for silent prayer.

Father,
watch over your family
and keep us safe in your care,
for all our hope is in you.

Grant this through our Lord Jesus Christ, your Son,
who lives and reigns with you and the Holy Spirit,
one God, for ever and ever.

PRAYER AFTER COMMUNION

Let us pray.

Pause for silent prayer, if this has not preceded.

God our Father,
you give us a share in the one bread and the one cup
and make us one in Christ.
Help us to bring your salvation and joy
to all the world.

We ask this through Christ our Lord.

SEXTO DOMINGO ORDINARIO

Oración del Día

Oremos.

Todos oran en silencio durante unos momentos.

Señor nuestro, que prometiste venir
y hacer tu morada en los corazones rectos y sinceros,
concédenos la rectitud y sinceridad de vida
que nos hagan dignos de esa presencia tuya.

Por nuestro Señor Jesucristo, tu Hijo,
que vive y reina contigo
en la unidad del Espíritu Santo y es Dios
por los siglos de los siglos.

Oración después de la Comunión

Oremos.

Todos oran en silencio durante unos momentos, a no ser que este silencio ya se haya hecho antes.

Señor, aviva cada vez más en nosotros
el deseo de recibir este pan eucarístico,
por medio del cual
nos comunicas tú la vida verdadera.

Por Jesucristo, nuestro Señor.

SIXTH SUNDAY IN ORDINARY TIME

PRAYER OF THE DAY

Let us pray
[that everything we do will be guided by God's law of love]

Pause for silent prayer.

God our Father,
you have promised to remain for ever
with those who do what is just and right.
Help us to live in your presence.

We ask this through our Lord Jesus Christ, your Son,
who lives and reigns with you and the Holy Spirit,
one God, for ever and ever.

PRAYER AFTER COMMUNION

Let us pray.

Pause for silent prayer, if this has not preceded.

Lord,
you give us food from heaven.
May we always hunger
for the bread of life.

Grant this through Christ our Lord.

SEPTIMO DOMINGO ORDINARIO

ORACIÓN DEL DÍA

Oremos.

Todos oran en silencio durante unos momentos.

Concédenos, Señor,
ser dóciles a las inspiraciones de tu Espíritu
para que realicemos siempre en nuestra vida
tu santa voluntad.

Por nuestro Señor Jesucristo, tu Hijo,
que vive y reina contigo
en la unidad del Espíritu Santo y es Dios
por los siglos de los siglos.

ORACIÓN DESPUÉS DE LA COMUNIÓN

Oremos.

Todos oran en silencio durante unos momentos, a no ser que este silencio ya se haya hecho antes.

Que el Cuerpo y la Sangre de Cristo,
que nos has dado, Señor, en este sacramento,
sean para todos nosotros
una prenda segura de vida eterna.

Por Jesucristo, nuestro Señor.

SEVENTH SUNDAY IN ORDINARY TIME

PRAYER OF THE DAY

Let us pray
[that God will make us more like Christ, his Son]

Pause for silent prayer.

Father,
keep before us the wisdom and love
you have revealed in your Son.
Help us to be like him
in word and deed,
for he lives and reigns with you and the Holy Spirit,
one God, for ever and ever.

PRAYER AFTER COMMUNION

Let us pray.

Pause for silent prayer, if this has not preceded.

Almighty God,
help us to live the example of love
we celebrate in this eucharist,
that we may come to its fulfillment in your presence.

We ask this through Christ our Lord.

OCTAVO DOMINGO ORDINARIO

ORACIÓN DEL DÍA

Oremos.

Todos oran en silencio durante unos momentos.

Concédenos, Señor,
que el curso de los acontecimientos del mundo
se desenvuelva, según tu voluntad,
en la justicia y en la paz,
y que tu Iglesia pueda servirte
con tranquilidad y alegría.

Por nuestro Señor Jesucristo, tu Hijo,
que vive y reina contigo
en la unidad del Espíritu Santo y es Dios
por los siglos de los siglos.

ORACIÓN DESPUÉS DE LA COMUNIÓN

Oremos.

Todos oran en silencio durante unos momentos, a no ser que este silencio ya
se haya hecho antes.

Te pedimos, Padre misericordioso,
que por este sacramento
con que ahora nos fortaleces,
nos hagas algún día, participar de la vida eterna.

Por Jesucristo, nuestro Señor.

EIGHTH SUNDAY IN ORDINARY TIME

PRAYER OF THE DAY

> **Let us pray**
> **[that God will bring peace to the world and freedom to his**
>   **Church]**
>
>> Pause for silent prayer.
>
> **Lord,**
> **guide the course of world events**
> **and give your Church the joy and peace**
> **of serving you in freedom.**
>
> **We ask this through our Lord Jesus Christ, your Son,**
> **who lives and reigns with you and the Holy Spirit,**
> **one God, for ever and ever.**

PRAYER AFTER COMMUNION

> **Let us pray.**
>
>> Pause for silent prayer, if this has not preceded.
>
> **God of salvation,**
> **may this sacrament which strengthens us here on earth**
> **bring us to eternal life.**
>
> **We ask this in the name of Jesus the Lord.**

NOVENO DOMINGO ORDINARIO

Oración del Día

Oremos.

Todos oran en silencio durante unos momentos.

**Nos acogemos, Señor, a tu providencia,
que nunca se equivoca,
y te pedimos humildemente que apartes de nosotros todo mal
y nos concedas aquello que pueda contribuir a nuestro bien.**

**Por nuestro Señor Jesucristo, tu Hijo,
que vive y reina contigo
en la unidad del Espíritu Santo y es Dios
por los siglos de los siglos.**

Oración después de la Comunión

Oremos.

Todos oran en silencio durante unos momentos, a no ser que este silencio ya
se haya hecho antes.

**Padre santo, tú que nos has alimentado
con el Cuerpo y la Sangre de tu Hijo,
guíanos por medio de tu Espíritu
a fin de que, no sólo con palabras, sino con toda nuestra vida
podamos demostrarte nuestro amor
y así merezeamos entrar al Reino de los cielos.**

Por Jesucristo, nuestro Señor.

NINTH SUNDAY IN ORDINARY TIME

Let us pray
[for God's care and protection]

Pause for silent prayer.

Father,
your love never fails.
Hear our call.
Keep us from danger
and provide for all our needs.

Grant this through our Lord Jesus Christ, your Son,
who lives and reigns with you and the Holy Spirit,
one God, for ever and ever.

PRAYER AFTER COMMUNION

Let us pray.

Pause for silent prayer, if this has not preceded.

Lord,
as you give us the body and blood of your Son,
guide us with your Spirit
that we may honor you
not only with our lips,
but also with the lives we lead,
and so enter your kingdom.

We ask this in the name of Jesus the Lord.

DECIMO DOMINGO ORDINARIO

ORACIÓN DEL DÍA

Oremos.

Todos oran en silencio durante unos momentos.

**Dios nuestro, de quien todo bien procede,
inspíranos propósitos de justicia y santidad
y concédenos tu ayuda
para poder cumplirlos.**

**Por nuestro Señor Jesucristo, tu Hijo,
que vive y reina contigo
en la unidad del Espíritu Santo y es Dios
por los siglos de los siglos.**

ORACIÓN DESPUÉS DE LA COMUNIÓN

Oremos.

Todos oran en silencio durante unos momentos, a no ser que este silencio ya
se haya hecho antes.

**Que la fuerza redentora de esta Eucaristía
nos proteja, Señor,
de nuestras malas inclinaciones
y nos guíe siempre por el camino de tus mandamientos.**

Por Jesucristo, nuestro Señor.

TENTH SUNDAY IN ORDINARY TIME

Let us pray
[for the guidance of the Holy Spirit]

Pause for silent prayer.

God of wisdom and love,
source of all good,
send your Spirit to teach us your truth
and guide our actions
in your way of peace.

We ask this through our Lord Jesus Christ, your Son,
who lives and reigns with you and the Holy Spirit,
one God, for ever and ever.

PRAYER AFTER COMMUNION

Let us pray.

Pause for silent prayer, if this has not preceded.

Lord,
may your healing love
turn us from sin
and keep us on the way that leads to you.

We ask this in the name of Jesus the Lord.

DECIMOPRIMER DOMINGO ORDINARIO

ORACIÓN DEL DÍA

Oremos.

Todos oran en silencio durante unos momentos.

Dios nuestro,
fuerza de todos los que en ti confían,
ayúdanos con tu gracia,
sin la cual nada puede nuestra humana debilidad,
para que podamos serte fieles
en la observancia de tus mandamientos.

Por nuestro Señor Jesucristo, tu Hijo,
que vive y reina contigo
en la unidad del Espíritu Santo y es Dios
por los siglos de los siglos.

ORACIÓN DESPUÉS DE LA COMUNIÓN

Oremos.

Todos oran en silencio durante unos momentos, a no ser que este silencio ya se haya hecho antes.

Que nuestra participación en este sacramento
signo de la unión de los fieles en ti,
contribuya, Señor,
a la unidad de tu Iglesia.

Por Jesucristo, nuestro Señor.

ELEVENTH SUNDAY IN ORDINARY TIME

Let us pray
[for the grace to follow Christ more closely]

Pause for silent prayer.

Almighty God,
our hope and our strength,
without you we falter.
Help us to follow Christ
and to live according to your will.

We ask this through our Lord Jesus Christ, your Son,
who lives and reigns with you and the Holy Spirit,
one God, for ever and ever.

PRAYER AFTER COMMUNION

Let us pray.

Pause for silent prayer, if this has not preceded.

Lord,
may this eucharist
accomplish in your Church
the unity and peace it signifies.

Grant this through Christ our Lord.

DECIMOSEGUNDO DOMINGO ORDINARIO

ORACIÓN DEL DÍA

Oremos.

Todos oran en silencio durante unos momentos.

**Padre misericordioso,
que nunca dejas de tu mano
a quienes has hecho arraigar en tu amistad,
concédenos vivir siempre movidos por tu amor
y un filial temor de ofenderte.**

**Por nuestro Señor Jesucristo, tu Hijo,
que vive y reina contigo
en la unidad del Espíritu Santo y es Dios
por los siglos de los siglos.**

ORACIÓN DESPUÉS DE LA COMUNIÓN

Oremos.

Todos oran en silencio durante unos momentos, a no ser que este silencio ya
se haya hecho antes.

**Señor, tú que nos has renovado
con el Cuerpo y la Sangre de tu Hijo,
concédenos que la participación en esta Eucaristía
nos ayude a obtener la plenitud de la redención.**

Por Jesucristo, nuestro Señor.

TWELFTH SUNDAY IN ORDINARY TIME

PRAYER OF THE DAY

Let us pray
[that we may grow in the love of God]

Pause for silent prayer.

Father,
guide and protector of your people,
grant us an unfailing respect for your name,
and keep us always in your love.

Grant this through our Lord Jesus Christ, your Son,
who lives and reigns with you and the Holy Spirit,
one God, for ever and ever.

PRAYER AFTER COMMUNION

Let us pray.

Pause for silent prayer, if this has not preceded.

Lord,
you give us the body and blood of your Son
to renew your life within us.
In your mercy, assure our redemption
and bring us to the eternal life
we celebrate in this eucharist.

We ask this through Christ our Lord.

DECIMOTERCER DOMINGO ORDINARIO

Oración del Día

Oremos.

Todos oran en silencio durante unos momentos.

Padre de bondad,
que por medio de tu gracia
nos has hecho hijos de la luz,
concédenos vivir fuera de las tinieblas del error
y permanecer siempre en el esplendor de la verdad.

Por nuestro Señor Jesucristo, tu Hijo,
que vive y reina contigo
en la unidad del Espíritu Santo y es Dios
por los siglos de los siglos.

Oración después de la Comunión

Oremos.

Todos oran en silencio durante unos momentos, a no ser que este silencio ya se haya hecho antes.

Que el Cuerpo y la Sangre de tu Hijo,
que hemos ofrecido en sacrificio
y recibido en comunión,
sean para nosotros principio de vida nueva,
a fin de que, unidos a ti por el amor,
demos frutos que permanezcan para siempre.

Por Jesucristo, nuestro Señor.

THIRTEENTH SUNDAY IN ORDINARY TIME

PRAYER OF THE DAY

Let us pray
[that Christ may be our light]

Pause for silent prayer.

Father,
you call your children
to walk in the light of Christ.
Free us from darkness
and keep us in the radiance of your truth.

We ask this through our Lord Jesus Christ, your Son,
who lives and reigns with you and the Holy Spirit,
one God, for ever and ever.

PRAYER AFTER COMMUNION

Let us pray.

Pause for silent prayer, if this has not preceded.

Lord,
may this sacrifice and communion
give us a share in your life
and help us bring your love to the world.

Grant this through Christ our Lord.

DECIMOCUARTO DOMINGO ORDINARIO

ORACIÓN DEL DÍA

Oremos.

> Todos oran en silencio durante unos momentos.

**Dios nuestro,
que por medio de la muerte de tu Hijo
has redimido al mundo de la esclavitud del pecado,
concédenos participar ahora de una santa alegría
y, después en el cielo, de la felicidad eterna.**

**Por nuestro Señor Jesucristo, tu Hijo,
que vive y reina contigo
en la unidad del Espíritu Santo y es Dios
por los siglos de los siglos.**

ORACIÓN DESPUÉS DE LA COMUNIÓN

Oremos.

> Todos oran en silencio durante unos momentos, a no ser que este silencio ya
> se haya hecho antes.

**Dios omnipotente y eterno,
que nos has alimentado
con el sacramento de tu amor,
concédenos vivir siempre en tu amistad
y agradecer continuamente tu misericordia.**

Por Jesucristo, nuestro Señor.

FOURTEENTH SUNDAY IN ORDINARY TIME

Let us pray
[for forgiveness through the grace of Jesus Christ]

Pause for silent prayer.

Father,
through the obedience of Jesus,
your servant and your Son,
you raised a fallen world.
Free us from sin
and bring us the joy that lasts for ever.

We ask this through our Lord Jesus Christ, your Son,
who lives and reigns with you and the Holy Spirit,
one God, for ever and ever.

PRAYER AFTER COMMUNION

Let us pray.

Pause for silent prayer, if this has not preceded.

Lord,
may we never fail to praise you
for the fullness of life and salvation
you give us in this eucharist.

We ask this through Christ our Lord.

DECIMOQUINTO DOMINGO ORDINARIO

ORACIÓN DEL DÍA

Oremos.

Todos oran en silencio durante unos momentos.

**Señor, tú que iluminas a los extraviados
con la luz de tu Evangelio
para que vuelvan al camino de la verdad,
concede a cuantos nos llamamos cristianos
imitar fielmente a Cristo
y rechazar lo que pueda alejarnos de él.**

**Por nuestro Señor Jesucristo, tu Hijo,
que vive y reina contigo
en la unidad del Espíritu Santo y es Dios
por los siglos de los siglos.**

ORACIÓN DESPUÉS DE LA COMUNIÓN

Oremos.

Todos oran en silencio durante unos momentos, a no ser que este silencio ya se haya hecho antes.

**Te suplicamos, Señor,
que esta Eucaristía que hemos recibido,
nos ayude a amarte más
y a servirte mejor cada día.**

Por Jesucristo, nuestro Señor.

FIFTEENTH SUNDAY IN ORDINARY TIME

PRAYER OF THE DAY

Let us pray
[that the gospel may be our rule of life]

Pause for silent prayer.

God our Father,
your light of truth
guides us to the way of Christ.
May all who follow him
reject what is contrary to the gospel.

We ask this through our Lord Jesus Christ, your Son,
who lives and reigns with you and the Holy Spirit,
one God, for ever and ever.

PRAYER AFTER COMMUNION

Let us pray.

Pause for silent prayer, if this has not preceded.

Lord,
by our sharing in the mystery of this eucharist,
let your saving love grow within us.

Grant this through Christ our Lord.

DECIMOSEXTO DOMINGO ORDINARIO

ORACIÓN DEL DÍA

Oremos.

Todos oran en silencio durante unos momentos.

Míranos, Señor, con amor
y multiplica en nosotros los dones de tu gracia
para que, llenos de fe, esperanza y caridad,
permanezcamos siempre fieles
en el cumplimiento de tus mandatos.

Por nuestro Señor Jesucristo, tu Hijo,
que vive y reina contigo
en la unidad del Espíritu Santo y es Dios
por los siglos de los siglos.

ORACIÓN DESPUÉS DE LA COMUNIÓN

Oremos.

Todos oran en silencio durante unos momentos, a no ser que este silencio ya se haya hecho antes.

Señor, tú que nos has concedido
participar en esta Eucaristía,
míranos con bondad y ayúdanos a vencer
nuestra fragilidad humana para poder vivir como hijos tuyos.

Por Jesucristo, nuestro Señor.

SIXTEENTH SUNDAY IN ORDINARY TIME

Prayer of the Day

Let us pray
[to be kept faithful in the service of God]

Pause for silent prayer.

Lord,
be merciful to your people.
Fill us with your gifts
and make us always eager to serve you
in faith, hope, and love.

Grant this through our Lord Jesus Christ, your Son,
who lives and reigns with you and the Holy Spirit,
one God, for ever and ever.

Prayer after Communion

Let us pray.

Pause for silent prayer, if this has not preceded.

Merciful Father,
may these mysteries
give us new purpose
and bring us to a new life in you.

We ask this in the name of Jesus the Lord.

DECIMOSEPTIMO DOMINGO ORDINARIO

ORACIÓN DEL DÍA

Oremos.

Todos oran en silencio durante unos momentos.

**Padre santo y todopoderoso,
protector de los que en ti confían,
ten misericordia de nosotros
y enséñanos a usar con sabiduría de los bienes de la tierra,
a fin de que no nos impidan alcanzar los del cielo.**

**Por nuestro Señor Jesucristo, tu Hijo,
que vive y reina contigo
en la unidad del Espíritu Santo y es Dios
por los siglos de los siglos.**

ORACIÓN DESPUÉS DE LA COMUNIÓN

Oremos.

Todos oran en silencio durante unos momentos, a no ser que este silencio ya se haya hecho antes.

**Señor, que esta Eucaristía,
memorial de la muerte y resurrección de tu Hijo,
nos ayude a corresponder
al don inefable de su amor
y a procurar cada día nuestra salvación eterna.**

Por Jesucristo, nuestro Señor.

SEVENTEENTH SUNDAY IN ORDINARY TIME

Let us pray
[that we will make good use of the gifts that God has given us]

Pause for silent prayer.

**God our Father and protector,
without you nothing is holy,
nothing has value.
Guide us to everlasting life
by helping us to use wisely
the blessings you have given to the world.**

**We ask this through our Lord Jesus Christ, your Son,
who lives and reigns with you and the Holy Spirit,
one God, for ever and ever.**

PRAYER AFTER COMMUNION

Let us pray.

Pause for silent prayer, if this has not preceded.

**Lord,
we receive the sacrament
which celebrates the memory
of the death and resurrection of Christ your Son.
May this gift bring us closer to our eternal salvation.**

We ask this through Christ our Lord.

DECIMOCTAVO DOMINGO ORDINARIO

ORACIÓN DEL DÍA

Oremos.

Todos oran en silencio durante unos momentos.

Señor, tú que eres nuestro creador
y quien amorosamente dispone toda nuestra vida,
renuévanos conforme a la imagen de tu Hijo
y ayúdanos a conservar siempre tu gracia.

Por nuestro Señor Jesucristo, tu Hijo,
que vive y reina contigo
en la unidad del Espíritu Santo y es Dios
por los siglos de los siglos.

ORACIÓN DESPUÉS DE LA COMUNIÓN

Oremos.

Todos oran en silencio durante unos momentos, a no ser que este silencio ya se haya hecho antes.

Protege, Señor, continuamente
a quienes renuevas y fortaleces con esta Eucaristía
y hazlos dignos de alcanzar
la salvación eterna.

Por Jesucristo, nuestro Señor.

EIGHTEENTH SUNDAY IN ORDINARY TIME

**Let us pray
[for the gift of God's forgiveness and love]**

Pause for silent prayer.

**Father of everlasting goodness,
our origin and guide,
be close to us
and hear the prayers of all who praise you.
Forgive our sins and restore us to life.
Keep us safe in your love.**

**Grant this through our Lord Jesus Christ, your Son,
who lives and reigns with you and the Holy Spirit,
one God, for ever and ever.**

PRAYER AFTER COMMUNION

Let us pray.

Pause for silent prayer, if this has not preceded.

**Lord,
you give us the strength of new life
by the gift of the eucharist.
Protect us with your love
and prepare us for eternal redemption.**

We ask this through Christ our Lord.

DECIMONOVENO DOMINGO ORDINARIO

ORACIÓN DEL DÍA

Oremos.

Todos oran en silencio durante unos momentos.

**Dios eterno y todopoderoso
a quien confiadamente podemos llamar ya Padre nuestro,
haz crecer en nuestros corazones
el espíritu de hijos adoptivos tuyos,
para que podamos gozar, después de esta vida,
de la herencia que nos has prometido.**

**Por nuestro Señor Jesucristo, tu Hijo,
que vive y reina contigo
en la unidad del Espíritu Santo y es Dios
por los siglos de los siglos.**

ORACIÓN DESPUÉS DE LA COMUNIÓN

Oremos.

Todos oran en silencio durante unos momentos, a no ser que este silencio ya
se haya hecho antes.

**Que la recepción de esta Eucaristía
nos confirme, Señor, en tu amor
y nos ayude a conseguir la vida eterna.**

Por Jesucristo, nuestro Señor.

NINETEENTH SUNDAY IN ORDINARY TIME

Let us pray
[in the Spirit that we may grow in the love of God]

Pause for silent prayer.

Almighty and ever-living God,
your Spirit made us your children,
confident to call you Father.
Increase your Spirit within us
and bring us to our promised inheritance.

Grant this through our Lord Jesus Christ, your Son,
who lives and reigns with you and the Holy Spirit,
one God, for ever and ever.

PRAYER AFTER COMMUNION

Let us pray.

Pause for silent prayer, if this has not preceded.

Lord,
may the eucharist you give us
bring us to salvation
and keep us faithful to the light of your truth.

We ask this in the name of Jesus the Lord.

VIGESIMO DOMINGO ORDINARIO

ORACIÓN DEL DÍA

Oremos.

Todos oran en silencio durante unos momentos.

**Enciende, Señor, nuestros corazones
con el fuego de tu amor
a fin de que, amándote en todo y sobre todo,
podamos obtener aquellos bienes
que no podemos nosotros ni siquiera imaginar
y has prometido tú a los que te aman.**

**Por nuestro Señor Jesucristo, tu Hijo,
que vive y reina contigo
en la unidad del Espíritu Santo y es Dios
por los siglos de los siglos.**

ORACIÓN DESPUÉS DE LA COMUNIÓN

Oremos.

Todos oran en silencio durante unos momentos, a no ser que este silencio ya se haya hecho antes.

**Tú que nos hecho partícipes de la vida de Cristo
en este sacramento,
transfórmanos, Señor, a imagen de tu Hijo,
para que participemos también de su gloria en el cielo.**

Por Jesucristo, nuestro Señor.

TWENTIETH SUNDAY IN ORDINARY TIME

Let us pray
[that the love of God may raise us beyond what we see to
the unseen glory of his kingdom]

Pause for silent prayer.

God our Father,
may we love you in all things and above all things
and reach the joy you have prepared for us
beyond all our imagining.

We ask this through our Lord Jesus Christ, your Son,
who lives and reigns with you and the Holy Spirit,
one God, for ever and ever.

PRAYER AFTER COMMUNION

Let us pray.

Pause for silent prayer, if this has not preceded.

God of mercy,
by this sacrament you make us one with Christ.
By becoming more like him on earth,
may we come to share his glory in heaven,
where he lives and reigns for ever and ever.

VIGESIMOPRIMER DOMINGO ORDINARIO

ORACIÓN DEL DÍA

Oremos.

Todos oran en silencio durante unos momentos.

**Dios nuestro,
tú que puedes darnos un mismo querer
y un mismo sentir,
concédenos a todos amar lo que nos mandas
y anhelar lo que nos prometes
para que, en medio de las preocupaciones de esta vida,
pueda encontrar nuestro corazón la felicidad verdadera.**

**Por nuestro Señor Jesucristo, tu Hijo,
que vive y reina contigo
en la unidad del Espíritu Santo y es Dios
por los siglos de los siglos.**

ORACIÓN DESPUÉS DE LA COMUNIÓN

Oremos.

Todos oran en silencio durante unos momentos, a no ser que este silencio ya se haya hecho antes.

**Completa, Señor, en nosotros
la obra redentora de tu amor
y danos la fortaleza y generosidad necesarias
para que podamos cumplir en todo tu santa voluntad.**

Por Jesucristo, nuestro Señor.

TWENTY-FIRST SUNDAY IN ORDINARY TIME

Let us pray
[that God will make us one in mind and heart]

Pause for silent prayer.

Father,
help us to seek the values
that will bring us lasting joy in this changing world.
In our desire for what you promise
make us one in mind and heart.

Grant this through our Lord Jesus Christ, your Son,
who lives and reigns with you and the Holy Spirit,
one God, for ever and ever.

PRAYER AFTER COMMUNION

Let us pray.

Pause for silent prayer, if this has not preceded.

Lord,
may this eucharist increase within us
the healing power of your love.
May it guide and direct our efforts
to please you in all things.

We ask this in the name of Jesus the Lord.

VIGESIMOSEGUNDO DOMINGO ORDINARIO

Oremos.

Todos oran en silencio durante unos momentos.

**Dios misericordioso,
de quien procede todo lo bueno,
inflámanos con tu amor y acércanos más a ti
a fin de que podamos crecer en tu gracia
y perseveremos en ella.**

**Por nuestro Señor Jesucristo, tu Hijo,
que vive y reina contigo
en la unidad del Espíritu Santo y es Dios
por los siglos de los siglos.**

ORACIÓN DESPUÉS DE LA COMUNIÓN

Oremos.

Todos oran en silencio durante unos momentos, a no ser que este silencio ya se haya hecho antes.

**Te rogamos, Señor, que este sacramento
con que nos has alimentado,
nos haga crecer en tu amor
y nos impulse a servirte en nuestros prójimos.**

Por Jesucristo, nuestro Señor.

TWENTY-SECOND SUNDAY IN ORDINARY TIME

Let us pray
[that God will increase our faith and bring to perfection the
gifts he has given us]

Pause for silent prayer.

Almighty God,
every good thing comes from you.
Fill our hearts with love for you,
increase our faith,
and by your constant care
protect the good you have given us.

We ask this through our Lord Jesus Christ, your Son,
who lives and reigns with you and the Holy Spirit,
one God, for ever and ever.

PRAYER AFTER COMMUNION

Let us pray.

Pause for silent prayer, if this has not preceded.

Lord,
you renew us at your table with the bread of life.
May this food strengthen us in love
and help us to serve you in each other.

We ask this in the name of Jesus the Lord.

VIGESIMOTERCER DOMINGO ORDINARIO

Oremos.

Todos oran en silencio durante unos momentos.

Señor, que te has dignado redimirnos
y hacernos hijos tuyos,
míranos siempre con amor de Padre
y haz que cuantos creemos en Cristo,
obtengamos la verdadera libertad y la herencia eterna.

Por nuestro Señor Jesucristo, tu Hijo,
que vive y reina contigo
en la unidad del Espíritu Santo y es Dios
por los siglos de los siglos.

ORACIÓN DESPUÉS DE LA COMUNIÓN

Oremos.

Todos oran en silencio durante unos momentos, a no ser que este silencio ya
se haya hecho antes.

Tú que nos has instruido con tu palabra
y alimentado con tu Eucaristía,
concédenos, Señor, aprovechar estos dones
para que vivamos aquí unidos a tu Hijo
y podamos, después, participar de su vida inmortal.

Por Jesucristo, nuestro Señor.

TWENTY-THIRD SUNDAY IN ORDINARY TIME

Let us pray
[that we may realize the freedom God has given us in mak-
ing us his sons and daughters]

Pause for silent prayer.

God our Father,
you redeem us
and make us your children in Christ.
Look upon us,
give us true freedom
and bring us to the inheritance you promised.

Grant this through our Lord Jesus Christ, your Son,
who lives and reigns with you and the Holy Spirit,
one God, for ever and ever.

PRAYER AFTER COMMUNION

Let us pray.

Pause for silent prayer, if this has not preceded.

Lord,
your word and your sacrament
give us food and life.
May this gift of your Son
lead us to share his life for ever.

We ask this through Christ our Lord.

VIGESIMOCUARTO DOMINGO ORDINARIO

ORACIÓN DEL DÍA

Oremos.

Todos oran en silencio durante unos momentos.

**Míranos, Señor, con ojos de misericordia
y haz que experimentemos vivamente tu amor
para que podamos servirte
con todas nuestras fuerzas.**

**Por nuestro Señor Jesucristo, tu Hijo,
que vive y reina contigo
en la unidad del Espíritu Santo y es Dios
por los siglos de los siglos.**

ORACIÓN DESPUÉS DE LA COMUNIÓN

Oremos.

Todos oran en silencio durante unos momentos, a no ser que este silencio ya
se haya hecho antes.

**Que la gracia de esta comunión
nos transforme, Señor, tan plenamente,
que no sea ya nuestro egoísmo, sino tu amor,
el que impulse, de ahora en adelante, nuestra vida.**

Por Jesucristo, nuestro Señor.

TWENTY-FOURTH SUNDAY IN ORDINARY TIME

PRAYER OF THE DAY

Let us pray
[that God will keep us faithful in his service]

Pause for silent prayer.

Almighty God,
our creator and guide,
may we serve you with all our heart
and know your forgiveness in our lives.

We ask this through our Lord Jesus Christ, your Son,
who lives and reigns with you and the Holy Spirit,
one God, for ever and ever.

PRAYER AFTER COMMUNION

Let us pray.

Pause for silent prayer, if this has not preceded.

Lord,
may the eucharist you have given us
influence our thoughts and actions.
May your Spirit guide and direct us in your way.

We ask this in the name of Jesus the Lord.

VIGESIMOQUINTO DOMINGO ORDINARIO

ORACIÓN DEL DÍA

Oremos.

Todos oran en silencio durante unos momentos.

**Dios nuestro, que en el amor a ti y a nuestro prójimo
has querido resumir toda tu ley,
concédenos descubrirte y amarte en nuestros hermanos
para que podamos alcanzar la vida eterna.**

**Por nuestro Señor Jesucristo, tu Hijo,
que vive y reina contigo
en la unidad del Espíritu Santo y es Dios
por los siglos de los siglos.**

ORACIÓN DESPUÉS DE LA COMUNIÓN

Oremos.

Todos oran en silencio durante unos momentos, a no ser que este silencio ya
se haya hecho antes.

**Concede siempre tu ayuda, Señor,
a quienes has alimentado con la Eucaristía,
a fin de que la gracia recibida en este sacramento,
transforme continuamente nuestra vida.**

Por Jesucristo, nuestro Señor.

TWENTY-FIFTH SUNDAY IN ORDINARY TIME

PRAYER OF THE DAY

Let us pray
[that we will grow in the love of God and of one another]

Pause for silent prayer.

Father,
guide us, as you guide creation
according to your law of love.
May we love one another
and come to perfection
in the eternal life prepared for us.

Grant this through our Lord Jesus Christ, your Son,
who lives and reigns with you and the Holy Spirit,
one God, for ever and ever.

PRAYER AFTER COMMUNION

Let us pray.

Pause for silent prayer, if this has not preceded.

Lord,
help us with your kindness.
Make us strong through the eucharist.
May we put into action
the saving mystery we celebrate.

We ask this in the name of Jesus the Lord.

VIGESIMOSEXTO DOMINGO ORDINARIO

Oración del Día

Oremos.

Todos oran en silencio durante unos momentos.

**Dios nuestro, que con tu perdón y tu misericordia,
nos das la prueba más delicada de tu omnipotencia,
apiádate de nosotros, pecadores,
para que no desfallezcamos en la lucha
por obtener el cielo que nos has prometido.**

**Por nuestro Señor Jesucristo, tu Hijo,
que vive y reina contigo
en la unidad del Espíritu Santo y es Dios
por los siglos de los siglos.**

Oración después de la Comunión

Oremos.

Todos oran en silencio durante unos momentos, a no ser que este silencio ya
se haya hecho antes.

**Que esta Eucaristía
renueve, Señor, nuestro cuerpo y nuestro espíritu
a fin de que podamos participar
de la herencia gloriosa de tu Hijo,
cuya muerte hemos anunciado y compartido.**

Por Jesucristo, nuestro Señor.

TWENTY-SIXTH SUNDAY IN ORDINARY TIME

PRAYER OF THE DAY

Let us pray
[for God's forgiveness and for the happiness it brings]

Pause for silent prayer.

Father,
you show your almighty power
in your mercy and forgiveness.
Continue to fill us with your gifts of love.
Help us to hurry toward the eternal life you promise
and come to share in the joys of your kingdom.

Grant this through our Lord Jesus Christ, your Son,
who lives and reigns with you and the Holy Spirit,
one God, for ever and ever.

PRAYER AFTER COMMUNION

Let us pray.

Pause for silent prayer, if this has not preceded.

Lord,
may this eucharist
in which we proclaim the death of Christ
bring us salvation
and make us one with him in glory,
for he is Lord for ever and ever.

VIGESIMOSEPTIMO DOMINGO ORDINARIO

Oración del Día

Oremos.

Todos oran en silencio durante unos momentos.

**Padre lleno de amor, que nos concedes siempre
más de lo que merecemos y deseamos,
perdona misericordiosamente nuestras ofensas
y otórganos aquellas gracias
que no hemos sabido pedirte y tú sabes que necesitamos.**

**Por nuestro Señor Jesucristo, tu Hijo,
que vive y reina contigo
en la unidad del Espíritu Santo y es Dios
por los siglos de los siglos.**

Oración después de la Comunión

Oremos.

Todos oran en silencio durante unos momentos, a no ser que este silencio ya
se haya hecho antes.

**Que esta comunión, Señor,
sacie nuestra hambre y nuestra sed de ti
y nos transforme en tu Hijo, Jesucristo,
que vive y reina por los siglos de los siglos.**

TWENTY-SEVENTH SUNDAY IN ORDINARY TIME

PRAYER OF THE DAY

Let us pray
[that God will forgive our failings and bring us peace]

Pause for silent prayer.

Father,
your love for us
surpasses all our hopes and desires.
Forgive our failings,
keep us in your peace
and lead us in the way of salvation.

We ask this through our Lord Jesus Christ, your Son,
who lives and reigns with you and the Holy Spirit,
one God, for ever and ever.

PRAYER AFTER COMMUNION

Let us pray.

Pause for silent prayer, if this has not preceded.

Almighty God,
let the eucharist we share
fill us with your life.
May the love of Christ
which we celebrate here
touch our lives and lead us to you.

We ask this in the name of Jesus the Lord.

VIGESIMOCTAVO DOMINGO ORDINARIO

ORACIÓN DEL DÍA

Oremos.

Todos oran en silencio durante unos momentos.

**Te pedimos, Señor,
que tu gracia nos inspire y acompañe siempre
para que podamos descubrirte en todos
y amarte y servirte en cada uno.**

**Por nuestro Señor Jesucristo, tu Hijo,
que vive y reina contigo
en la unidad del Espíritu Santo y es Dios
por los siglos de los siglos.**

ORACIÓN DESPUÉS DE LA COMUNIÓN

Oremos.

Todos oran en silencio durante unos momentos, a no ser que este silencio ya se haya hecho antes.

**Te pedimos, Señor, humildemente,
que el Cuerpo y la Sangre de tu Hijo
que hemos recibido en alimento,
nos comuniquen su misma vida.**

Por Jesucristo, nuestro Señor.

TWENTY-EIGHTH SUNDAY IN ORDINARY TIME

PRAYER OF THE DAY

Let us pray
[that God will help us to love one another]

Pause for silent prayer.

Lord,
our help and guide,
make your love the foundation of our lives.
May our love for you express itself
in our eagerness to do good for others.

Grant this through our Lord Jesus Christ, your Son,
who lives and reigns with you and the Holy Spirit,
one God, for ever and ever.

PRAYER AFTER COMMUNION

Let us pray.

Pause for silent prayer, if this has not preceded.

Almighty Father,
may the body and blood of your Son
give us a share in his life,
for he is Lord for ever and ever.

VIGESIMONOVENO DOMINGO ORDINARIO

ORACIÓN DEL DÍA

Oremos.

Todos oran en silencio durante unos momentos.

**Dios todopoderoso y eterno,
haz que nuestra voluntad sea siempre dócil a la tuya
y que te sirvamos con un corazón sincero.**

**Por nuestro Señor Jesucristo, tu Hijo,
que vive y reina contigo
en la unidad del Espíritu Santo y es Dios
por los siglos de los siglos.**

ORACIÓN DESPUÉS DE LA COMUNIÓN

Oremos.

Todos oran en silencio durante unos momentos, a no ser que este silencio ya
se haya hecho antes.

**Que esta celebración eucarística
nos comunique, Señor, nuevas fuerzas
para cumplir tu voluntad en esta vida
y nos confirme en la esperanza de tu Reino.**

Por Jesucristo, nuestro Señor.

TWENTY-NINTH SUNDAY IN ORDINARY TIME

Let us pray
[for the gift of simplicity and joy in our service of God and man]

Pause for silent prayer.

Almighty and ever-living God,
our source of power and inspiration,
give us strength and joy
in serving you as followers of Christ,
who lives and reigns with you and the Holy Spirit,
one God, for ever and ever.

PRAYER AFTER COMMUNION

Let us pray.

Pause for silent prayer, if this has not preceded.

Lord,
may this eucharist help us to remain faithful.
May it teach us the way to eternal life.

Grant this through Christ our Lord.

TRIGESIMO DOMINGO ORDINARIO

Oración del Día

Oremos.

Todos oran en silencio durante unos momentos.

**Aumenta, Señor, en nosotros
la fe, la esperanza y la caridad
para que cumplamos con amor tus mandamientos
y podamos conseguir, así,
el cielo que nos tienes prometido.**

**Por nuestro Señor Jesucristo, tu Hijo,
que vive y reina contigo
en la unidad del Espíritu Santo y es Dios
por los siglos de los siglos.**

Oración después de la Comunión

Oremos.

Todos oran en silencio durante unos momentos, a no ser que este silencio ya se haya hecho antes.

**Concédenos, Señor, que este memorial
de la muerte y resurrección de tu Hijo
nos haga morir de veras al pecado
y renacer a una nueva vida.**

Por Jesucristo, nuestro Señor.

THIRTIETH SUNDAY IN ORDINARY TIME

Let us pray
[for the strength to do God's will]

Pause for silent prayer.

Almighty and ever-living God,
strengthen our faith, hope, and love.
May we do with loving hearts
what you ask of us
and come to share the life you promise.

We ask this through our Lord Jesus Christ, your Son,
who lives and reigns with you and the Holy Spirit,
one God, for ever and ever.

PRAYER AFTER COMMUNION

Let us pray.

Pause for silent prayer, if this has not preceded.

Lord,
bring to perfection within us
the communion we share in this sacrament.
May our celebration have an effect in our lives.

We ask this in the name of Jesus the Lord.

TRIGESIMOPRIMER DOMINGO ORDINARIO

ORACIÓN DEL DÍA

Oremos.

Todos oran en silencio durante unos momentos.

**Dios omnipotente y misericordioso,
de cuya mano proviene
el don de servirte y de alabarte,
ayúdanos a vencer en esta vida
cuanto pueda separarnos de ti.**

**Por nuestro Señor Jesucristo, tu Hijo,
que vive y reina contigo
en la unidad del Espíritu Santo y es Dios
por los siglos de los siglos.**

ORACIÓN DESPUÉS DE LA COMUNIÓN

Oremos.

Todos oran en silencio durante unos momentos, a no ser que este silencio ya se haya hecho antes.

**Continúa, Señor, en nosotros
tu obra de salvación
por medio de esta Eucaristía
para que, cada vez más unidos a Cristo en esta vida,
merezcamos vivir con él eternamente.**

Por Jesucristo, nuestro Señor.

THIRTY-FIRST SUNDAY IN ORDINARY TIME

Let us pray
[that our lives will reflect our faith]

Pause for silent prayer.

God of power and mercy,
only with your help
can we offer you fitting service and praise.
May we live the faith we profess
and trust your promise of eternal life.

Grant this through our Lord Jesus Christ, your Son,
who lives and reigns with you and the Holy Spirit,
one God, for ever and ever.

PRAYER AFTER COMMUNION

Let us pray.

Pause for silent prayer, if this has not preceded.

Lord,
you give us new hope in this eucharist.
May the power of your love
continue its saving work among us
and bring us to the joy you promise.

We ask this in the name of Jesus the Lord.

TRIGESIMOSEGUNDO DOMINGO ORDINARIO

ORACIÓN DEL DÍA

Oremos.

Todos oran en silencio durante unos momentos.

**Ayúdanos, Señor,
a dejar en tus manos paternales
todas nuestras preocupaciones,
a fin de que podamos entregarnos
con mayor libertad a tu servicio.**

**Por nuestro Señor Jesucristo, tu Hijo,
que vive y reina contigo
en la unidad del Espíritu Santo y es Dios
por los siglos de los siglos.**

ORACIÓN DESPUÉS DE LA COMUNIÓN

Oremos.

Todos oran en silencio durante unos momentos, a no ser que este silencio ya
se haya hecho antes.

**Te damos gracias, Señor,
por habernos alimentado
con el Cuerpo y la Sangre de tu Hijo
y te rogamos que la fuerza del Espíritu Santo,
que nos has comunicado en este sacramento,
permanezca en nosotros y transforme toda nuestra vida.**

Por Jesucristo, nuestro Señor.

THIRTY-SECOND SUNDAY IN ORDINARY TIME

PRAYER OF THE DAY

**Let us pray
[for health of mind and body]**

Pause for silent prayer.

**God of power and mercy,
protect us from all harm.
Give us freedom of spirit
and health in mind and body
to do your work on earth.**

**We ask this through our Lord Jesus Christ, your Son,
who lives and reigns with you and the Holy Spirit,
one God, for ever and ever.**

PRAYER AFTER COMMUNION

Let us pray.

Pause for silent prayer, if this has not preceded.

**Lord,
we thank you for the nourishment you give us
through your holy gift.
Pour out your Spirit upon us
and in the strength of this food from heaven
keep us single-minded in your service.**

We ask this in the name of Jesus the Lord.

TRIGESIMOTERCER DOMINGO ORDINARIO

Oración del Día

Oremos.

Todos oran en silencio durante unos momentos.

**Concédenos, Señor, tu ayuda
para entregarnos fielmente a tu servicio
porque sólo en el cumplimiento de tu voluntad
podremos encontrar la felicidad verdadera.**

**Por nuestro Señor Jesucristo, tu Hijo,
que vive y reina contigo
en la unidad del Espíritu Santo y es Dios
por los siglos de los siglos.**

Oración después de la Comunión

Oremos.

Todos oran en silencio durante unos momentos, a no ser que este silencio ya
se haya hecho antes.

**Señor, que nuestra participación en esta Eucaristía
que tu Hijo nos mandó celebrar como memorial suyo,
nos una siempre con el vínculo de tu amor.**

Por Jesucristo, nuestro Señor.

THIRTY-THIRD SUNDAY IN ORDINARY TIME

PRAYER OF THE DAY

Let us pray
[that God will help us to be faithful]

Pause for silent prayer.

Father of all that is good,
keep us faithful in serving you,
for to serve you is our lasting joy.

We ask this through our Lord Jesus Christ, your Son,
who lives and reigns with you and the Holy Spirit,
one God, for ever and ever.

PRAYER AFTER COMMUNION

Let us pray.

Pause for silent prayer, if this has not preceded.

Father,
may we grow in love
by the eucharist we have celebrated
in memory of the Lord Jesus,
who is Lord for ever and ever.

NUESTRO SEÑOR JESUCRISTO
REY DEL UNIVERSO
(Ultimo domingo del tiempo ordinario)

ORACIÓN DEL DÍA

Oremos.

Todos oran en silencio durante unos momentos.

**Dios todopoderoso y eterno,
que quisiste fundar todas las cosas
en tu Hijo muy amado, Rey del universo,
haz que toda creatura, liberada de la esclavitud,
sirva a tu majestad y te alabe eternamente.**

**Por nuestro Señor Jesucristo, tu Hijo,
que vive y reina contigo
en la unidad del Espíritu Santo y es Dios
por los siglos de los siglos.**

ORACIÓN DESPUÉS DE LA COMUNIÓN

Oremos.

Todos oran en silencio durante unos momentos, a no ser que este silencio ya
se haya hecho antes.

**Alimentados con el pan que da la vida eterna,
te pedimos, Señor,
que quienes nos gloriamos en obedecer aquí
los mandatos de Cristo,
Rey del universo,
podamos vivir con él eternamente en el cielo.**

Por Jesucristo, nuestro Señor.

CHRIST THE KING

(Last Sunday in Ordinary Time)

PRAYER OF THE DAY

Let us pray
[that all men will acclaim Jesus as Lord]

Pause for silent prayer.

Almighty and merciful God,
you break the power of evil
and make all things new
in your Son Jesus Christ, the King of the universe.
May all in heaven and earth acclaim your glory
and never cease to praise you.

We ask this through our Lord Jesus Christ, your Son,
who lives and reigns with you and the Holy Spirit,
one God, for ever and ever.

PRAYER AFTER COMMUNION

Let us pray.

Pause for silent prayer, if this has not preceded.

Lord,
you give us Christ, the King of all creation,
as food for everlasting life.
Help us to live by his gospel
and bring us to the joy of his kingdom,
where he lives and reigns for ever and ever.

LA PRESENTACION DEL SEÑOR

(2 de febrero)

ORACIÓN DEL DÍA

Oremos.

Todos oran en silencio durante unos momentos.

**Dios todopoderoso y eterno,
mira a tus fieles reunidos hoy
para celebrar la presentación en el templo
de tu Hijo Jesucristo,
y concédenos que podamos presentarnos ante ti
plenamente renovados en el espíritu.**

**Por nuestro Señor Jesucristo, tu Hijo,
que vive y reina contigo
en la unidad del Espíritu Santo y es Dios
por los siglos de los siglos.**

ORACIÓN DESPUÉS DE LA COMUNIÓN

Oremos.

Todos oran en silencio durante unos momentos, a no ser que este silencio ya
se haya hecho antes.

**Señor, tú que colmaste las esperanzas
del anciano Simeón
de no morir antes de ver al Mesías,
completa en nosotros la obra de tu gracia
por medio de esta comunión,
para que sepamos buscar siempre
a Cristo en esta vida
y podamos llegar a contemplarlo en la eternidad.**

Por Jesucristo, nuestro Señor.

PRESENTATION OF THE LORD
(February 2)

PRAYER OF THE DAY

Let us pray.

Pause for silent prayer.

**All-powerful Father,
Christ your Son became man for our sake
and was presented in the temple.
May he free our hearts from sin
and bring us into your presence.**

**We ask this through our Lord Jesus Christ, your Son,
who lives and reigns with you and the Holy Spirit,
one God, for ever and ever.**

PRAYER AFTER COMMUNION

Let us pray.

Pause for silent prayer, if this has not preceded.

**Lord,
you fulfilled the hope of Simeon,
who did not die
until he had been privileged to welcome the Messiah.
May this communion perfect your grace in us
and prepare us to meet Christ
when he comes to bring us into everlasting life,
for he is Lord for ever and ever.**

LA NATIVIDAD DE SAN JUAN BAUTISTA
(24 de junio)

ORACIÓN DEL DÍA

Oremos.

Todos oran en silencio durante unos momentos.

**Dios nuestro, que enviaste a san Juan Bautista
para prepararle a Cristo, el Señor,
un pueblo dispuesto a recibirlo,
alegra ahora a tu Iglesia
con la abundancia de los dones del Espíritu
y guíala por el camino de la salvación y de la paz.**

**Por nuestro Señor Jesucristo, tu Hijo,
que vive y reina contigo
en la unidad del Espíritu Santo y es Dios
por los siglos de los siglos.**

ORACIÓN DESPUÉS DE LA COMUNIÓN

Oremos.

Todos oran en silencio durante unos momentos, a no ser que este silencio ya se haya hecho antes.

**Señor, que la comunión que hemos recibido
al celebrar el nacimiento del precursor de tu Hijo,
renueve en nosotros el amor y la fidelidad a Jesucristo,
que vive y reina por los siglos de los siglos.**

BIRTH OF JOHN THE BAPTIST
(June 24)

Let us pray
[that God will give us joy and peace]

Pause for silent prayer.

God our Father,
you raised up John the Baptist
to prepare a perfect people for Christ the Lord.
Give your Church joy in spirit
and guide those who believe in you
into the way of salvation and peace.

We ask this through our Lord Jesus Christ, your Son,
who lives and reigns with you and the Holy Spirit,
one God, for ever and ever.

PRAYER AFTER COMMUNION

Let us pray.

Pause for silent prayer, if this has not preceded.

Lord,
you have renewed us with this eucharist,
as we celebrate the feast of John the Baptist,
who foretold the coming of the Lamb of God.
May we welcome your Son as our Savior,
for he gives us new life,
and is Lord for ever and ever.

SAN PEDRO Y SAN PABLO, APOSTOLES
(29 de junio)

ORACIÓN DEL DÍA

Oremos.

Todos oran en silencio durante unos momentos.

**Dios nuestro, que nos llenas de santa alegría
con la solemnidad de los santos Apóstoles Pedro y Pablo,
haz que tu Iglesia se mantenga siempre fiel
a las enseñanzas de estos Apóstoles,
de quienes recibió el primer anuncio de la fe.**

**Por nuestro Señor Jesucristo, tu Hijo,
que vive y reina contigo
en la unidad del Espíritu Santo y es Dios
por los siglos de los siglos.**

ORACIÓN DESPUÉS DE LA COMUNIÓN

Oremos.

Todos oran en silencio durante unos momentos, a no ser que este silencio ya
se haya hecho antes.

**Tú que nos has alimentado con esta Eucaristía,
haz, Señor, que la participación perseverante
en el memorial de la muerte y resurrección de tu Hijo,
y la fidelidad a la doctrina de los Apóstoles
nos conserven unidos en tu amor.**

Por Jesucristo, nuestro Señor.

PETER AND PAUL, APOSTLES
(June 29)

PRAYER OF THE DAY

Let us pray
[that we will remain true to the faith of the apostles]

Pause for silent prayer.

God our Father,
today you give us the joy
of celebrating the feast of the apostles Peter and Paul.
Through them your Church first received the faith.
Keep us true to their teaching.

Grant this through our Lord Jesus Christ, your Son,
who lives and reigns with you and the Holy Spirit,
one God, for ever and ever.

PRAYER AFTER COMMUNION

Let us pray.

Pause for silent prayer, if this has not preceded.

Lord,
renew the life of your Church
with the power of this sacrament.
May the breaking of bread
and the teaching of the apostles
keep us united in your love.

We ask this in the name of Jesus the Lord.

LA TRANSFIGURACION DEL SEÑOR

(6 de agosto)

ORACIÓN DEL DÍA

Oremos.

Todos oran en silencio durante unos momentos.

**Dios nuestro,
que en la Transfiguración gloriosa de tu Hijo unigénito
fortaleciste nuestra fe con el testimonio de Moisés y Elías
y nos dejaste entrever la gloria que nos espera, como hijos
tuyos,
concédenos seguir el Evangelio de Cristo
para compartir con él la herencia de tu Reino.**

**Por nuestro Señor Jesucristo, tu Hijo,
que vive y reina contigo
en la unidad del Espíritu Santo y es Dios
por los siglos de los siglos.**

ORACIÓN DESPUÉS DE LA COMUNIÓN

Oremos.

Todos oran en silencio durante unos momentos, a no ser que este silencio ya
se haya hecho antes.

**Que la comunión que hemos recibido
nos asemeje, Señor,
cada día más a tu Hijo,
cuya gloria quisiste manifestarnos
en su Transfiguración.**

Por Jesucristo, nuestro Señor.

TRANSFIGURATION OF THE LORD
(August 6)

Let us pray
[that we may hear the Lord Jesus and share his everlasting life]

Pause for silent prayer.

God our Father,
in the transfigured glory of Christ your Son,
you strengthen our faith
by confirming the witness of your prophets,
and show us the splendor
of your beloved sons and daughters.
As we listen to the voice of your Son,
help us to become heirs to eternal life with him
who lives and reigns with you and the Holy Spirit,
one God, for ever and ever.

PRAYER AFTER COMMUNION

Let us pray.

Pause for silent prayer, if this has not preceded.

Lord,
you revealed the true radiance of Christ
in the glory of his transfiguration.
May the food we receive from heaven
change us into his image.

We ask this in the name of Jesus the Lord.

LA ASUNCION DE LA SANTISIMA VIRGEN MARIA

(15 de agosto)

ORACIÓN DEL DÍA

Oremos.

Todos oran en silencio durante unos momentos.

**Dios todopoderoso y eterno,
que hiciste subir al cielo en cuerpo y alma
a la inmaculada Virgen María, Madre de tu Hijo,
concédenos vivir en este mundo
sin perder de vista los bienes del cielo
y con la esperanza de disfrutar eternamente de su gloria.**

**Por nuestro Señor Jesucristo, tu Hijo,
que vive y reina contigo
en la unidad del Espíritu Santo y es Dios
por los siglos de los siglos.**

ORACIÓN DESPUÉS DE LA COMUNIÓN

Oremos.

Todos oran en silencio durante unos momentos, a no ser que este silencio ya se haya hecho antes.

**Tú que nos has hecho partícipes
de este sacramento de vida eterna,
concédenos, Señor, por intercesión de la Virgen María,
en este día de su Asunción al cielo,
alcanzar la gloria de la resurrección.**

Por Jesucristo, nuestro Señor.

ASSUMPTION OF THE VIRGIN MARY
(August 15)

Let us pray
[that we will join Mary, the mother of the Lord, in the glory
of heaven]

Pause for silent prayer.

All-powerful and ever-living God,
you raised the sinless Virgin Mary,
mother of your Son,
body and soul to the glory of heaven.
May we see heaven as our final goal
and come to share her glory.

We ask this through our Lord Jesus Christ, your Son,
who lives and reigns with you and the Holy Spirit,
one God, for ever and ever.

PRAYER AFTER COMMUNION

Let us pray.

Pause for silent prayer, if this has not preceded.

Lord,
may we who receive this sacrament of salvation
be led to the glory of heaven
by the prayers of the Virgin Mary.

We ask this in the name of Jesus the Lord.

LA SANTA CRUZ

(14 de septiembre)

Oremos.

Todos oran en silencio durante unos momentos.

**Dios nuestro, que quisiste que tu Hijo
muriera en la Cruz para la salvación del género humano,
concédenos aceptar por su amor
la cruz del sufrimiento aquí en la tierra,
para poder gozar en el cielo los frutos de su redención.**

**Por nuestro Señor Jesucristo, tu Hijo,
que vive y reina contigo
en la unidad del Espíritu Santo y es Dios
por los siglos de los siglos.**

Oración después de la Comunión

Oremos.

Todos oran en silencio durante unos momentos, a no ser que este silencio ya
se haya hecho antes.

**Señor nuestro Jesucristo,
tú que nos has redimido por medio de tu Cruz
y nos has hecho partícipes de tu Cuerpo y de tu Sangre,
concédenos participar también de la gloria de tu resurrección.**

Tú que vives y reinas por los siglos de los siglos.

HOLY CROSS
(September 14)

PRAYER OF THE DAY

Let us pray
[that the death of Christ on the cross will bring us to the
    glory of the resurrection]

Pause for silent prayer.

God our Father,
in obedience to you
your only Son accepted death on the cross
for the salvation of mankind.
We acknowledge the mystery of the cross on earth.
May we receive the gift of redemption in heaven.

We ask this through our Lord Jesus Christ, your Son,
who lives and reigns with you and the Holy Spirit,
one God, for ever and ever.

PRAYER AFTER COMMUNION

Let us pray.

Pause for silent prayer, if this has not preceded.

Lord Jesus Christ,
you are the holy bread of life.
Bring to the glory of the resurrection
the people you have redeemed by the wood of the cross,
for you are Lord for ever and ever.

TODOS LOS SANTOS
(1 de noviembre)

Oración del Día

Oremos.

Todos oran en silencio durante unos momentos.

**Dios omnipotente y eterno,
que otorgas a tu Iglesia la alegría de celebrar,
en esta solemnidad,
los méritos y la gloria de todos los santos,
concede a tu pueblo,
por esta multitud de intercesores,
la abundancia de tu misericordia.**

**Por nuestro Señor Jesucristo, tu Hijo,
que vive y reina contigo
en la unidad del Espíritu Santo y es Dios
por los siglos de los siglos.**

Oración después de la Comunión

Oremos.

Todos oran en silencio durante unos momentos, a no ser que este silencio ya se haya hecho antes.

**Dios nuestro, fuente única de toda santidad
y admirable en todos tus santos,
haz que este sacramento
nos encienda en el fuego de tu amor
y nos prepare para la alegría de tu Reino.**

Por Jesucristo, nuestro Señor.

ALL SAINTS
(November 1)

Let us pray
[that the prayers of all the saints will bring us forgiveness
for our sins]

Pause for silent prayer.

Father, all-powerful and ever-living God,
today we rejoice in the holy men and women
of every time and place.
May their prayers bring us your forgiveness and love.

We ask this through our Lord Jesus Christ, your Son,
who lives and reigns with you and the Holy Spirit,
one God, for ever and ever.

PRAYER AFTER COMMUNION

Let us pray.

Pause for silent prayer, if this has not preceded.

Father, holy one,
we praise your glory reflected in the saints.
May we who share at this table
be filled with your love
and prepared for the joy of your kingdom,
where Jesus is Lord for ever and ever.

LA CONMEMORACION DE TODOS LOS FIELES DIFUNTOS

(2 de noviembre)

ORACIÓN DEL DÍA

Oremos.

Todos oran en silencio durante unos momentos.

Escucha, Señor, nuestras súplicas y haz que,
al proclamar nuestra fe
en la resurrección de tu Hijo,
se avive también nuestra esperanza
en que tus siervos resucitarán.

Por nuestro Señor Jesucristo, tu Hijo,
que vive y reina contigo
en la unidad del Espíritu Santo y es Dios
por los siglos de los siglos.

ORACIÓN DESPUÉS DE LA COMUNIÓN

Oremos.

Todos oran en silencio durante unos momentos, a no ser que este silencio ya se haya hecho antes.

Por este memorial de la muerte y resurrección USA
de Cristo que hemos celebrado,
concede, Señor, a tus siervos difuntos
llegar a la mansión de la luz y de la paz.

Por Jesucristo, nuestro Señor.

COMMEMORATION OF ALL THE FAITHFUL DEPARTED
(ALL SOULS)

(November 2)

PRAYER OF THE DAY

Let us pray
[for all our departed brothers and sisters]

Pause for silent prayer.

Merciful Father,
hear our prayers and console us.
As we renew our faith in your Son,
whom you raised from the dead,
strengthen our hope that all our departed
brothers and sisters
will share in his resurrection,
who lives and reigns with you and the Holy Spirit,
one God, for ever and ever.

PRAYER AFTER COMMUNION

Let us pray.

Pause for silent prayer, if this has not preceded.

Lord God,
may the death and resurrection of Christ
which we celebrate in this eucharist
bring the departed faithful to the peace of your
eternal home.

We ask this in the name of Jesus the Lord.

LA DEDICACION DE LA BASILICA DE LETRAN
(9 de noviembre)

Oremos.

Todos oran en silencio durante unos momentos.

**Señor, tú que edificas
con piedras vivas y escogidas
el templo eterno de tu gloria,
derrama sobre tu Iglesia
los dones del Espíritu Santo,
para que tu pueblo fiel
llegue un día a transformarse en la Jerusalén celestial.**

**Por nuestro Señor Jesucristo, tu Hijo,
que vive y reina contigo
en la unidad del Espíritu Santo y es Dios
por los siglos de los siglos.**

ORACIÓN DESPUÉS DE LA COMUNIÓN

Oremos.

Todos oran en silencio durante unos momentos, a no ser que este silencio ya
se haya hecho antes.

**Señor y Dios nuestro, que has querido darnos en tu Iglesia
un signo temporal de la Jerusalén celeste,
concédenos, por esta comunión,
ser transformados aquí en templos de tu gracia
y entrar un día en el Reino de tu gloria.**

Por Jesucristo, nuestro Señor.

DEDICATION OF THE LATERAN BASILICA
(November 9)

Let us pray

Pause for silent prayer.

**God our Father,
from living stones, your chosen people,
you built an eternal temple to your glory.
Increase the spiritual gifts you have given to your Church,
so that your faithful people may continue to grow
into the new and eternal Jerusalem.**

**We ask this through our Lord Jesus Christ, your Son,
who lives and reigns with you and the Holy Spirit,
one God, for ever and ever.**

PRAYER AFTER COMMUNION

Let us pray.

Pause for silent prayer, if this has not preceded.

**Father,
you make your Church on earth
a sign of the new and eternal Jerusalem.
By sharing in this sacrament
may we become the temple of your presence
and the home of your glory.**

Grant this in the name of Jesus the Lord.

LA INMACULADA CONCEPCION DE LA VIRGEN MARIA
(8 de diciembre)

ORACIÓN DEL DÍA

Oremos.

Todos oran en silencio durante unos momentos.

**Dios todopoderoso,
que por la inmaculada concepción de la Virgen María
preparaste una morada digna para tu Hijo
y, en atención a los méritos de la muerte redentora de Cristo,
la preservaste de toda mancha de pecado,
concédenos, por su maternal intercesión,
vivir en tu presencia sin pecado.**

**Por nuestro Señor Jesucristo, tu Hijo,
que vive y reina contigo
en la unidad del Espíritu Santo y es Dios
por los siglos de los siglos.**

ORACIÓN DESPUÉS DE LA COMUNIÓN

Oremos.

Todos oran en silencio durante unos momentos, a no ser que este silencio ya
se haya hecho antes.

**Que el Cuerpo y la Sangre de tu Hijo
que hemos recibido,
nos ayuden, Señor, a superar la debilidad
que nos dejó el pecado original,
del cual, por singular privilegio,
preservaste a la santísima Virgen María
en su inmaculada concepción.**

Por Jesucristo, nuestro Señor.

IMMACULATE CONCEPTION OF THE VIRGIN MARY
(December 8)

Let us pray
[that through the prayers of the sinless Virgin Mary, God
will free us from our sins]

Pause for silent prayer.

Father,
you prepared the Virgin Mary
to be the worthy mother of your Son.
You let her share beforehand
in the salvation Christ would bring by his death,
and kept her sinless from the first moment of her conception.
Help us by her prayers
to live in your presence without sin.

We ask this through our Lord Jesus Christ, your Son,
who lives and reigns with you and the Holy Spirit,
one God, for ever and ever.

PRAYER AFTER COMMUNION

Let us pray.

Pause for silent prayer, if this has not preceded.

Lord our God,
in your love, you chose the Virgin Mary
and kept her free from sin.
May this sacrament of your love
free us from our sins.

Grant this through Christ our Lord.

APENDICE IV

ORACIONES ADICIONALES
DESPUES DE LA COMUNION

APPENDIX IV

ADDITIONAL PRAYERS AFTER COMMUNION

ORACIONES ADICIONALES DESPUES DE LA COMUNION

162   Cuando una celebración de la Oración de la Mañana o de la Tarde o una Liturgia de la Palabra concluye con la sagrada comunión, se puede usar una de las siguientes Oraciones después de la Comunión o la Oración después de la Comunión asignada para el día en el Apéndice III (véase los núms. 79, 114, 151 anteriores).

Oremos.

A **Señor nuestro Jesucristo, que en este sacramento admirable**
nos dejaste el memorial de tu pasión,
concédenos venerar de tal modo
los sagrados misterios de tu Cuerpo y de tu Sangre,
que experimentemos constantemente en nosotros
el fruto de tu redención.

Tú, que vives y reinas por los siglos de los siglos.

Todos responden:

Amén.

B **Señor, que por el misterio pascual de tu Hijo**
realizaste la redención de los hombres,
concédenos avanzar por el camino de la salvación
a quienes, celebrando los sacramentos,
proclamamos con fe
la muerte y resurrección de Cristo.

Que vive y reina por los siglos de los siglos.

C **Derrama, Señor, sobre nosotros**
tu Espíritu de caridad
para que, alimentados por el mismo pan del cielo,
permanezcamos unidos en el mismo amor.

Por Jesucristo, nuestro Señor.

ADDITIONAL PRAYERS AFTER COMMUNION

162　When holy communion concludes a celebration of Morning or Evening Prayer or a Liturgy of the Word, one of the following Prayers after Communion or the Prayer after Communion assigned for the day in Appendix III may be used (see above, nos. 79, 114, 151).

Let us pray.

A　**Lord Jesus Christ,**
　you gave us the eucharist
　as the memorial of your suffering and death.
　May our worship of this sacrament of your body and blood
　help us to experience the salvation you won for us
　and the peace of the kingdom
　where you live with the Father and the Holy Spirit,
　one God, for ever and ever.

　　　All respond:

Amen.

B　**Father,**
　you have brought to fulfillment the work of our redemption
　through the Easter mystery of Christ your Son.
　May we who faithfully proclaim his death and resurrection
　in these sacramental signs
　experience the constant growth of your salvation
　in our lives.

　We ask this through Christ our Lord.

C　**Lord,**
　you have nourished us with one bread from heaven.
　Fill us with your Spirit,
　and make us one in peace and love.

　We ask this through Christ our Lord.

D   Te rogamos, Señor,
     que nos santifique nuestra participación en esta celeración
     para que, en el Cuerpo y en la Sangre de Cristo,
     se estreche cada vez más
     la fraternidad universal de todos los hombres.

     Por Jesucristo, nuestro Señor.

E   Alimentados por este pan del cielo,
     te pedimos, Señor,
     por la comunión de tu Sacramento,
     nos des sabiduría para sopesar los bienes de la tierra
     amando intensamente los del cielo.

     Por Jesucristo, nuestro Señor.

F   Te damos gracias, Señor,
     porque al darnos en este Sacramento
     el Cuerpo glorioso de tu Hijo
     nos haces partícipes, ya en este mundo,
     de los bienes eternos de tu reino.

     Por Jesucristo, nuestro Señor.

G   Te suplicamos, Dios todopoderoso,
     que concedas a quienes alimentas
     con tus Sacramentos
     la gracia de poder servirte
     llevando una vida según tu voluntad.

     Por Jesucristo, nuestro Señor.

H   Oh Dios,
     que has querido hacernos partícipes
     de un mismo pan y de un mismo cáliz;
     concédenos vivir tan unidos en Cristo
     que fructifiquemos con gozo
     para la salvación de los hombres.

     Por Jesucristo, nuestro Señor.

D   Lord,
    may our sharing at this holy table make us holy.
    By the body and blood of Christ
    join all your people in brotherly love.

    We ask this through Christ our Lord.

E   Father,
    you give us food from heaven.
    By our sharing in this mystery
    teach us to judge wisely the things of earth
    and to love the things of heaven.

    Grant this through Christ our Lord.

F   Lord,
    we give thanks for these holy mysteries
    which bring to us here on earth
    a share in the life to come,
    through Christ our Lord.

G   All-powerful God,
    you renew us with your sacraments.
    Help us to thank you by lives of faithful service.

    We ask this through Christ our Lord.

H   God our Father,
    you give us a share in the one bread and the one cup
    and make us one in Christ.
    Help us to bring your salvation and joy to all the world.

    We ask this through Christ our Lord.

I   Saciados con el pan del cielo,
    te pedimos, Señor,
    que el amor con que nos alimentas
    fortalezca nuestros corazones
    y nos mueva a servirte en nuestros hermanos.

    Por Jesucristo, nuestro Señor.

J   Alimentados por este pan del cielo,
    te hacemos presente, Señor, nuestra acción de gracias,
    implorando de tu misericordia
    que el Espíritu Santo mantenga siempre vivo
    el amor a la verdad
    en quienes han recibido la fuerza de lo alto.

    Por Jesucristo, nuestro Señor.

K   Después de comer el mismo pan
    te rogamos, Señor, humildemente
    que nos mantengas en tu amor
    y siempre caminemos
    como hombres nuevos en una vida nueva.

    Por Jesucristo, nuestro Señor.

    Durante el tiempo Pascual son especialmente apropiadas las siguientes oraciones:

L   Derrama, Señor, sobre nosotros
    tu Espíritu de caridad,
    para que vivamos siempre unidos en tu amor
    los que hemos participado
    en el mismo Sacramento pascual.

    Por Jesucristo, nuestro Señor.

I   Lord,
you renew us at table with the bread of life.
May this food strengthen us in love
and help us to serve you in each other.

We ask this in the name of Jesus the Lord.

J   Lord,
we thank you for the nourishment you give us
through your holy gift.
Pour out your Spirit upon us
and in the strength of this food from heaven
keep us single-minded in your service.

We ask this in the name of Jesus the Lord.

K   Lord,
we are renewed by the breaking of one bread.
Keep us in your love
and help us to live the new life Christ won for us.

Grant this in the name of Jesus the Lord.

During the Easter season the following prayers are especially appropriate:

L   Lord,
you have nourished us with your Easter sacraments.
Fill us with your Spirit
and make us one in peace and love.

We ask this through Christ our Lord.

M   Te pedimos, Señor,
    que la participación en los Sacramentos de tu Hijo
    nos libre de nuestros antiguos pecados
    y nos transforme en hombres nuevos.

    Por Jesucristo, nuestro Señor.

N   Dios todopoderoso y eterno,
    que en la resurrección de Jesucristo
    nos has hecho renacer a la vida eterna;
    haz que los sacramentos pascuales
    den en nosotros fruto abundante,
    y que el alimento de salvación que acabamos de recibir
    fortalezca nuestras vidas.

    Por Jesucristo, nuestro Señor.

M   Lord,
may this sharing in the sacrament of your Son
free us from our old life of sin
and make us your new creation.

We ask this in the name of Jesus the Lord.

N   Almighty and ever-living Lord,
you restored us to life
by raising Christ from death.
Strengthen us by this Easter sacrament;
may we feel its saving power in our daily life.

We ask this through Christ our Lord.

APENDICE V
BENDICIONES

APPENDIX V
BLESSINGS

BENDICIONES

163   Para concluir la celebración, un líder que es diácono puede usar una de las bendiciones solemnes u oraciones sobre el pueblo de Dios que se encuentran en el Sacramentario, o una de las bendiciones siguientes.

Después del saludo **El Señor esté con ustedes** el diácono dice **Inclinen la cabeza e imploren la bendición de Dios.** Luego extiende las manos sobre la asamblea y da la bendición.

A   Diácono:

Que el Señor los bendiga y los guarde.

℞. Amén.

Diácono:

Que haga resplandecer su rostro sobre ustedes
y les muestre su misericordia.

℞. Amén.

Diácono:

Que vuelva su mirada hacia ustedes
y les conceda su paz.

℞. Amén.

Diácono:

La bendición de Dios todopoderoso,
Padre, Hijo, ✠ y Espíritu Santo,
descienda sobre ustedes.

℞. Amén.

B   **Que la paz de Dios,**
que sobrepasa todo anhelo y esfuerzo humano,
custodie su corazón y su inteligencia
en el amor y conocimiento de Dios
y de su Hijo Jesucristo, nuestro Señor.

℞. Amén.

BLESSINGS

Blessings for Use by Deacons

163 A leader who is a deacon may use one of the solemn blessings or prayers over the people given in the Sacramentary, or one of the following blessings, to conclude the celebration.

After the greeting, **The Lord be with you,** the deacon says: **Bow your heads and pray for God's blessing.** He then extends his hands over the people and gives the blessing.

A   Deacon:

May the Lord bless you and keep you.

℞. Amen.

Deacon:

**May his face shine upon you
and be gracious to you.**

℞. Amen.

Deacon:

**May he look upon you with kindness,
and give you his peace.**

℞. Amen.

Deacon:

**May almighty God bless you,
the Father, and the Son, ✝ and the Holy Spirit.**

℞. Amen.

B   **May the peace of God
which is beyond all understanding
keep your hearts and minds
in the knowledge and love of God
and of his Son, our Lord Jesus Christ.**

℞. Amen.

La bendición de Dios todopoderoso,
Padre, Hijo, ✝ y Espíritu Santo,
descienda sobre ustedes.

℞. Amén.

C   Que Dios todopoderoso
los bendiga con su misericordia
y les conceda la sabiduría que salva.

℞. Amén.

Que aumente en ustedes la fe
y los haga perseverar en las buenas obras.

℞. Amén.

Que enderece hacia sí sus pasos
y les muestre el camino del amor y de la paz.

℞. Amén.

La bendición de Dios todopoderoso,
Padre, Hijo, ✝ y Espíritu Santo,
descienda sobre ustedes.

℞. Amén.

D   Que el Dios de todo consuelo
disponga en su paz sus días
y los llene de sus bendiciones.

℞. Amén.

Que los libre de toda perturbación
y afiance en su amor sus corazones.

℞. Amén.

Que llenos de fe, de esperanza y de caridad,
pasen ustedes por la vida haciendo el bien
y puedan alcanzar la felicidad eterna.

℞. Amén.

May almighty God bless you,
the Father, and the Son, ✝ and the Holy Spirit.

℟. Amen.

C   May almighty God bless you in his mercy,
and make you always aware of his saving wisdom.

℟. Amen.

May he strengthen your faith with proofs of his love,
so that you will persevere in good works.

℟. Amen.

May he direct your steps to himself,
and show you how to walk in charity and peace.

℟. Amen.

May almighty God bless you,
the Father, and the Son, ✝ and the Holy Spirit.

℟. Amen.

D   May the God of all consolation
bless you in every way
and grant you peace all the days of your life.

℟. Amen.

May he free you from all anxiety
and strengthen your hearts in his love.

℟. Amen.

May he enrich you with his gifts of faith, hope, and love,
so that what you do in this life
will bring you to the happiness of everlasting life.

℟. Amen.

**La bendición de Dios todopoderoso,
Padre, Hijo, ☩ y Espíritu Santo,
descienda sobre ustedes.**

℟. Amén.

E **Que Dios omnipotente
aleje de ustedes toda adversidad
y les conceda la abundancia de sus bendiciones.**

℟. Amén.

**Que los haga atentos y dóciles a su palabra
para que lleguen a poseer los goces sempiternos.**

℟. Amén.

**Que comprendiendo lo que es bueno y recto,
avancen ustedes siempre por el camino de los mandamientos
y lleguen a ser coherederos de los santos.**

℟. Amén.

**La bendición de Dios todopoderoso,
Padre, Hijo, ☩ y Espíritu Santo,
descienda sobre ustedes.**

℟. Amén.

BENDICIONES QUE PERSONAS LAICAS PUEDEN USAR

164 Un/a líder que es una persona laica puede concluir la celebración haciendo la señal de la cruz sobre sí mismo/a mientras dice una de las siguientes fórmulas.

A **El Señor nos bendiga,
nos guarde de todo mal
y nos lleve a la vida eterna.**

℟. Amén.

**May almighty God bless you,
the Father, and the Son, ✝ and the Holy Spirit.**

℞. Amen.

E   **May almighty God keep you from all harm
and bless you with every good gift.**

℞. Amen.

**May he set his Word in your heart
and fill you with lasting joy.**

℞. Amen.

**May you walk in his ways,
always knowing what is right and good,
until you enter your heavenly inheritance.**

℞. Amen.

**May almighty God bless you,
the Father, and the Son, ✝ and the Holy Spirit.**

℞. Amen.

BLESSINGS FOR USE BY LAYPERSONS

164   A leader who is a layperson may conclude a celebration by signing himself or herself with the sign of the cross while saying one of the following:

A   **May the Lord bless us,
protect us from all evil
and bring us to everlasting life.**

℞. Amen.

B   **Dios omnipotente y misericordioso
nos bendiga y nos guarde,
el Padre, y el Hijo, y el Espíritu Santo.**

℟. Amén.

C   **Que el Señor nos bendiga y nos guarde de todo mal.**

℟. Amén.

**Que haga resplandecer su rostro sobre nosotros
y nos muestre su misericordia.**

℟. Amén.

**Que vuelva su mirada hacia nosotros,
y nos conceda su paz.**

℟. Amén.

B   **May the almighty and merciful God bless and protect us, the Father, and the Son, and the Holy Spirit.**

      ℟. Amen.

C   **May the Lord bless us and keep us.**

      ℟. Amen.

      **May his face shine upon us
and be gracious to us.**

      ℟. Amen.

      **May he look upon us with kindness,
and give us his peace.**

      ℟. Amen.

APPENDIX VI

DIRECTORY FOR SUNDAY CELEBRATIONS
IN THE ABSENCE OF A PRIEST

CONGREGATION FOR DIVINE WORSHIP

Prot. 691/86

The *Directory for Sunday Celebrations in the Absence of a Priest* is a response to the convergence of several factors. The first of these is the fact that it is not everywhere and always possible to have a complete liturgical celebration of Sunday (no. 2). A second factor is the request over the past few years from several conferences of bishops that the Holy See issue guidelines for this de facto situation (no. 7). A third factor is a matter of experience: in the light of the actual situation and its circumstances the Holy See and many bishops in their local Churches have already turned their attention to Sunday celebrations in the absence of a priest. The *Directory* has profited from such experience in regard to its assessment of the advantages and at the same time the possible limitations of the sort of celebration in question.

The fundamental point of the entire *Directory* is to ensure, in the best way possible and in every situation, the Christian celebration of Sunday. This means remembering that the Mass remains the proper way of celebrating Sunday, but also means recognizing the presence of important elements even when Mass cannot be celebrated.

The intent of the present document is not to encourage, much less facilitate unnecessary or contrived Sunday assemblies without the celebration of the eucharist. The intent rather is simply to guide and to prescribe what should be done when real circumstances require the decision to have Sunday celebrations in the absence of a priest (nos. 21–22).

The first part of the *Directory* is completely devoted to a summary of the meaning of Sunday and its point of departure is art. 106 of the Constitution on the Liturgy *Sacrosanctum Concilium* (no. 8).

The second part prescribes the conditions necessary for the decision in a diocese to schedule as a regular occurrence Sunday assemblies in the absence of a priest. From a practical and directive point of view this is the most important part of this document. The document envisions the collaboration of the laity in the cases in question; this is an example of responsibilities that parish priests (pastors) can entrust to lay members of their community.

The third part of the Directory is a brief description of the rite for Sunday celebrations of the word along with distribution of communion.

As with similar documents, the application of this *Directory* depends on all the bishops, each acting in accord with the situation of his Church; in matters involving norms for an entire region, the application of the *Directory* depends on the conference of bishops.

What matters above all is ensuring that communities involved in the situation in question have the opportunity to gather together on Sunday, and in a way that coincides with the celebration of the liturgical year (no. 36), and that unites such communities with a community that is celebrating the eucharist with their own parish priest (pastor) (no. 42).

As Pope Paul Vl (no. 21) and Pope John Paul II (no. 50) have stated, the purpose of all pastoral endeavor concerned with Sunday is that it be celebrated and regarded in accord with Christian tradition.

PREFACE

1.   From the day of Pentecost, after the coming of the Holy Spirit, the Church of Christ has always faithfully come together to celebrate the paschal mystery on the day called "the Lord's Day" in memory of the Lord's resurrection. In the Sunday assembly the Church reads in all the Scriptures those things that concern Christ[1] and celebrates the eucharist as the memorial of the death and resurrection of the Lord until he comes.

2.   But a complete celebration of the Lord's Day is not always possible. There have been and still are many of the faithful for whom "because of the lack of a priest or some other serious reason, participation in the eucharistic celebration is not possible."[2]

3.   In some regions, after their first evangelization, the bishops have put catechists in charge of gathering the faithful together on Sunday and, in the form of a devotional exercise, of leading them in prayer. In such cases the number of Christians grew and they were scattered in so many and such widely separated places that a priest could not reach them every Sunday.

4.   In other places the faithful were completely blocked from gathering on Sunday, either because of the persecution of Christians or because of other severe restrictions of religious freedom. Like the Christians of old, who held fast to the Sunday assembly even in the face of martyrdom,[3] the faithful today, even when deprived of the presence of an ordained minister, also strive to gather on Sunday for prayer either within a family or in small groups.

5.   On other grounds today, namely, the scarcity of priests, in many places not every parish can have its own eucharistic celebration each Sunday. Further, for various social and economic reasons some parishes have many fewer members. As a consequence many priests are assigned to celebrate Mass several times on Sunday in many, widely scattered churches. But this practice is regarded as not always satisfactory either to the parishes lacking their own parish priest (pastor) or to the priests involved.

6.   In some local Churches, then, because of the conditions indicated, the bishops have judged it necessary to arrange for other Sunday celebrations in the absence of a priest, so that in the best way possible the weekly gathering of the faithful can be continued and the Christian tradition regarding Sunday preserved.

---

[1] See Luke 24:17.

[2] *Codex Iuris Canonici*, 1983 (hereafter, *CIC*), can. 1248, §2.

[3] See *Acta Martyrum Bytiniae*, in D. Ruiz Bueno, *Actas de los Martires*, Biblioteca de Autores Cristianos (BAC) 75 (Madrid, 1951), 973.

It is by no means unusual, particularly in mission territories, for the faithful themselves, aware of the importance of the Lord's Day and with the help of catechists and religious, to gather to listen to the word of God, to pray, and, in some cases, even to receive communion.

7. The Congregation for Divine Worship has considered these matters, reviewed the documents already published by the Holy See,[4] and acceded to the wishes of the conferences of bishops. Therefore the Congregation regards it as opportune to recall elements of the teaching on the meaning of Sunday, to lay down the conditions for the lawfulness of such celebrations in dioceses, and to provide guidelines for carrying out such celebrations correctly.

It will be the responsibility of the conferences of bishops, as circumstances suggest, to determine these norms in greater detail, to adapt them to the culture and conditions of their people, and to report their decisions to the Apostolic See.

---

[4] See SC Rites, Instruction *Inter Oecumenici* (26 September 1964), no. 37: *Acta Apostolicae Sedis* (hereafter, *AAS*) 56 (1964), 884–885; *Documents on the Liturgy, 1963–1979: Conciliar, Papal, and Curial Texts* (hereafter, *DOL*) 23, no. 329. *CIC*, can. 1248, §2.

CHAPTER I

SUNDAY AND ITS OBSERVANCE

8.   "By a tradition handed down from the apostles and having its origin from the very day of Christ's resurrection, the Church celebrates the paschal mystery every eighth day, which, with good reason, bears the name of the Lord's Day or Sunday."[5]

9.   Evidence of the gathering of the faithful on the day which the New Testament itself already designates as the Lord's Day[6] appears explicitly in documents of the first and second centuries.[7] Outstanding among such evidence is the testimony of Saint Justin: "On this day which is called Sunday, all who live in the cities or in the country gather together in one place."[8] But the day of gathering for Christians did not coincide with the day of rest in the Greek or Roman calendar and therefore even the gathering on this day was a sign to fellow citizens of the Christians' identity.

10.   From the earliest centuries pastors had never failed to counsel their people on the need to gather together on Sunday. "Because you are Christ's members, do not scatter from the church by not coming together . . . do not neglect your Savior or separate him from his members. Do not shatter or scatter the Body of Christ. . . ."[9] Vatican Council II recalled this teaching in the following words: "On this day Christ's faithful must gather together, so that, by hearing the word of God and taking part in the eucharist, they may call to mind the passion, resurrection, and glorification of the Lord Jesus and may thank God, who 'has begotten them again unto a living hope through the resurrection of Jesus Christ from the dead' (1 Peter 1:3)."[10]

11.   Saint Ignatius of Antioch pointed out the importance of the Sunday celebration for the life of the faithful: "Christians no longer observe the sabbath day but live according to the Lord's Day, on which our life was restored through Jesus Christ and his death."[11] In their "sense of the faith" (sensus fidelium) the faithful, now as in the past, have held the Lord's Day in such high regard that they have never willingly omitted its observance even in times of persecution or in the midst of cultures alien or hostile to the Christian faith.

---

[5] Vatican Council II, Constitution on the Liturgy *Sacrosanctum Concilium* (hereafter, *SC*), art. 106: *DOL* 1, no. 106. See also *ibid.*, Appendix, Declaration of the Second Vatican Ecumenical Council on Revision of the Calendar: *DOL* 1, no. 131.

[6] See Revelation 1:10. See also John 20:19, 26; Acts 20:7-12; 1 Corinthians 16:2; Hebrews 10:24-25.

[7] Didache 14, 1: F. X. Funk, ed., *Doctrina duodecim Apostolorum* (1887), p. 42.

[8] Saint Justin, *Apologia* I, 67: PG 6, 430.

[9] *Didascalia Apostolorum* 2, 59, 1–3: F. X. Funk, ed., *Didascalia et Constitutiones Apostolorum* (1905) vol. 1, p. 170.

[10] *SC*, art. 106: *DOL* 1, no. 106.

[11] Saint Ignatius of Antioch, *Ad Magnesios* 9, 1: F. X. Funk ed., *Didascalia et Constitutiones Apostolorum* (1905) vol. 1, p. 199.

12. The following are the principal requisites for the Sunday assembly of the faithful.

a.   the gathering of the faithful to manifest the Church, not simply on their own initiative but as called together by God, that is, as the people of God in their organic structure, presided over by a priest, who acts in the person of Christ;

b.   their instruction in the paschal mystery through the Scriptures that are proclaimed and that are explained by a priest or deacon;

c.   the celebration of the eucharistic sacrifice, by which the paschal mystery is expressed, and which is carried out by the priest in the person of Christ and offered in the name of the entire Christian people.

13.   Pastoral efforts should have this aim above all that the sacrifice of the Mass on Sunday be regarded as the only true actualization of the Lord's paschal mystery[12] and as the most complete manifestation of the Church: "Hence the Lord's Day is the first holyday of all and should be proposed to the devotion of the faithful and taught to them. . . . Other celebrations, unless they be truly of greatest importance, shall not have precedence over the Sunday, the foundation and core of the whole liturgical year."[13]

14.   Such principles should be set before the faithful and instilled in them right from the beginning of their Christian formation, in order that they may willingly fulfill the precept to keep this day holy and may understand why they are brought together for the celebration of the eucharist by the call of the Church[14] and not simply by their personal devotion. In this way the faithful will be led to experience the Lord's Day as a sign of the divine transcendence over all human works, and not as simply a day off from work; in virtue of the Sunday assembly they will more deeply perceive themselves to be members of the Church and will show this outwardly.

15.   In the Sunday assembly, as also in the life of the Christian community, the faithful should find both active participation and a true spirit of community, as well as the opportunity to be renewed spiritually under the guidance of the Holy Spirit. In this way, too, they will be protected against the attractions of sects that promise relief from the pain of loneliness and a more complete fulfillment of religious aspirations.

---

[12] See Paul VI, Address to bishops of central France, 26 March 1977: *AAS* 69 (1977), 465; "The goal must always be the celebration of the sacrifice of the Mass, the only true actualization of the Lord's paschal mystery" (tr., *DOL* 449, no. 38:2).

[13] *SC*, art. 106: *DOL* 1, no. 106.

[14] See *SC* Rites, Instruction *Eucharisticum mysterium* (25 May 1967), no. 25: *AAS* 59 (1967), 555; *DOL* 179, no. 25.

16.   Finally, pastoral effort should concentrate on measures which have as their purpose "that the Lord's Day becomes in fact a day of joy and of freedom from work."[15] In this way Sunday will stand out in today's culture as a sign of freedom and consequently as a day established for the well being of the human person, which clearly is a higher value than commerce or industrial production."[16]

17.   The word of God, the eucharist, and the ministry of the priest are gifts that the Lord presents to the Church, his Bride, and they are to be received and to be prayed for as divine graces. The Church, which possesses these gifts above all in the Sunday assembly, thanks God for them in that same assembly and awaits the joy of its complete rest in the day of the Lord "before the throne of God and before the Lamb."[17]

---

[15] *SC*, art. 106: *DOL* 1, no. 106.

[16] See "Le sens du dimanche dans une societé pluralists Reflexions pastorales de la Conference des eveques du Canada," *La Documentation Catholique,* no. 1935 (1987), 273–276.

[17] Revelation 7:9.

CHAPTER II

CONDITIONS FOR HOLDING SUNDAY CELEBRATIONS IN THE ABSENCE OF A PRIEST

18.   Whenever and wherever Mass cannot be celebrated on Sunday, the first thing to be ascertained is whether the faithful can go to a church in a place nearby to participate there in the eucharistic mystery. At the present time this solution is to be recommended and to be retained where it is in effect; but it demands that the faithful, rightly imbued with a fuller understanding of the Sunday assembly, respond with good will to a new situation.

19.   The aim is that the riches of Sacred Scripture and of the Church's prayer be amply provided to the faithful gathered on Sundays in various ways even apart from Mass. For the faithful should not be deprived of the readings that are read at Mass in the course of a year, nor of the prayers of the liturgical seasons.

20.   Among the forms of celebration found in liturgical tradition when Mass is not possible, a celebration of the word of God is particularly recommended,[18] and also its completion, when possible, by eucharistic communion. In this way the faithful can be nourished by both the word of God and the body of Christ. "By hearing the word of God the faithful learn that the marvels it proclaims reach their climax in the paschal mystery, of which the Mass is a sacramental memorial and in which they share by communion."[19] Further, in certain circumstances the Sunday celebration can be combined with the celebration of one or more of the sacraments and especially of the sacramentals and in ways that are suited to the needs of each community.

21.   It is imperative that the faithful be taught to see the substitutional character of these celebrations, which should not be regarded as the optimal solution to new difficulties nor as a surrender to mere convenience.[20] Therefore a gathering or assembly of this kind can never be held on a Sunday in places where Mass has already been celebrated or is to be celebrated or was celebrated on the preceding Saturday evening, even if the Mass is celebrated in a different language. Nor is it right to have more than one assembly of this kind on any given Sunday

---

[18] See *SC*, art. 35, 4: *DOL* 1, no. 35.

[19] The Roman Ritual, *Holy Communion and Worship of the Eucharist outside Mass*, no. 26.

[20] See Paul VI, Address to bishops of central France, 26 March 1977: *AAS* 69 (1977): "Proceed judiciously, but without multiplying this type of Sunday assembly, as though it were the ideal solution and the last chance" (tr., *DOL* 449, no. 3842).

22. Any confusion between this kind of assembly and a eucharistic celebration must be carefully avoided. Assemblies of this kind should not take away but rather increase the desire of the faithful to take part in the celebration of the eucharist, and should make them more eager to be present at the celebration of the eucharist.

23. The faithful are to understand that the eucharistic sacrifice cannot take place without a priest and that the eucharistic communion which they may receive in this kind of assembly is closely connected with the sacrifice of the Mass. On that basis the faithful can be shown how necessary it is to pray that God will "give the Church more priests and keep them faithful in their love and service."[21]

24. It belongs to the diocesan bishop, after hearing the council of presbyters, to decide whether Sunday assemblies without the celebration of the eucharist should be held on a regular basis in his diocese. It belongs also to the bishop, after considering the place and persons involved, to set out both general and particular norms for such celebrations. These assemblies are therefore to be conducted only in virtue of their convocation by the bishop and only under the pastoral ministry of the parish priest (pastor).

25. "No Christian community is ever built up unless it has its roots and center in the eucharistic liturgy."[22] Therefore before the bishop decides on having Sunday assemblies without celebration of the eucharist the following, in addition to the status of parishes (see no. 5), should be considered: the possibility of recourse to priests, even religious priests, who are not directly assigned to the care of souls and the frequency of Masses in the various parishes and churches.[23] The preeminence of the celebration of the eucharist, particularly on Sunday, over other pastoral activities is to be respected.

26. Either personally or through his representatives the bishop will, by an appropriate catechesis, instruct the diocesan community on the causes requiring provision of these celebrations, pointing out the seriousness of the issue and urging the community's support and cooperation. The bishop is to appoint a delegate or a special committee to see to it that these celebrations are carried out correctly; he is also to choose those who are to promote these celebrations, and to see to it that these people receive the necessary instruction. But the bishop's concern is always to be that several times a year the faithful involved have the opportunity to participate in the celebration of the eucharist.

---

[21] *The Roman Missal (Sacramentary)*, Masses and Prayers for Various Needs and Occasions, I. For the Church, 9. For Priestly Vocations, prayer over the gifts.

[22] Vatican Council II, Decree on the Ministry and Life of Priests *Presbyterorum ordinis*, no. 6: DOL 18, no. 261.

[23] See SC Rites, Instruction *Eucharisticum mysterium* (25 May 1967), no. 26: *AAS* 59 (1967), 555; *DOL* 179, no. 1255.

27. It is the duty of the parish priest (pastor) to inform the bishop about the opportuneness of such celebrations in his territory, to prepare the faithful for them, to visit them during the week, and at a convenient time to celebrate the sacraments for them, particularly the sacrament of penance. In this way the communities involved will come to realize that their assembly on Sunday is not an assembly "without a priest," but an assembly "in the absence of a priest," or, better still, an assembly "in expectation of a priest."

28. When Mass cannot be celebrated the parish priest (pastor) is to ensure that holy communion be given. He is also to see to it that there is a celebration of the eucharist in due time in each community. The consecrated hosts are to be renewed often and kept in a safe place.

29. As the primary assistants of priests, deacons are called in a special way to lead these Sunday assemblies. Since the deacon has been ordained for the nurture and increase of the people of God, it belongs to him to lead the prayers, to proclaim the gospel, to preach the homily, and to give communion.[24]

30. In the absence of both a priest and a deacon, the parish priest (pastor) is to appoint laypersons, who are to be entrusted with the care of these celebrations, namely, with leading the prayers, with the ministry of the word, and with giving holy communion.

Those to be chosen first by the parish priest (pastor) are readers and acolytes who have been duly instituted for the service of the altar and of the word of God. If there are no such instituted ministers available, other laypersons, both men and women, may be appointed; they can carry out this responsibility in virtue of their baptism and confirmation.[25] Such persons are to be chosen in view of the consistency of their way of life with the Gospel and in the expectation of their being acceptable to the community of the faithful. Appointment is usually to be for a definite time and is to be made known publicly to the community. It is fitting that there be a celebration in which prayers are offered to God on behalf of those appointed.[26]

The parish priest (pastor) is to see to the suitable and continuous instruction of these laypersons and to prepare with them worthy celebrations (see Chapter III).

31. The laypersons appointed should regard the office entrusted to them not so much as an honor but as a responsibility and above all as a service to their brothers and sisters under the authority of the parish priest (pastor). For theirs is not a proper office but a suppletory office, since they exercise it "where the need of the Church suggests in the absence of ministers."[27]

---

[24] See Paul VI, Motu proprio *Ad pascendum* (15 August 1972), no. 1: *AAS* 64 (1972), 534; *DOL* 319, no. 2576.

[25] See *CIC*, can. 230, §3.

[26] See The Roman Ritual, *Book of Blessings*, ch. 4, I, B.

[27] *CIC*, can. 230, §3.

Those who are appointed to such an office "should do all of, but only, those parts which pertain to that office."[28] They should carry out their office with sincere devotion and the decorum demanded by such a responsibility and rightly expected of them by God's people.[29]

32.   When on a Sunday a celebration of the word of God along with the giving of holy communion is not possible, the faithful are strongly urged to devote themselves to prayer "for a suitable time either individually or with the family or, if possible, with a group of families."[30] In these circumstances the telecast of liturgical services can provide useful assistance.

33.   Particularly to be kept in mind is the possibility of celebrating some part of the liturgy of the hours, for example, morning prayer or evening prayer, during which the Sunday readings of the current year can be inserted. For "when the people are invited to the liturgy of the hours and come together in unity of heart and voice, they show forth the Church in its celebration of the mystery of Christ."[31] At the end of such a celebration communion may be given (see no. 46).

34.   "The grace of the Redeemer is not lacking for individual members of the faithful or entire communities that, because of persecution or a lack of priests, are deprived of celebration of the eucharist for a short time or even for a long period. They can be moved by a deep desire for the sacrament and be united in prayer with the whole Church. Then when they call upon the Lord and raise their minds and hearts to him, through the power of the Holy Spirit they enter into communion with Christ and with the Church, his living Body . . . and therefore they receive the fruits of the eucharist."[32]

---

[28] *SC*, art. 28: *DOL* 1, no. 28.

[29] See *SC*, art. 29: *DOL* 1, no. 29.

[30] *CIC*, can. 1248, §2.

[31] General Instruction of the Liturgy of the Hours (hereafter, *GILH*), no. 22: *DOL* 426, no. 3452.

[32] Congregation for the Doctrine of the Faith, *Epistle . . . on certain questions regarding the minister of the eucharist*, 6 August 1983: *AAS* 75 (1983), 1007.

CHAPTER III

ORDER OF CELEBRATION

35. The order to be followed in a Sunday celebration that does not include Mass consists of two parts, the celebration of the word of God and the giving of holy communion. Nothing that is proper to Mass, and particularly the presentation of the gifts and the eucharistic prayer, is to be inserted into the celebration. The order of celebration is to be arranged in such a way that it is truly conducive to prayer and conveys the image not of a simple meeting but of a genuine liturgical assembly.

36. As a rule the texts for the prayers and readings for each Sunday or solemnity are to be taken from *The Roman Missal (Sacramentary)* and the *Lectionary for Mass*. In this way the faithful will follow the cycle of the liturgical year and will pray and listen to the word of God in communion with the other communities of the Church.

37. In preparing the celebration the parish priest (pastor) together with the appointed laypersons may make adaptations suited to the number of those who will take part in the celebration, the ability of the leaders (animators), and the kind of instruments available for the music and the singing.

38. When a deacon presides at the celebration, he acts in accord with his ministry in regard to the greetings, the prayers, the gospel reading and homily, the giving of communion, and the dismissal and blessing. He wears the vestments proper to his ministry, that is, the alb with stole, and, as circumstances suggest, the dalmatic. He uses the presidential chair.

39. A layperson who leads the assembly acts as one among equals, in the way followed in the liturgy of the hours when not presided over by an ordained minister, and in the case of blessings when the minister is a layperson ("May the Lord bless us . . ."; "Let us praise the Lord . . ."). The layperson is not to use words that are proper to a priest or deacon and is to omit rites that are too readily associated with the Mass, for example, greetings—especially "The Lord be with you"—and dismissals, since these might give the impression that the layperson is a sacred minister.[33]

---

[33] See *GILH*, no. 258: *DOL* 426, no. 3688; see also The Roman Ritual, *Book of Blessings*, nos. 48, 119, 130, 181.

---

40. The lay leader wears vesture that is suitable for his or her function or the vesture prescribed by the bishop.[34] He or she does not use the presidential chair, but another chair prepared outside the sanctuary.[35] Since the altar is the table of sacrifice and of the paschal banquet, its only use in this celebration is for the rite of communion, when the consecrated bread is placed on it before communion is given.

Preparation of the celebration should include careful attention to a suitable distribution of offices, for example, for the readings, the singing, etc., and also to the arrangement and decoration of the place of celebration.

41. The following is an outline of the elements of the celebration.

a.   Introductory rites. The purpose of these is to form the gathered faithful into a community and for them to dispose themselves for the celebration.

b.   Liturgy of the word. Here God speaks to his people, to disclose to them the mystery of redemption and salvation; the people respond through the profession of faith and the general intercessions.

c.   Thanksgiving. Here God is blessed for his great glory (see no. 45).

d.   Communion rites. These are an expression and accomplishment of communion with Christ and with his members, especially with those who on this same day take part in the eucharistic sacrifice.

e.   Concluding rites. These point to the connection existing between the liturgy and the Christian life.

The conference of bishops, or the individual bishop himself, may, in view of the conditions of the place and the people involved, determine more precisely the details of the celebration, using resources prepared by the national or diocesan liturgical committee, but the general structure of the celebration should not be changed unnecessarily.

42. In the introduction at the beginning of the celebration, or at some other point, the leader should make mention of the community of the faithful with whom the parish priest (pastor) is celebrating the eucharist on that Sunday and urge the assembly to unite itself in spirit with that community.

43. In order that the participants may retain the word of God, there should be an explanation of the readings or a period of silence for reflection on what has been heard. Since only a priest or a deacon may give a homily,[36] it is desirable that the parish priest (pastor) prepare a homily and give it to the leader of the assembly to be read. But in this matter the decisions of the conference of bishops are to be followed.

---

[34] See The Roman Ritual, *Holy Communion and Worship of the Eucharist outside Mass*, no. 20: *DOL* 266, no. 2098.
[35] See *GILH*, no. 258: *DOL* 426, no. 3688.
[36] See *CIC*, can. 766–767.

44. The general intercessions are to follow an established series of intentions.[37] Intentions for the whole diocese that the bishop may have proposed are not to be omitted. There should also often be intentions for vocations to sacred orders, for the bishop, and for the parish priest (pastor).

45. The thanksgiving may follow either one of the ways described here.

1. After the general intercessions or after holy communion, the leader invites all to an act of thanksgiving, in which the faithful praise the glory and mercy of God. This can be done by use of a psalm (for example, Psalms 100, 113, 118, 136, 147, 150), a hymn (for example, the *Gloria*), a canticle (for example, the Canticle of Mary), or a litanic prayer. The leader and the faithful stand and, facing the altar, together recite the thanksgiving.

2. After the Lord's Prayer, the leader of the assembly goes to the tabernacle or other place where the eucharist is reserved and, after making a reverence, places the ciborium with the holy eucharist on the altar. Then while kneeling before the altar he or she together with all the faithful sing or recite a hymn, psalm, or litany, which in this case is directed to Christ in the eucharist.

But this thanksgiving is not in any way to take the form of the eucharistic prayer, the texts of prefaces or eucharistic prayers from *The Roman Missal (Sacramentary)* are not to be used, and all danger of confusion is to be removed.

46. For the communion rite the provisions given in The Roman Ritual for communion outside Mass are to be observed.[38] The faithful are to be frequently reminded that even when they receive communion outside Mass they are united to the eucharistic sacrifice.

47. For communion, if at all possible, bread consecrated that same Sunday in a Mass celebrated elsewhere is used; a deacon or layperson brings it in a ciborium or pyx and places it in the tabernacle before the celebration. Bread consecrated at the last Mass celebrated in the place of assembly may also be used. Before the Lord's Prayer the leader goes to the tabernacle or place where the eucharist is reserved, takes the vessel with the body of the Lord, and places it upon the table of the altar, then introduces the Lord's Prayer—unless the act of thanksgiving mentioned in no. 45, 2 is to take place at this point.

---

[37] See *General Instruction of the Roman Missal,* nos. 45–47: DOL 208, nos. 1435–1437.

[38] See The Roman Ritual, *Holy Communion and Worship of the Eucharist outside Mass,* ch. 1: DOL 266, nos. 2092–2103.

48. The Lord's Prayer is always recited or sung by all, even if there is to be no communion. The sign of peace may be exchanged. After communion, "a period of silence may be observed or a psalm or song of praise may be sung."[39] A thanksgiving as described in no. 45, 1 may also take place here.

49. Before the conclusion of the assembly, announcements or notices related to the life of the parish or the diocese are read.

50. "Too much importance can never be attached to the Sunday assembly, whether as the source of the Christian life of the individual and of the community, or as a sign of God's intent to gather the whole human race together in Christ.

"All Christians must share the conviction that they cannot live their faith or participate—in the manner proper to them—in the universal mission of the Church unless they are nourished by the eucharistic bread. They should be equally convinced that the Sunday assembly is a sign to the world of the mystery of communion, which is the eucharist."[40]

On 21 May 1988 this Directory, prepared by the Congregation for Divine Worship, was approved and confirmed by Pope John Paul II, who also ordered its publication.

Office of the Congregation for Divine Worship, Solemnity of the Body and Blood of Christ, 2 June 1988.

Paul Augustin Cardinal Mayer, O.S.B.
Prefect

✠ Vergilio Noé
Titular Archbishop of Voncaria
Secretary

---

[39] *Ibid.*, no. 37.
[40] John Paul II, Address to the bishops of France on the occasion of their *ad limina* visit, 27 March 1987.